Edmund Gosse, Thomas Gray

Works

In Prose and Verse

Edmund Gosse, Thomas Gray

Works
In Prose and Verse

ISBN/EAN: 9783744685504

Printed in Europe, USA, Canada, Australia, Japan

Cover: Foto ©Thomas Meinert / pixelio.de

More available books at **www.hansebooks.com**

THE WORKS

OF

THOMAS GRAY

In Prose and Verse

EDITED BY

EDMUND GOSSE

CLARK LECTURER ON ENGLISH LITERATURE AT THE UNIVERSITY OF CAMBRIDGE

IN FOUR VOLS.—VOL. II.

LETTERS.—I.

London

MACMILLAN AND CO.

1884

LETTERS

[The *Letters* of Gray were first published in 1775, by Mason, who took the liberty of amending and omitting portions of the text, and of inserting interpolations of his own. A better and a much fuller text was published by Mitford in 1816. The letters addressed to the Rev. Norton Nicholls appeared in 1843, and in 1853 Mitford published an additional volume of new letters, chiefly addressed to Mason. In the following pages I have followed Mitford's latest collations, except as regards the very numerous letters addressed to Wharton, which are all printed here directly from Gray's holographs in the *Egerton MSS.*—*Ed.*]

CONTENTS.

LETTERS.

I.—TO RICHARD WEST.[1]

Cantabr. May 8, 1736.

MY DEAR WEST—My letter enjoys itself before it is opened, in imagining the confusion you will be in when you hear that a coach and six is just stopped at Christ Church gates, and desires to speak with you, with a huddle of things in it, as different as ever met together in Noah's Ark; a fat one and a lean one, and one that can say a little with his mouth and a great deal with his pen, and one that can neither speak nor write. But you will see them; joy be with you! I hope too I shall shortly see you, at least *in congratulatione Oxoniensi.*

[1] Richard West (1717-1742), was the only son of a Lord Chancellor of Ireland, of the same name, who died in 1726. His poems were collected by Gray, but not printed until after that writer's death. West possessed a tender elegiac vein of no great depth, but was a sound scholar. He, Gray, Walpole, and Ashton formed a "quadruple alliance" of friendship at Eton, whence West proceeded to Oxford and the other three to Cambridge.—[*Ed.*]

My dear West, I more than ever regret you: it would be the greatest of pleasure to me to know what you do, what you read, how you spend your time, etc., and to tell you what I do not do, not read, and how I do not, for almost all the employment of my hours may be best explained by negatives. Take my word and experience upon it, doing nothing is a most amusing business, and yet neither something nor nothing give me any pleasure. For this little while last past I have been playing with Statius; we yesterday had a game at quoits together. You will easily forgive me for having broke his head,[1] as you have a little pique to him.

I will not plague you too much, and so break the affair in the middle, and give you leave to resume your Aristotle instead of your friend and servant,

T. Gray.

II.—TO RICHARD WEST.

When you have seen one of my days, you have seen a whole year of my life; they go round and round like the blind horse in the mill, only he has the satisfaction of fancying he makes a progress and gets some ground; my eyes are open enough to see the same dull prospect, and to know that having

[1] West replied: "I agree with you that you have broke Statius' head, but it is in like manner as Apollo broke Hyacinth's, you have foiled him infinitely at his own weapon."—[*Ed.*]

made four-and-twenty steps more, I shall be just where I was; I may, better than most people, say my life is but a span, were I not afraid lest you should not believe that a person so short-lived could write even so long a letter as this; in short, I believe I must not send you the history of my own time, till I can send you that also of the reformation. However, as the most undeserving people in the world must sure have the vanity to wish somebody had a regard for them, so I need not wonder at my own, in being pleased that you care about me. You need not doubt, therefore, of having a first row in the front box of my little heart, and I believe you are not in danger of being crowded there; it is asking you to an old play, indeed, but you will be candid enough to excuse the whole piece for the sake of a few tolerable lines.

Cambridge, May 8, 1736.

III.—TO THE REV. GEORGE BIRKETT.

October 8 [1736 ?].

Sir—As I shall stay only a fortnight longer in town, I'll beg you to give yourself the trouble of writing out my Bills, and sending 'em, that I may put myself out of your Debt, as soon as I come down: if Piazza[1] should come to you, you'll be so good as to satisfie him: I protest, I forget what I owe him, but

[1] Hieronimo Bartolomeo Piazza, a renegade Dominican friar, Gray's Italian master at Cambridge.—[*Ed.*]

he is honest enough to tell you right. My father and mother desires me to send their compliments, and I beg you'd believe me,—S$^{r.}$, your most obedt. humble servt., T. GRAY.

IV.—TO RICHARD WEST.

YOU must know that I do not take degrees, and, after this term, shall have nothing more of college impertinences to undergo,[1] which I trust will be some pleasure to you, as it is a great one to me. I have endured lectures daily and hourly since I came last, supported by the hopes of being shortly at full liberty to give myself up to my friends and classical companions, who, poor souls! though I see them fallen into great contempt with most people here, yet I cannot help sticking to them, and out of a spirit of obstinacy (I think) love them the better for it; and indeed, what can I do else? Must I plunge into metaphysics? Alas, I cannot see in the dark; nature has not furnished me with the optics of a cat. Must I pore upon mathematics? Alas, I cannot see in too much light; I am no eagle. It is very possible that two and two make four, but I would not give four farthings to demonstrate this ever so clearly; and if

[1] "In December 1736 there was an attempt at rebellion; he declined to take degrees, and announced his intention of quitting college; but as we hear no more of this, and as he stayed two years longer at Cambridge, we may believe that this was overruled."—Gosse, *Life of Gray*, pp. 19, 20. Gray took no degree till the winter of 1742.

these be the profits of life, give me the amusements of it. The people I behold all around me, it seems, know all this and more, and yet I do not know one of them who inspires me with any ambition of being like him. Surely it was of this place, now Cambridge,[1] but formerly known by the name of Babylon, that the prophet spoke when he said, "The wild beasts of the desert shall dwell there, and their houses shall be full of doleful creatures, and owls shall build there, and satyrs shall dance there; their forts and towers shall be a den for ever, a joy of wild asses; there shall the great owl make her nest, and lay and hatch and gather under her shadow; it shall be a court of dragons; the screech owl also shall rest there, and find for herself a place of rest." You see here is a pretty collection of desolate animals, which is verified in this town to a tittle, and perhaps it may also allude to your habitation, for you know all types may be taken by abundance of handles; however, I defy your owls to match mine.

If the default of your spirits and nerves be nothing but the effect of the hyp, I have no more to say. We all must submit to that wayward queen; I too in no small degree own her sway,

> I feel her influence while I speak her power.

But if it be a real distemper, pray take more care of your health, if not for your own at least for our sakes,

[1] Gray was of the same opinion in 1742, when he wrote his splenetic *Hymn to Ignorance.*—[*Ed.*]

and do not be so soon weary of this little world: I do not know what[1] refined friendships you may have contracted in the other, but pray do not be in a hurry to see your acquaintance above; among your terrestrial familiars, however, though I say it, that should not say it, there positively is not one that has a greater esteem for you than yours most sincerely, etc.

Peterhouse, December 1736.

V.—TO HORACE WALPOLE.[2]

YOU can never weary me with the repetition of anything that makes me sensible of your kindness; since that has been the only idea of any social happiness that I have almost ever received, and which (begging your pardon for thinking so differently from you in such cases) I would by no means have parted with for an exemption from all the uneasiness mixed with it: but it would be unjust to imagine my taste was any rule for yours; for which reason my letters are shorter and less frequent than they would be, had I any materials but myself to entertain you with. Love

[1] This thought is very juvenile, but perhaps he meant to ridicule the affected manner of Mrs. Rowe's letters of the dead to the living; a book which was, I believe, published about this time.—[*Mason.*]

[2] Horace Walpole, Earl of Orford (1717-1797), entered Eton on the 26th of April 1727, and became the school-fellow of Gray, whose friendship he retained, with a certain interval, throughout the life of the latter. When this letter was written, Walpole had been nearly two years at King's College, Cambridge; but at the moment was, doubtless, in London for Christmas.—[*Ed.*]

and brown sugar must be a poor regale for one of your goût, and alas! you know I am by trade a grocer. Scandal (if I had any) is a merchandise you do not profess dealing in; now and then, indeed, and to oblige a friend, you may perhaps slip a little out of your pocket, as a decayed gentlewoman would a piece of right mecklin, or a little quantity of run tea, but this only now and then, not to make a practice of it. Monsters appertaining to this climate you have seen already, both wet and dry. So you perceive within how narrow bounds my pen is circumscribed, and the whole contents of my share in our correspondence may be reduced under the two heads of 1st, you; 2dly, I; the first is, indeed, a subject to expatiate upon, but you might laugh at me for talking about what I do not understand; the second is so tiny, so tiresome, that you shall hear no more of it, than that it is ever yours.

Peterhouse, December 23, 1736.

VI.—FRAGMENT OF A LETTER TO RICHARD WEST.

March 1737.

. . . I LEARN Italian like any dragon, and in two months am got through the 16th Book of Tasso, whom I hold in great admiration; I want you to learn too, that I may know your opinion of him; nothing can be easier than that language to any one who knows Latin and French already, and there are few so copious and expressive. . . . My college has set me a versifying on a public occasion (viz. those verses which are called tripos) on the theme of *Luna est habitabilis.*

VII.—TO RICHARD WEST.

After a month's expectation of you, and a fortnight's despair, at Cambridge, I am come to town, and to better hopes of seeing you. If what you sent me last[1] be the product of your melancholy, what may I not expect from your more cheerful hours? For by this time the ill health that you complain of is (I hope) quite departed; though, if I were self-interested, I ought to wish for the continuance of anything that could be the occasion of so much pleasure to me. Low spirits are my true and faithful companions;[2] they get up with me, go to bed with me, make journeys and returns as I do; nay, and pay visits, and will even affect to be jocose, and force a feeble laugh with me; but most commonly we sit alone together, and are the prettiest insipid company in the

[1] A very touching elegy in Latin, "Ad Amicos," sent by West to Gray and Walpole from Christ Church on the 4th of July 1737.—[*Ed.*]

[2] So Flaubert says in writing to George Sand: "Je suis submergé par une mélancolie noire, qui revient à propos de tout et de rien, plusieurs fois dans la journée. Puis, ça se passe et ça recommence. Il y a peut-être trop longtemps que je n'ai écrit?" There is much in what is recorded of the temperament of Flaubert which may help us to comprehend Gray.—[*Ed.*]

world. However, when you come, I believe they must undergo the fate of all humble companions, and be discarded. Would I could turn them to the same use that you have done, and make an Apollo of them. If they could write such verses with me, not hartshorn, nor spirit of amber, nor all that furnishes the closet of an apothecary's widow, should persuade me to part with them. But, while I write to you, I hear the bad news of Lady Walpole's death on Saturday night last. Forgive me if the thought of what my poor Horace must feel on that account, obliges me to have done in reminding you that I am yours, etc.

London, August 22, 1737.

VIII.—TO HORACE WALPOLE.

I WAS hindered in my last, and so could not give you all the trouble I would have done. The description of a road, which your coach wheels have so often honoured, it would be needless to give you; suffice it that I arrived safe at my uncle's,[1] who is a great hunter in imagination; his dogs take up every chair in the house, so I am forced to stand at this present writing; and though the gout forbids him galloping after them in the field, yet he continues still to regale his ears and nose with their comfortable noise and stink. He holds me mighty cheap, I perceive, for walking when I should ride, and reading when I

[1] His mother's brother, Robert Antrobus, of Burnham.

should hunt. My comfort amidst all this is, that I have at the distance of half a mile, through a green lane, a forest (the vulgar call it a common) all my own, at least as good as so, for I spy no human thing in it but myself. It is a little chaos of mountains and precipices; mountains, it is true, that do not ascend much above the clouds, nor are the declivities quite so amazing as Dover cliff; but just such hills as people who love their necks as well as I do may venture to climb, and crags that give the eye as much pleasure as if they were more dangerous. Both vale and hill are covered with most venerable beeches, and other very reverend vegetables, that, like most other ancient people, are always dreaming out their old stories to the winds,

> And as they bow their hoary tops relate,
> In murm'ring sounds, the dark decrees of fate;
> While visions, as poetic eyes avow,
> Cling to each leaf, and swarm on every bough.

At the foot of one of these squats ME I (il penseroso), and there grow to the trunk for a whole morning. The timorous hare and sportive squirrel gambol around me like Adam in Paradise, before he had an Eve; but I think he did not use to read Virgil, as I commonly do there. In this situation I often converse with my Horace, aloud, too, that is, talk to you, but I do not remember that I ever heard you answer me. I beg pardon for taking all the conversation to myself, but it is entirely your own fault. We have old Mr. Southern[1] at a gentleman's house a little way off, who often comes to see us; he is now seventy-seven years old, and has almost wholly lost his memory; but is as agreeable as an old man can be, at least I persuade myself so when I look at him, and think of Isabella and Oroonoko. I shall be in town in about three weeks. Adieu.

September 1737.

IX.—TO HORACE WALPOLE.[2]

I SYMPATHISE with you in the sufferings which you foresee are coming upon you. We are both at present, I imagine, in no very agreeable situation; for my part I am under the misfortune of having nothing to do, but it is a misfortune which, thank my stars, I can pretty well bear. You are in a confusion of wine, and roaring, and hunting, and tobacco, and, heaven be praised, you too can pretty well bear it; while our evils are no more I believe we shall not much repine. I imagine, how-

[1] Thomas Southerne (1660-1746), the last survivor of the Restoration dramatists. His two best tragedies were *The Fatal Marriage*, 1694, of which Isabella was the heroine, and *Oroonoko*, 1696, to both of which Gray presently refers. Southerne lived nine years after this interview.—[*Ed.*]

[2] At this time with his father at Houghton.—[*Mason.*] Houghton Hall, in Norfolk, the seat of Sir Robert Walpole. It was famous for its gallery of pictures, which were sold to the Empress of Russia in 1779. In 1789 the hall was burned down.—[*Ed.*]

ever, you will rather choose to converse with the living dead, that adorn the walls of your apartments, than with the dead living that deck the middles of them; and prefer a picture of still life to the realities of a noisy one, and as I guess, will imitate what you prefer, and for an hour or two at noon will stick yourself up as formal as if you had been fixed in your frame for these hundred years, with a pink or rose in one hand, and a great seal ring on the other. Your name, I assure you, has been propagated in these countries by a convert of yours, one * *, he has brought over his whole family to you; they were before pretty good Whigs, but now they are absolute Walpolians. We have hardly anybody in the parish but knows exactly the dimensions of the hall and saloon at Houghton, and begin to believe that the lanthorn[1] is not so great a consumer of the fat of the land as disaffected persons have said. For your reputation, we keep to ourselves your not hunting nor drinking hogan, either of which here would be sufficient to lay your honour in the dust. To-morrow se'nnight I hope to be in town, and not long after at Cambridge. I am, etc.

Burnham, September 1737.

[1] A lanthorn for eighteen candles, of copper-gilt, hung in the hall at Houghton. It became a favourite object of Tory satire at the time; see the *Craftsman*. This lanthorn was afterwards sold to the Earl of Chesterfield. See Walpole's *Works*, vol. ii. p. 263; and *Letters to H. Mann*, vol. ii. p. 368. —[*Mit.*]

X.—TO RICHARD WEST.

[This letter began with the *Sapphic Ode to Mr. West*, and ended with the *Alcaic Fragment.*]

. . . .

OHE! amicule noster, et unde, sodes tu μουσοπάτακτος adeò repente evasisti? jam rogitaturum credo. Nescio hercle, sic planè habet. Quicquid enim nugarum ἐπὶ σχολῆς inter ambulandum in palimpsesto scriptitavi, hisce te maxumè impertiri[1] visum est, quippe quem probare, quod meum est, aut certè ignoscere solitum probè novi: bonâ tuâ veniâ sit si fortè videar in fine subtristior; nam risui jamdudum salutem dixi; etiam paulò mœstitiæ studiosiorem factum scias, promptumque, Καινοῖς παλαιὰ δακρύοις στένειν κακά.

. . . .

Sed de me satis. Cura ut valeas.

June 1738.

XI.—TO HORACE WALPOLE.

MY DEAR SIR—I should say[2] Mr. Inspector-General of the Exports and Imports; but that appellation would

[1] This is a strange construction, and in all probability incorrectly copied.—[*Ed.*]

[2] Mr. Walpole was just named to that post, which he exchanged soon after for that of Usher of the Exchequer.—[*Mason.*]

make but an odd figure in conjunction with the three familiar monosyllables above written, for

> Non benè conveniunt nec in unâ sede morantur
> Majestas & amor.[1]

Which is, being interpreted, Love does not live at the Custom-house; however, by what style, title, or denomination soever you choose to be dignified or distinguished hereafter, these three words will stick by you like a burr, and you can no more get quit of these and your Christian name than St. Anthony could of his pig. My motions at present (which you are pleased to ask after), are much like those of a pendulum or (Dr. Longically[2] speaking) oscillatory. I swing from Chapel or Hall home, and from home to Chapel or Hall. All the strange incidents that happen in my journeys and returns I shall be sure to acquaint you with; the most wonderful is, that it now rains exceedingly, this has refreshed the prospect,[3] as the way for the most part lies between green fields on either hand, terminated with buildings at some distance, castles, I presume, and of great

[1] *Ovidii Met.*, II. v. 6.

[2] Dr. Roger Long (1680-1770) was Master of Pembroke College during the greater part of Gray's Cambridge career. He was Professor of Astronomy and Geography from 1749 to his death. His personal whimsicalities and vanities are frequently referred to in Gray's Letters.—[*Ed.*] Dr. Long was at this time reading lectures in experimental philosophy.—[*Mason.*]

[3] All that follows is a humorously-hyperbolic description of the quadrangle of Peterhouse.—[*Mason.*]

antiquity. The roads are very good, being, as I suspect, the works of Julius Cæsar's army, for they still preserve, in many places, the appearance of a pavement in pretty good repair, and, if they were not so near home, might perhaps be as much admired as the Via Appia; there are at present several rivulets to be crossed, and which serve to enliven the view all around. The country is exceeding fruitful in ravens and such black cattle; but, not to tire you with my travels, I abruptly conclude. —Yours, etc.

August 1738.

XII.—TO RICHARD WEST.

I AM coming away all so fast, and leaving behind me without the least remorse, all the beauties of Sturbridge Fair. Its white bears may roar, its apes may wring their hands, and crocodiles cry their eyes out, all's one for that; I shall not once visit them, nor so much as take my leave. The university has published a severe edict against schismatical congregations, and created half a dozen new little procterlings to see its orders executed, being under mighty apprehensions lest Henley[1] and his gilt tub should come to the Fair and seduce their young ones; but their pains are to small purpose, for lo, after all, he is not coming.

[1] The Rev. John Henley (1692-1756), known as Orator Henley, a prominent preacher and political lecturer.

I am at this instant in the very agonies of leaving college, and would not wish the worst of my enemies a worse situation. If you knew the dust, the old boxes, the bedsteads, and tutors that are about my ears, you would look upon this letter as a great effort of my resolution and unconcernedness in the midst of evils. I fill up my paper with a loose sort of version of that scene in Pastor Fido that begins, Care selve beati.

September 1738.

XIII.—TO MRS. DOROTHY GRAY.

Amiens, April 1, N. S., 1739.

As we made a very short journey to-day, and came to our inn early, I sit down to give you some account of our expedition. On the 29th (according to the style here) we left Dover at twelve at noon, and with a pretty brisk gale, which pleased everybody mighty well, except myself, who was extremely sick the whole time; we reached Calais by five. The weather changed, and it began to snow hard the minute we got into the harbour, where we took the boat and soon landed. Calais is an exceeding old, but very pretty town, and we hardly saw anything there that was not so new and so different from England, that it surprised us agreeably. We went the next morning to the great Church, and were at high Mass (it being Easter Monday). We saw also the Convents of the Capuchins, and the Nuns of St. Dominic; with these last we held much conversation, especially with an English Nun, a Mrs. Davis, of whose work I sent you by the return of the Pacquet, a letter-case to remember her by. In the afternoon we took a post-chaise (it still snowing very hard) for Boulogne, which was only eighteen miles farther. This chaise is a strange sort of conveyance, of much greater use than beauty, resembling an ill-shaped chariot, only with the door opening before instead of the side; three horses draw it, one between the shafts, and the other two on each side, on one of which the postillion rides, and drives too.[1] This vehicle will, upon occasion, go fourscore miles a-day, but Mr. Walpole, being in no hurry, chooses to make easy journeys of it, and they are easy ones indeed; for the motion is much like that of a sedan, we go about six miles an hour, and commonly change horses at the end of it. It is true they are no very graceful steeds, but they go well, and through roads which they say are bad for France, but to me they seem gravel walks and bowling-greens; in short, it would be the finest travelling in the world were it not for the inns, which are mostly terrible places indeed. But to describe our progress somewhat more regularly, we came into Boulogne when it was almost dark, and went out pretty early on Tuesday morning; so that all I can say about it is, that it is a large, old, fortified town, with more English in it than French.

[1] This was before the introduction of post-chaises here, else it would not have appeared a circumstance worthy notice.—[*Mason.*]

On Tuesday we were to go to Abbéville, seventeen leagues, or fifty-one short English miles; but by the way we dined at Montreuil, much to our hearts' content, on stinking mutton cutlets, addled eggs, and ditch water. Madame the hostess made her appearance in long lappets of bone lace and a sack of linsey-woolsey. We supped and lodged pretty well at Abbeville, and had time to see a little of it before we came out this morning. There are seventeen convents in it, out of which we saw the chapels of Minims and the Carmelite Nuns. We are now come farther thirty miles to Amiens, the chief city of the province of Picardy. We have seen the cathedral, which is just what that of Canterbury must have been before the Reformation. It is about the same size, a huge Gothic building, beset on the outside with thousands of small statues, and within adorned with beautiful painted windows, and a vast number of chapels dressed out in all their finery of altar-pieces, embroidery, gilding, and marble. Over the high altar are preserved, in a very large wrought shrine of massy gold, the relicks of St. Firmin, their patron saint. We went also to the chapels of the Jesuits and Ursuline Nuns, the latter of which is very richly adorned. To-morrow we shall lie at Clermont, and next day reach Paris. The country we have passed through hitherto has been flat, open, but agreeably diversified with villages, fields well-cultivated, and little rivers. On every hillock is a windmill, a crucifix, or a Virgin Mary dressed in flowers, and a sarcenet robe; one sees not many people or carriages on the road; now and then indeed you meet a strolling friar, a countryman with his great muff, or a woman riding astride on a little ass, with short petticoats, and a great head-dress of blue wool. . . .

XIV.—TO RICHARD WEST.

Paris, April 12, 1739.

ENFIN donc me voici à Paris. Mr. Walpole is gone out to supper at Lord Conway's,[1] and here I remain alone, though invited too. Do not think I make a merit of writing to you preferably to a good supper; for these three days we have been here, have actually given me an aversion to eating in general. If hunger be the best sauce to meat, the French are certainly the worst cooks in the world; for what tables we have seen have been so delicately served, and so profusely, that, after rising from one of them, one imagines it impossible ever to eat again. And now, if I tell you all I have in my head, you will believe me mad, mais n'importe, courage, allons! for if I wait till my head grow clear and settle a little, you may stay long enough for a letter. Six days have we been coming hither, which other people do in two; they

[1] Francis Seymour Conway, second Baron Conway (died 1794), Walpole's cousin; he was afterwards created Earl of Hertford. A gentle and admirable person, afterwards sent, as being "a man of the first character and quality," as our Ambassador to Paris.—[*Ed.*]

have not been disagreeable ones; through a fine, open country, admirable roads, and in an easy conveyance; the inns not absolutely intolerable, and images quite unusual presenting themselves on all hands. At Amiens we saw the fine cathedral, and ate paté de perdrix; passed through the park of Chantilly by the Duke of Bourbon's palace, which we only beheld as we passed; broke down at Lusarche; stopt at St. Denis, saw all the beautiful monuments of the Kings of France, and the vast treasures of the abbey, rubies, and emeralds as big as small eggs, crucifixes, and vows, crowns and reliquaries, of inestimable value; but of all their curiosities the thing the most to our tastes, and which they indeed do the justice to esteem the glory of their collection, was a vase of an entire onyx, measuring at least five inches over, three deep, and of great thickness. It is at least two thousand years old, the beauty of the stone and sculpture upon it (representing the mysteries of Bacchus) beyond expression admirable; we have dreamed of it ever since. The jolly old Benedictine, that showed us the treasures, had in his youth been ten years a soldier; he laughed at all the relics, was very full of stories, and mighty obliging. On Saturday evening we got to Paris, and were driving through the streets a long while before we knew where we were. The minute we came, voilà Milors Holdernesse,[1] Conway and his brother; all stayed supper,

[1] Robert d'Arcy, fourth Earl of Holdernesse (died 1778). Mason, in 1754, became his chaplain.

and till two o'clock in the morning, for here nobody ever sleeps; it is not the way. Next day go to dine at my Lord Holdernesse's, there was the Abbé Prevôt,[1] author of the *Cleveland*, and several other pieces much esteemed: the rest were English. At night we went to the Pandore; a spectácle literally, for it is nothing but a beautiful piece of machinery of three scenes. The first represents the chaos, and by degrees the separation of the elements. The second, the temple of Jupiter, the giving of the box to Pandora. The third, the opening of the box, and all the mischiefs that ensued. An absurd design, but executed in the highest perfection, and that in one of the finest theatres in the world; it is the grande sale des machines in the Palais des Tuileries. Next day dined at Lord Waldegrave's; then to the opera. Imagine to yourself for the drama four acts entirely unconnected with each other, each founded on some little history, skilfully taken out of an ancient author, *e.g.* Ovid's *Metamorphoses*, etc., and with great address converted into a French piece of gallantry. For instance, that which I saw, called the *Ballet de la Paix*,[2] had its first act built upon the story of Nireus. Homer

[1] Antoine François Prevôst d'Exiles (1697-1763), the famous writer of romances, who had, at the time of Gray's visit, just published the eighth and last volume of his scandalous *Histoire de M. Cleveland*, begun at Amsterdam in 1732. His masterpiece, the *Manon Lescaut*, dates from 1733.—[*Ed.*]

[2] Produced on the 29th of May 1738, and the most successful ballet of the period. The words were by Roy, the music by Rebel and Francœur.—[*Ed.*]

having said he was the handsomest man of his time, the poet, imagining such a one could not want a mistress, has given him one. These two come in and sing sentiment in lamentable strains, neither air nor recitative; only, to one's great joy, they are every now and then interrupted by a dance, or (to one's great sorrow) by a chorus that borders the stage from one end to the other, and screams, past all power of simile to represent. The second act was Baucis and Philemon. Baucis is a beautiful young shepherdess, and Philemon her swain. Jupiter falls in love with her, but nothing will prevail upon her; so it is all mighty well, and the chorus sing and dance the praises of Constancy. The two other acts were about Iphis and Ianthe, and the judgment of Paris. Imagine, I say, all this transacted by cracked voices, trilling divisions upon two notes and a half, accompanied by an orchestra of humstrums, and a whole house more attentive than if Farinelli[1] sung, and you will almost have formed a just notion of the thing. Our astonishment at their absurdity you can never conceive; we had enough to do to express it by screaming an hour louder than the whole dramatis personæ. We have also seen twice the Comédie Françoise; first, the *Mahomet Second*, a tragedy that has had a great run of late; and the thing itself does not want its beauties, but the actors are beyond measure delightful. Mademoiselle Gaus-

[1] Carlo Broschi, called Farinelli (1705-1782), the greatest sopranist of Europe in the eighteenth century. His successes in England were immortalised by Hogarth's satire.—[*Ed.*]

sin[1] (M. Voltaire's Zara) has with a charming (though little) person the most pathetic tone of voice, the finest expression in her face, and most proper action imaginable. There is also a Dufrêne,[2] who did the chief character, a handsome man and a prodigious fine actor. The second we saw was the *Philosophe Marié*,[3] and here they performed as well in comedy; there is a Mademoiselle Quinault,[4] somewhat in Mrs. Clive's way, and a Monsieur Grandval,[5] in the nature of Wilks, who is the genteelest thing in the world. There are several more would be much admired in England, and many (whom we have not seen) much celebrated here.

[1] Jeanne Catherine Gaussem, called La Gaussin (1711-1767), a very popular actress, who had appeared first in 1731. She was considered the best heroine for heroic plays of that age, and Voltaire wrote for her the parts of Zaïre and Alzire.—[*Ed.*]

[2] Abraham Alexis Quinault-Dufresne (1690-1767), the famous comedian, distinguished alike for his talent, his vanity, and his eccentricity.—[*Ed.*]

[3] A delightful comedy in verse by Néricault Destouches (1680-1754), perhaps the best comic dramatist of that age. It was brought out at the Comédie Française on the 15th of February 1727, and its plot was founded on the poet's own secret marriage with Dorothy Johnston in London, in 1723.—[*Ed.*]

[4] Of the many actresses of this name, this was probably Jeanne Françoise Quinault, called Quinault cadette (1699-1783), sister of the actor Quinault-Dufresne. She was a woman of strong literary proclivities, and after her retirement in 1741 her *salon* became one of the principal centres for the meetings of the Encyclopedists.—[*Ed.*]

[5] Racot de Grandval (1710-1784), son of the dramatist, and himself a famous comedian. He afterwards enjoyed a great success as the author of a series of abominable farces.—[*Ed.*]

Great part of our time is spent in seeing churches and palaces full of fine pictures, etc., the quarter of which is not yet exhausted. For my part, I could entertain myself this month merely with the common streets and the people in them. . . .

XV.—TO RICHARD WEST.

Paris, May 22, 1739.

After the little particulars aforesaid I should have proceeded to a journal of our transactions for this week past, should have carried you post from hence to Versailles, hurried you through the gardens to Trianon, back again to Paris, so away to Chantilly. But the fatigue is perhaps more than you can bear, and moreover I think I have reason to stomach your last piece of gravity. Supposing you were in your soberest mood, I am sorry you should think me capable of ever being so dissipé, so evaporé, as not to be in a condition of relishing anything you could say to me. And now, if you have a mind to make your peace with me, arouse ye from your megrims and your melancholies, and (for exercise is good for you) throw away your night-cap, call for your jack-boots, and set out with me, last Saturday evening, for Versailles—and so at eight o'clock, passing through a road speckled with vines, and villas, and hares, and partridges, we arrive at the great avenue, flanked on either hand with a double row of trees about half a mile long, and with the palace itself to terminate the view; facing which, on each side of you is placed a semicircle of very handsome buildings, which form the stables. These we will not enter into, because you know we are no jockeys. Well! and is this the great front of Versailles? What a huge heap of littleness! it is composed, as it were, of three courts, all open to the eye at once, and gradually diminishing till you come to the royal apartments, which on this side present but half a dozen windows and a balcony. This last is all that can be called a front, for the rest is only great wings. The hue of all this mass is black, dirty red, and yellow; the first proceeding from stone changed by age; the second, from a mixture of brick; and the last, from a profusion of tarnished gilding. You cannot see a more disagreeable tout-ensemble; and, to finish the matter, it is all stuck over in many places with small busts of a tawny hue between every two windows. We pass through this to go into the garden,[1] and here the case is indeed altered; nothing can be vaster and more magnificent than the back front; before it a very spacious terrace spreads itself, adorned with two large basons; these are bordered and lined (as most of the others) with white marble, with handsome statues of bronze reclined on their edges. From hence you descend a huge flight of steps into a semi-

1 "The garden is littered with statues and fountains, each of which has its tutelary deity. In particular, the elementary god of fire solaces himself in one. In another, Enceladus, in lieu of a mountain, is overwhelmed with many waters. . . . In short, 'tis a garden for a great child."—[*Walpole to West.*]

circle formed by woods, that are cut all around into niches, which are filled with beautiful copies of all the famous antique statues in white marble. Just in the midst is the bason of Latona; she and her children are standing on the top of a rock in the middle, on the sides of which are the peasants, some half, some totally changed into frogs, all which throw out water at her in great plenty. From this place runs on the great alley, which brings you into a complete round, where is the bason of Apollo, the biggest in the gardens. He is rising in his car out of the water, surrounded by nymphs and tritons, all in bronze, and finely executed, and these, as they play, raise a perfect storm about him; beyond this is the great canal, a prodigious long piece of water, that terminates the whole: all this you have at one coup d'œil in entering the garden, which is truly great. I cannot say as much of the general taste of the place: everything you behold savours too much of art; all is forced, all is constrained about you; statues and vases sowed everywhere without distinction; sugar loaves and minced pies of yew; scrawl work of box, and little squirting jets-d'eau, besides a great sameness in the walks, cannot help striking one at first sight, not to mention the silliest of labyrinths, and all Æsop's fables in water; since these were designed in usum Delphini only. Here then we walk by moonlight, and hear the ladies and the nightingales sing. Next morning, being Whitsunday, make ready to go to the Installation of nine Knights du Saint

Esprit, Cambis[1] is one: high mass celebrated with music, great crowd, much incense, King, Queen, Dauphin, Mesdames, Cardinals, and Court: Knights arrayed by his Majesty; reverences before the altar, not bows but curtsies; stiff hams: much tittering among the ladies; trumpets, kettle-drums, and fifes. My dear West, I am vastly delighted with Trianon, all of us with Chantilly; if you would know why, you must have patience, for I can hold my pen no longer, except to tell you that I saw *Britannicus* last night; all the characters, particularly Agrippina and Nero, done to perfection; to-morrow Phædra and Hippolitus. We are making you a little bundle of petites pieces; there is nothing in them, but they are acting at present; there are too Crebillon's *Letters*,[2] and *Amusemens sur le langage des Bêtes*, said[3] to be of one Bougeant, a Jesuit; they are both esteemed, and lately come out. This day se'nnight we go to Rheims.

1 The Marquis de Cambis-Velleron (1706-1772), the Pope's Lieutenant-General in France, equally famous as a brilliant soldier and as a fanatical collector of illuminated MSS. and rare first editions. Gray mentions him, no doubt, because he had just returned from an embassy in England.—[*Ed.*]

2 Evidently the *Lettres de la Marquise M*** au Comte de R****, of Crébillon *fils*. It is odd to find Gray speaking of this book, published in 1732, as new; he had probably just met with the second edition, published in 1738.—[*Ed.*]

3 The conjecture was right. *L'Amusement philosophique sur le langage des Bêtes*, which had then just appeared, was the work of the Jesuit scribbler Guillaume Hyacinthe Bougeant (1690-1743), who was banished to La Flèche for writing it, almost immediately after Gray left Paris.—[*Ed.*]

XVI.—TO MRS. DOROTHY GRAY.

Rheims, June 21, N. S., 1739.

WE have now been settled almost three weeks in this city, which is more considerable upon account of its size and antiquity, than from the number of its inhabitants, or any advantages of commerce. There is little in it worth a stranger's curiosity, besides the cathedral church, which is a vast Gothic building of a surprising beauty and lightness, all covered over with a profusion of little statues, and other ornaments. It is here the Kings of France are crowned by the Archbishop of Rheims, who is the first Peer, and the Primate of the kingdom. The holy vessel made use of on that occasion, which contains the oil, is kept in the church of St. Nicasius [1] hard by, and is believed to have been brought by an angel from heaven at the coronation of Clovis, the first Christian king. The streets in general have but a melancholy aspect, the houses all old; the public walks run along the side of a great moat under the ramparts, where one hears a continual croaking of frogs; the country round about is one great plain covered with vines, which at this time of the year afford no very pleasing prospect, as being not above a foot high. What pleasures the

[1] The church of St. Nicaise, a masterpiece of the thirteenth century, was destroyed at the Revolution. The *trésor* here described by Gray was saved, and is now preserved in the Cathedral, in the chapel of St. Jean. The holy vessel mentioned here is the so-called Chalice of St. Remi, a fine example of Byzantine enamel on gold.—[*Ed.*]

place denies to the sight, it makes up to the palate; since you have nothing to drink but the best champaigne in the world, and all sorts of provisions equally good. As to other pleasures, there is not that freedom of conversation among the people of fashion here, that one sees in other parts of France; for though they are not very numerous in this place, and consequently must live a good deal together, yet they never come to any great familiarity with one another. As my Lord Conway had spent a good part of his time among them, his brother, and we with him, were soon introduced into all their assemblies. As soon as you enter, the lady of the house presents each of you a card, and offers you a party at quadrille; you sit down, and play forty deals without intermission, excepting one quarter of an hour, when everybody rises to eat of what they call the gouter, which supplies the place of our tea, and is a service of wine, fruits, cream, sweetmeats, crawfish and cheese. People take what they like, and sit down again to play; after that, they make little parties to go to the walks together, and then all the company retire to their separate habitations. Very seldom any suppers or dinners are given; and this is the manner they live among one another; not so much out of any aversion they have to pleasure, as out of a sort of formality they have contracted by not being much frequented by people who have lived at Paris. It is sure they do not hate gaiety any more than the rest of their country-people, and can enter into diversions, that are once proposed, with a good grace enough: for instance, the other evening we happened to be got together in a company of eighteen people, men and women of the best fashion here, at a garden in the town to walk; when one of the ladies bethought herself of asking, Why should not we sup here? Immediately the cloth was laid by the side of a fountain under the trees, and a very elegant supper served up; after which another said, Come, let us sing; and directly began herself. From singing we insensibly fell to dancing, and singing in a round; when somebody mentioned the violins, and immediately a company of them was ordered. Minuets were begun in the open air, and then came country-dances, which held till four o'clock next morning; at which hour the gayest lady there proposed, that such as were weary should get into their coaches, and the rest of them should dance before them with the music in the van; and in this manner we paraded through all the principal streets of the city, and waked everybody in it. Mr. Walpole had a mind to make a custom of the thing, and would have given a ball in the same manner next week; but the women did not come into it; so I believe it will drop, and they will return to their dull cards, and usual formalities. We are not to stay above a month longer here, and shall then go to Dijon, the chief city of Burgundy, a very splendid and very gay town; at least such is the present design.

XVII.—TO PHILIP GRAY.

Dijon, Friday, September 11, N. S., 1739.

We have made three short days' journey of it from Rheims hither, where we arrived the night before last. The road we have passed through has been extremely agreeable; it runs through the most fertile part of Champaigne by the side of the river Marne, with a chain of hills on each hand at some distance, entirely covered with woods and vineyards, and every now and then the ruins of some old castle on their tops. We lay at St. Dizier the first night, and at Langres the second, and got hither the next evening time enough to have a full view of this city in entering it. It lies in a very extensive plain covered with vines and corn, and consequently is plentifully supplied with both. I need not tell you that it is the chief city of Burgundy, nor that it is of great antiquity; considering which one should imagine it ought to be larger than one finds it. However, what it wants in extent is made up in beauty and cleanliness, and in rich convents and churches, most of which we have seen. The palace of the States is a magnificent new building, where the Duke of Bourbon is lodged when he comes every three years to hold that assembly, as governor of the Province. A quarter of a mile out of the town is a famous Abbey of Carthusians, which we are just returned from seeing. In their chapel are the tombs of the ancient Dukes of Burgundy, that were so powerful, till at the death of Charles the

Bold, the last of them, this part of his dominions was united by Lewis XI. to the crown of France. To-morrow we are to pay a visit to the Abbot of the Cistercians, who lives a few leagues off, and who uses to receive all strangers with great civility; his Abbey is one of the richest in the kingdom; he keeps open house always, and lives with great magnificence. We have seen enough of this town already to make us regret the time we spent at Rheims; it is full of people of condition, who seem to form a much more agreeable society than we found in Champaigne; but as we shall stay here but two or three days longer, it is not worth while to be introduced into their houses. On Monday or Tuesday we are to set out for Lyons, which is two days' journey distant, and from thence you shall hear again from me.

XVIII.—TO RICHARD WEST.

Lyons, September 18, N. S., 1739.

SCAVEZ vous bien, mon cher ami, que je vous hais, que je vous deteste? voila des termes un peu forts; and that will save me, upon a just computation, a page of paper and six drops of ink; which, if I confined myself to reproaches of a more moderate nature, I should be obliged to employ in using you according to your deserts. What! to let anybody reside three months at Rheims, and write but once to them? Please to consult *Tully de Amicit.* page 5, line 25, and you will find it said in express terms, "Ad amicum inter Remos relegatum mense uno quinquies scriptum esto;" nothing more plain or less liable to false interpretations. Now because, I suppose, it will give you pain to know we are in being, I take this opportunity to tell you that we are at the ancient and celebrated Lugdunum, a city situated upon the confluence of the Rhône and Saône (Arar, I should say) two people, who though of tempers extremely unlike, think fit to join hands here, and make a little party to travel to the Mediterranean in company; the lady comes gliding along through the fruitful plains of Burgundy, incredibili lenitate, ita ut oculis in utram partem fluit judicari non possit; the gentleman runs all rough and roaring down from the mountains of Switzerland to meet her; and with all her soft airs she likes him never the worse. She goes through the middle of the city in state, and he passes incog. without the walls, but waits for her a little below. The houses here are so high, and the streets so narrow, as would be sufficient to render Lyons the dismalest place in the world, but the number of people, and the face of commerce diffused about it, are, at least, as sufficient to make it the liveliest. Between these two sufficiencies, you will be in doubt what to think of it; so we shall leave the city and proceed to its environs, which are beautiful beyond expression. It is surrounded with mountains, and those mountains all bedropped and bespeckled with houses, gardens, and plantations of the rich Bourgeois, who have from thence a prospect of the city in the vale below on the one hand, on the other the rich plains of the Lyonnois, with the rivers winding among them, and the Alps, with the mountains of Dauphiné, to bound the view. All yesterday morning we were busied in climbing up Mount Fourvière, where the ancient city stood perched at such a height, that nothing but the hopes of gain could certainly ever persuade their neighbours to pay them a visit. Here are the ruins of the Emperors' palaces, that resided here, that is to say, Augustus and Severus; they consist in nothing but great masses of old wall, that have only their quality to make them respected. In a vineyard of the Minims are remains of a theatre: the Fathers, whom they belong to, hold them in no esteem at all, and would have showed us their sacristy and chapel instead of them. The Ursuline Nuns have in their garden some Roman baths, but we having the misfortune to be men, and heretics, they did not think proper to admit us. Hard by are eight arches of a most magnificent aqueduct, said to be erected by Antony, when his legions were quartered here. There are many other parts of it dispersed up and down the country, for it brought the water from a river many leagues off in La Forez. Here are remains too of Agrippa's seven great roads which met at Lyons; in some places they lie twelve feet deep in the ground. In short, a thousand matters that you shall not know, till you give me a description of the Païs de Tombridge, and the effect its waters have upon you.

XIX.—TO MRS. DOROTHY GRAY.

Lyons, October 13, N. S., 1739.

It is now almost five weeks since I left Dijon, one of the gayest and most agreeable little cities of France, for Lyons, its reverse in all these particulars. It is the second in the kingdom in bigness and rank, the streets excessively narrow and nasty; the houses immensely high and large (that, for instance, where we are lodged, has twenty-five rooms on a floor, and that for five stories); it swarms with inhabitants like Paris itself, but chiefly a mercantile people, too much given up to commerce to think of their own, much less of a stranger's diversions. We have no acquaintance in the town, but such English as happen to be passing through here, on their way to Italy and the south, which at present happen to be near thirty in number. It is a fortnight since we set out from hence upon a little excursion to Geneva. We took the longest road, which lies through Savoy, on purpose to see a famous monastery, called the grand Chartreuse, and had no reason to think our time lost. After having travelled seven days very slow (for we did not change horses, it being impossible for a chaise to go post in these roads) we arrived at a little village, among the mountains of Savoy, called Échelles; from thence we proceeded on horses, who are used to the way, to the mountain of the Chartreuse. It is six miles to the top; the road runs winding up it, commonly not six feet broad; on one hand is the rock, with woods of pine-trees[1] hanging overhead; on the other, a monstrous precipice, almost perpendicular, at the bottom of which rolls a torrent, that sometimes tumbling among the fragments of stone that have fallen from on high, and sometimes precipitating itself down vast descents with a noise like thunder, which is still made greater by the echo from the mountains on each side, concurs to form one of the most solemn, the most romantic, and the most astonishing scenes I ever beheld: add to this the strange views made by the craggs and cliffs on the other hand; the cascades that in many places throw themselves from the very summit down into the vale, and the river below; and many other particulars impossible to describe; you will conclude we had no occasion to repent our pains. This place St. Bruno[2] chose to retire to, and upon its very top founded the aforesaid convent, which is the superior of the whole order. When we came there, the two fathers, who are commissioned to entertain strangers (for the rest must neither speak one to another, nor to any one else), received us very kindly; and set before us a repast of dried fish, eggs, butter and fruits, all excellent in their kind, and extremely neat. They pressed us to spend the night there, and to stay some days with them; but this we could not do, so they led us about their house, which is, you must think,

[1] Not *pine-trees*, but beech and firs.—[*Mit.*]

[2] St. Bruno (1030?-1101) founded "the aforesaid convent" about 1086.—[*Ed.*]

like a little city; for there are 100 fathers, besides 300 servants, that make their clothes, grind their corn, press their wine, and do everything among themselves: the whole is quite orderly and simple; nothing of finery, but the wonderful decency, and the strange situation, more than supply the place of it. In the evening we descended by the same way, passing through many clouds that were then forming themselves on the mountain's side. Next day we continued our journey by Chamberry, which, though the chief city of the duchy, and residence of the King of Sardinia, when he comes into this part of his dominions, makes but a very mean and insignificant appearance; we lay at Aix, once famous for its hot baths, and the next night at Annecy; the day after, by noon, we got to Geneva. I have not time to say anything about it, nor of our solitary journey back again. . . .

XX.—TO PHILIP GRAY.

Lyons, October 25, N. S., 1739.

In my last I gave you the particulars of our little journey to Geneva: I have only to add that we stayed about a week, in order to see Mr. Conway settled there: I do not wonder so many English choose it for their residence; the city is very small, neat, prettily built, and extremely populous; the Rhône runs through the middle of it, and it is surrounded with new fortifications, that give it a military compact air; which, joined to the happy, lively countenances of the inhabitants, and an exact discipline always as strictly observed as in time of war, makes the little republic appear a match for a much greater power; though perhaps Geneva, and all that belongs to it, are not of equal extent with Windsor and its two parks. To one that has passed through Savoy, as we did, nothing can be more striking than the contrast, as soon as he approaches the town. Near the gates of Geneva runs the torrent Arve, which separates it from the King of Sardinia's dominions; on the other side of it lies a country naturally, indeed, fine and fertile; but you meet with nothing in it but meagre, ragged, bare-footed peasants, with their children, in extreme misery and nastiness; and even of these no great numbers. You no sooner have crossed the stream I have mentioned, but poverty is no more; not a beggar, hardly a discontented face to be seen; numerous and well-dressed people swarming on the ramparts; drums beating, soldiers, well clothed and armed, exercising; and folks, with business in their looks, hurrying to and fro; all contribute to make any person, who is not blind, sensible what a difference there is between the two governments, that are the causes of one view and the other. The beautiful lake, at one end of which the town is situated; its extent; the several states that border upon it; and all its pleasures, are too well known for me to mention them. We sailed upon it as far as the dominions of Geneva extend, that is, about two leagues and a half on each side; and landed at several of the little houses of pleasure, that the inhabitants have built all about it, who received us with much politeness. The same night we ate part of a trout, taken in the lake, that weighed thirty-seven pounds; as great a monster as it appeared to us, it was esteemed there nothing extraordinary, and they assured us, it was not uncommon to catch them of fifty pounds; they are dressed here and sent post to Paris upon some great occasions; nay, even to Madrid, as we were told. The road we returned through was not the same we came by. We crossed the Rhône at Seyssel, and passed for three days among the mountains of Bugey, without meeting with anything new: at last we came out into the plains of La Bresse, and so to Lyons again. Sir Robert has written to Mr. Walpole, to desire he would go to Italy; which he has resolved to do; so that all the scheme of spending the winter in the south of France is laid aside, and we are to pass it in a much finer country. You may imagine I am not sorry to have this opportunity of seeing the place in the world that best deserves it. Besides as the Pope (who is eighty-eight, and has been lately at the point of death) cannot probably last a great while, perhaps we may have the fortune to be present at the election of a new one, when Rome will be in all its glory. Friday next we certainly begin our journey; in two days we shall come to the foot of the Alps, and six more we shall be in passing them. Even here the winter is begun; what then must it be among those vast snowy mountains where it is hardly ever summer? We are, however, as well armed as possible against the cold, with muffs, hoods, and masks of beaver, fur-boots, and bear skins. When we arrive at Turin, we shall rest after the fatigues of the journey. . . .

XXI.—TO MRS. DOROTHY GRAY.

Turin, November 7, N. S., 1739.

I AM this night arrived here, and have just set down to rest me after eight days' tiresome journey. For the three first we had the same road we before passed through to go to Geneva; the fourth we turned out of it, and for that day and the next travelled rather among than upon the Alps; the way commonly running through a deep valley by the side of the river Arve, which works itself a passage, with great difficulty and a mighty noise, among vast quantities of rocks, that have rolled down from the mountain-tops. The winter was so far advanced, as in great measure to spoil the beauty of the prospect; however, there was still somewhat fine remaining amidst the savageness and horror of the place: the sixth we began to go up several of these mountains; and as we were passing one, met with an odd accident enough: Mr. Walpole had a little fat black spaniel,[1] that he was very fond of,

[1] "It was called 'Tory,' an odd name enough for a dog of his."—[*MS. note by Bennet, Bishop of Cloyne.*]

which he sometimes used to set down, and let it run by the chaise side. We were at that time in a very rough road, not two yards broad at most; on one side was a great wood of pines, and on the other a vast precipice; it was noonday, and the sun shone bright, when all of a sudden, from the wood-side (which was as steep upwards as the other part was downwards), out rushed a great wolf, came close to the head of the horses, seized the dog by the throat, and rushed up the hill again with him in his mouth. This was done in less than a quarter of a minute; we all saw it, and yet the servants had not time to draw their pistols, or do anything to save the dog.[1] If he had not been there, and the creature had thought fit to lay hold of one of the horses; chaise, and we, and all must inevitably have tumbled above fifty fathoms perpendicular down the precipice. The seventh we came to Lanebourg,[2] the last town in Savoy; it lies at the foot of the famous Mount Cenis, which is so situated as to allow no room for any way but over the very top of it. Here the chaise was forced to be pulled to pieces, and the baggage and that to be carried by mules. We ourselves were wrapped up in our furs, and seated upon a sort of matted chair without legs, which is carried upon poles in the manner of a bier, and so begun to

[1] This odd incident might have afforded Mr. Gray a subject for an ode, which would have been a good companion to that on the death of a favourite cat.—[*Mason.*]

[2] Lanslebourg.—[*Ed.*]

ascend by the help of eight men. It was six miles to the top, where a plain opens itself about as many more in breadth, covered perpetually with very deep snow, and in the midst of that a great lake of unfathomable depth, from whence a river takes its rise, and tumbles over monstrous rocks quite down the other side of the mountain. The descent is six miles more, but infinitely more steep than the going up; and here the men perfectly fly down with you, stepping from stone to stone with incredible swiftness in places where none but they could go three paces without falling. The immensity of the precipices, the roaring of the river and torrents that run into it, the huge craggs covered with ice and snow, and the clouds below you and about you, are objects it is impossible to conceive without seeing them; and though we had heard many strange descriptions of the scene, none of them at all came up to it. We were but five hours in performing the whole, from which you may judge of the rapidity of the men's motion. We are now got into Piedmont, and stopped a little while at La Ferriere, a small village about three-quarters of the way down, but still among the clouds, where we began to hear a new language spoken round about us; at last we got quite down, went through the Pas de Suse, a narrow road among the Alps, defended by two fortresses, and lay at Bussoleno. Next evening through a fine avenue of nine miles in length, as straight as a line, we arrived at this city, which, as you know, is the capital of the Principality, and the residence of the King of Sardinia. . . .[1] We shall stay here, I believe, a fortnight, and proceed for Genoa, which is three or four days' journey to go post.—I am, etc.

XXII.—TO RICHARD WEST.

Turin, November 16, N. S., 1739.

After eight days' journey through Greenland, we arrived at Turin. You approach it by a handsome avenue of nine miles long, and quite straight. The entrance is guarded by certain vigilant dragons, called Douâniers, who mumbled us for some time. The city is not large, as being a place of strength, and consequently confined within its fortifications; it has many beauties and some faults; among the first are streets all laid out by the line, regular uniform buildings, fine walks that surround the whole, and in general a good lively clean appearance: but the houses are of brick plastered, which is apt to want repairing; the windows of oiled paper, which is apt to be torn; and everything very slight, which is apt to tumble down. There is an excellent Opera, but it is only in the Carnival: Balls every night, but only in the Carnival: Masquerades too, but only

[1] That part of the letter here omitted, contained only a description of the city; which, as Mr. Gray has given it to Mr. West in the following letter, and that in a more lively manner, I thought it unnecessary to insert: a liberty I have taken in other parts of this correspondence in order to avoid repetitions.—[*Mason.*]

in the Carnival. This Carnival lasts only from Christmas to Lent; one-half of the remaining part of the year is passed in remembering the last, the other in expecting the future Carnival. We cannot well subsist upon such slender diet, no more than upon an execrable Italian Comedy, and a Puppet-Show,[1] called *Rappresentazione d'un' anima dannata*, which, I think, are all the present diversions of the place; except the Marquise de Cavaillac's Conversazione, where one goes to see people play at Ombre and Taroc,[2] a game with 72 cards all painted with suns, and moons, and devils and monks. Mr. Walpole has been at court; the family are at present at a country palace, called La Venerie. The palace here in town is the very quintessence of gilding and looking-glass; inlaid floors, carved pannels, and painting, wherever they could stick a brush. I own I have not, as yet, anywhere met with those grand and simple works of Art, that are to amaze one, and whose sight one is

[1] Spence was at Turin a month later, and saw the same Puppet-Show. He thus describes it to his mother: "In spite of the excellence of the actors, the greatest part of the entertainment to me was the countenances of the people in the pit and boxes. When the devils were like to carry off the damned soul, everybody was in the utmost consternation; and when St. John spoke so obligingly to her, they were ready to cry out for joy. When the Virgin appeared on the stage, everybody looked respectful; and on several words spoke by the actors, they pulled off their hats and crossed themselves. What can you think of a people, when their very farces are religious, and when they are so religiously received?" December 2, 1739.—[*Ed.*]

[2] *Tarocco*, a game also called *minchiate*, and still in vogue. —[*Ed.*]

to be the better for: but those of Nature have astonished me beyond expression. In our little journey up to the Grande Chartreuse, I do not remember to have gone ten paces without an exclamation, that there was no restraining. Not a precipice, not a torrent, not a cliff, but is pregnant with religion and poetry. There are certain scenes that would awe an atheist into belief, without the help of other argument. One need not have a very fantastic imagination to see spirits there at noonday; you have Death perpetually before your eyes, only so far removed, as to compose the mind without frighting it. I am well persuaded St. Bruno was a man of no common genius, to choose such a situation for his retirement; and perhaps should have been a disciple of his, had I been born in his time. You may believe Abelard and Heloïse were not forgot upon this occasion. If I do not mistake, I saw you too every now and then at a distance along the trees; il me semble, que j'ai vu ce chien de visage[1] là quelque part. You seemed to call to me from the other side of the precipice, but the noise of the river below was so great, that I really could not distinguish what you said; it seemed to have a cadence like verse. In your next you will be so good to let me know what it was. The week we have since passed among the Alps, has not equalled the single day upon that mountain, because the winter

[1] Mr. West, with whom I was much acquainted when a schoolboy, and never saw after, was a most worthy character, tall and slim, of a pale and meagre look and complexion, and promised not half what he performed.—[*Cole.*]

was rather too far advanced, and the weather a little foggy. However, it did not want its beauties; the savage rudeness of the view is inconceivable without seeing it: I reckoned in one day, thirteen cascades, the least of which was, I dare say, one hundred feet in height. I had Livy in the chaise with me, and beheld his "Nives cœlo propè immistæ, tecta informia imposita rupibus, pecora jumentaque torrida frigore, homines intonsi & inculti, animalia inanimaque omnia rigentia gelu; omnia, confragosa, præruptaque." The creatures that inhabit them are, in all respects, below humanity; and most of them, especially women, have the tumidum guttur, which they call goscia.[1] Mont Cenis, I confess, carries the permission[2] mountains have of being frightful rather too far; and its horrors were accompanied with too much danger to give one time to reflect upon their beauties. There is a family of the Alpine monsters I have mentioned, upon its very top, that in the middle of winter calmly lay in their stock of provisions and firing, and so are buried in their hut for a month or two under the snow. When we were down it, and got a little way into Piedmont, we began to find "Apricos quosdam colles, rivosque prope sylvas, & jam humano cultu digniora loca." I read Silius Italicus too, for the first time; and wished for you according to custom. We set out for Genoa in two days' time.

[1] Or rather, *il gozzo*.—[*Ed.*]

[2] A phrase borrowed from Madame de Sevigné, who quotes a *bon mot* on Pelisson, qu'il abusoit de la permission qu'ont les hommes, d'être laids.—[*Mason.*]

XXIII.—TO RICHARD WEST.

Genoa, November 21, 1739.

Horridos tractus, Boreæque linquens
Regna Taurini fera, molliorem
Advehor brumam, Genuæque amantes
Litora soles.

At least if they do not, they have a very ill taste: for I never beheld anything more amiable. Only figure to yourself a vast semicircular basin, full of fine blue sea, and vessels of all sorts and sizes, some sailing out, some coming in, and others at anchor; and all round it palaces, and churches peeping over one another's heads, gardens, and marble terraces full of orange and cypress trees, fountains, and trellis-works covered with vines, which altogether compose the grandest of theatres. This is the first coup d'œil, and is almost all I am yet able to give you an account of, for we arrived late last night. To-day was, luckily, a great festival, and in the morning we resorted to the church of the Madonna delle Vigne, to put up our little orisons (I believe I forgot to tell you, that we have been some time converts to the holy Catholic church); we found our Lady richly dressed out, with a crown of diamonds on her own head, another upon the child's, and a constellation of wax lights burning before them: shortly after came the Doge, in his robes of crimson damask, and a cap of the same, followed by the Senate in black. Upon his approach began a fine concert of music, and among the rest two eunuchs' voices, that were a perfect feast to ears that had heard nothing but French operas for a year. We listened to this, and breathed nothing but incense for two hours. The Doge is a very tall, lean, stately, old figure, called Constantino Balbi; and the Senate seem to have been made upon the same model. They said their prayers, and heard an absurd white friar preach, with equal devotion. After this we went to the Annonciata, a church built by the family Lomellini, and belonging to it; which is, indeed, a most stately structure, the inside wholly marble of various kinds, except where gold and painting take its place. From hence to the Palazzo Doria. I should make you sick of marble, if I told you how it was lavished here upon the porticoes, the balustrades, and terraces, the lowest of which extends quite to the sea. The inside is by no means answerable to the outward magnificence; the furniture seems to be as old as the founder of the family.[1] There great embossed silver tables tell you, in bas-relief, his victories at sea; how he entertained the Emperor Charles, and how he refused the sovereignty of the Commonwealth when it was offered him; the rest is old-fashioned velvet chairs, and Gothic tapestry. The rest of the day has been spent, much to our hearts' content, in cursing French music and architecture, and in singing the praises of Italy. We find this place so very fine, that we are in fear of finding nothing finer. We are fallen in love with the

[1] The famous Andrea Doria.

Mediterranean Sea, and hold your lakes and your rivers in vast contempt. This is

> "The happy country where huge lemons grow," [1]

as Waller says; and I am sorry to think of leaving it in a week for Parma, although it be

> The happy country where huge cheeses grow.

XXIV.—TO MRS. DOROTHY GRAY.

Bologna, December 9, N. S., 1739.

OUR journey hither has taken up much less time than I expected. We left Genoa (a charming place, and one that deserved a longer stay) the week before last; crossed the mountains, and lay that night at Tortona, the next at St. Giovanni, and the morning after came to Piacenza. That city (though the capital of a Duchy) made so frippery an appearance, that instead of spending some days there, as had been intended, we only dined, and went on to Parma; stayed there all the following day, which was passed in visiting the famous works of Correggio in the Dome, and other churches. The fine gallery of pictures, that once belonged to the Dukes of Parma, is no more here; the King of Naples has carried it all thither, and the city had not merit enough to detain us any longer, so we proceeded through Reggio to

[1] This line occurs in the first canto of *The Battle of the Summer Islands.* To be precise, what Waller says is:

> "That happy Island where huge Lemons grow."

[*Ed.*]

Modena; this, though the residence of its Duke, is an ill-built melancholy place, all of brick, as are most of the towns in this part of Lombardy: he himself lives in a private manner, with very little appearance of a court about him; he has one of the noblest collections of paintings in the world, which entertained us extremely well the rest of that day and a part of the next; and in the afternoon we came to Bologna. So now you may wish us joy of being in the dominions of his Holiness. This is a populous city, and of great extent. All the streets have porticoes on both sides, such as surround a part of Covent Garden, a great relief in summer-time in such a climate; and from one of the principal gates to a church of the Virgin (where is a wonder-working picture, at three miles distance), runs a corridore of the same sort, lately finished, and indeed a most extraordinary performance. The churches here are more remarkable for their paintings than architecture, being mostly old structures of brick; but the palaces are numerous, and fine enough to supply us with somewhat worth seeing from morning till night. The country of Lombardy, hitherto, is one of the most beautiful imaginable; the roads broad, and exactly straight, and on either hand vast plantations of trees, chiefly mulberries and olives, and not a tree without a vine twining about it and spreading among its branches. This scene, indeed, which must be the most lovely in the world during the proper season, is at present all deformed by the winter, which here is rigorous enough for the time it lasts; but one still sees the skeleton of a charming place, and reaps the benefit of its product, for the fruits and provisions are admirable; in short, you find everything that luxury can desire in perfection. We have now been here a week, and shall stay some little time longer. We are at the foot of the Appennine mountains; it will take up three days to cross them, and then we shall come to Florence, where we shall pass the Christmas. Till then we must remain in a state of ignorance as to what is doing in England, for our letters are to meet us there. If I do not find four or five from you alone, I shall wonder.

XXV.—TO MRS. DOROTHY GRAY.

Florence, December 19, N. S., 1739.

We spent twelve days at Bologna, chiefly (as most travellers do) in seeing sights; for as we knew no mortal there, and as it is no easy matter to get admission into any Italian house, without very particular recommendations, we could see no company but in public places; and there are none in that city but the churches. We saw, therefore, churches, palaces, and pictures from morning to night; and the 15th of this month set out for Florence, and began to cross the Appennine mountains; we travelled among and upon them all that day, and, as it was but indifferent weather, were commonly in the middle of thick clouds, that utterly deprived us of a sight of their beauties. For this vast chain of hills has its beauties, and all the valleys are cultivated; even the mountains themselves are many of them so within a little of their very tops. They are not so horrid as the Alps, though pretty near as high; and the whole road is admirably well kept, and paved throughout, which is a length of fourscore miles and more. We left the Pope's dominions, and lay that night in those of the Grand Duke at Fiorenzuolo, a paltry little town at the foot of Mount Giogo, which is the highest of them all. Next morning we went up it; the post-house is upon its very top, and usually involved in clouds, or half-buried in the snow. Indeed there was none of the last at the time we were there, but it was still a dismal habitation. The descent is most excessively steep, and the turnings very short and frequent; however, we performed it without any danger, and in coming down could dimly discover Florence, and the beautiful plain about it, through the mists, but enough to convince us, it must be one of the noblest prospects upon earth in summer. That afternoon we got thither; and Mr. Mann,[1] the resident, had sent his servant to meet us at the gates, and conduct us to his house. He is the best and most obliging person in the world. The next night we were introduced at the Prince of Craon's assembly (he has the chief power here in the Grand Duke's absence). The princess, and he, were extremely civil to the name of Walpole, so we were asked to stay

[1] Afterwards Sir Horace Mann, and Envoy Extraordinary at the same Court.

supper, which is as much as to say, you may come and sup here whenever you please; for after the first invitation this is always understood. We have also been at the Countess Suarez's, a favourite of the late Duke, and one that gives the first movement to everything gay that is going forward here. The news is every day expected from Vienna of the Great Duchess's delivery; if it be a boy, here will be all sorts of balls, masquerades, operas, and illuminations; if not, we must wait for the Carnival, when all those things come of course. In the meantime it is impossible to want entertainment, the famous gallery, alone, is an amusement for months; we commonly pass two or three hours every morning in it, and one has perfect leisure to consider all its beauties. You know it contains many hundred antique statues, such as the whole world cannot match, besides the vast collection of paintings, medals, and precious stones, such as no other prince was ever master of; in short, all that the rich and powerful house of Medicis has in so many years got together.[1] And besides this city abounds with so many palaces and churches, that you can hardly place yourself anywhere without having some fine one in view, or at least some statue or fountain, magnificently adorned; these undoubtedly are far more numerous than Genoa can pretend to;

[1] He catalogued and made occasional short remarks on the pictures, etc., which he saw here, as well as at other places, many of which are in my possession, but it would have swelled this work too much if I had inserted them.—[*Mason.*] They were afterwards, in 1843, printed by Mitford.—[*Ed.*]

yet, in its general appearance, I cannot think that Florence equals it in beauty. Mr. Walpole is just come from being presented to the Electress Palatine Dowager; she is a sister of the late Great Duke's; a stately old lady, that never goes out but to church, and then she has guards, and eight horses to her coach. She received him with much ceremony, standing under a huge black canopy, and, after a few minutes talking, she assured him of her goodwill, and dismissed him. She never sees anybody but thus in form; and so she passes her life, poor woman! . . .

XXVI.—TO RICHARD WEST.

Florence, January 15, 1740.

I THINK I have not yet told you how we left that charming place Genoa: how we crossed a mountain of green marble, called Buchetto: how we came to Tortona, and waded through the mud to come to Castel St. Giovanni, and there ate mustard and sugar with a dish of crows' gizzards. Secondly, how we passed the famous plains; "Quâ Trebie,"[1] etc. Nor, thirdly, how we passed through Piacenza, Parma, Modena, entered the territories of the Pope; stayed twelve days at Bologna; crossed the Appennines, and afterwards arrived at Florence. None of these things have I told you, nor do I intend to tell you,

[1] Here follow the verses beginning "Qua Trebie glaucas," etc. etc.—[*Ed.*]

till you ask me some questions concerning them. No not even of Florence itself, except that it is as fine as possible, and has everything in it that can bless the eyes. But, before I enter into particulars, you must make your peace both with me and the Venus de Medicis, who, let me tell you, is highly and justly offended at you for not inquiring, long before this, concerning her symmetry and proportions.[1] . . .

XXVII.—TO THOMAS WHARTON.

Proposals for Printing by Subscription, in

THIS LARGE

LETTER,

THE TRAVELS OF T. G. GENT.

WHICH WILL CONSIST OF THE FOLLOWING PARTICULARS.

CHAP. I.

THE Author arrives at Dover; his conversation with the Mayor of that Corporation. Sets out in the pacquet-boat, grows very sick; the Author spews, a very minute account of all the circumstances thereof: his arrival at Calais; how the inhabitants of that country speak French, and are said to be all Papishes; the Author's reflections thereupon.

[1] West responded by sending a graceful little elegy in the manner of Tibullus, in which he acknowledged how justly "irata nobis est Medicæa Venus," but attempted to deprecate that anger.—[*Ed.*]

II.

How they feed him with soupe, and what soupe is. How he meets with a capucin; and what a capucin is. How they shut him up in a post-chaise, and send him to Paris; he goes wondring along during six days; and how there are trees, and houses just as in England. Arrives at Paris without knowing it.

III.

Full account of the river Seine, and of the various animals and plants its borders produce. Description of the little creature called an Abbé, its parts, and their uses; with the reasons why they will not live in England, and the methods, that have been used to propagate them there. A cut of the inside of a nunnery; its structure, wonderfully adapted to the use of the animals, that inhabit it; a short account of them, how they propagate without the help of a male, and how they eat up their own young ones, like cats and rabbits. Supposed to have both sexes in themselves, like a snail. Dissection of a Duchess with copper-plates, very curious.

IV.

Goes to the opera; grand orchestra of humstrums, bag-pipes, salt-boxes, tabors and pipes. Anatomy of a French ear, shewing the formation of it to be entirely different from that of an English one, and that sounds have a directly contrary effect upon one and the other. Farinelli, at Paris said to have a fine manner, but no voice. Grand ballet, in which there is no seeing the dance for petticoats. Old women with flowers, and jewels stuck in the curls of their grey hair; red-heeled shoes and roll-ups innumerable, hoops, and panniers immeasurable, paint unspeakable. Tables, wherein is calculated with the utmost exactness, the several degrees of red, now in use, from the rising blush of an Advocate's wife to the flaming crimson of a princess of the Blood; done by a limner in great vogue.

V.

The author takes unto him a taylour; his character. How he covers him with silk, and fringe, and widens his figure with buckram a yard on each side; waistcoat, and breeches so strait, he can neither breathe nor walk. How the barber curls him en bequille, and à la negligée, and ties a vast solitaire about his neck; how the milliner lengthens his ruffles to his fingers' ends, and sticks his two arms into a muff. How he cannot stir; and how they cut him in proportion to his clothes.

VI.

He is carried to Versailles; despises it infinitely. A dissertation upon taste. Goes to an Installation in the Chapel Royal; enter the King and fifty fiddlers solus; kettle-drums and trumpets, queens, and dauphins, princesses, and cardinals, incense, and the mass. Old knights making curtsies; Holy Ghosts, and fiery tongues.

VII.

Goes into the country to Rheims, in Champagne, stays there three months; what he did there (he must beg the reader's pardon, but) he has really forgot.

VIII.

Proceeds to Lyons. Vastness of that city. Can't see the streets for houses.[1] How rich it is, and how much it stinks. Poem upon the confluence of the Rhone and the Sâone, by a friend of the Author's; very pretty.

IX.

Makes a journey into Savoy, and in his way visits the Grand Chartreuse; he is set astride upon a mule's back, and begins to climb up the mountains. Rocks and torrents beneath; pine-trees, and snows above; horrors, and terrors on all sides. The Author dies of the fright.

X.

He goes to Geneva. His mortal antipathy to a presbyterian, and the cure for it. Returns to Lyons; gets a surfeit with eating ortolans, and lampreys; is advised to go into Italy for the benefit of the air.

[1] From the *Menagiana*, vol. i. p. 13. "Mons. Le Duc de M. disoit, que les maisons de Paris étoient si hautes, qu'elles empêchoient de voir la ville." See also Bishop Hall's *Satires* (Singer's ed.), p. 72.—[*Mit.*]

XI.

Sets out the latter end of November to cross the Alps. He is devoured by a wolf, and how it is to be devoured by a wolf. The seventh day he comes to the foot of Mount Cenis. How he is wrap'd up in[1] bear-skins, and beaver-skins, boots on his legs, caps on his head, muffs on his hands, and taffety over his eyes; he is placed on a bier, and is carried to heaven by the savages blindfold. How he lights among a certain fat nation, called Clouds: how they are always in a sweat, and never speak, but they f—t; how they

[1] In a letter from Walpole to West, dated Turin, Nov. 11, 1737.—" 'So,' as the song says, 'we are in fair Italy!' I wonder we are, for on the highest precipice of Mount Cenis, the devil of Discord, in the similitude of sour wine, had got amongst our Alpine savages and set them a-fighting, with Gray and me in the chairs: they rushed him by me on a crag where there was scarce room for a cloven foot; the least slip had tumbled us into such a fog, and such an eternity, as we should never have found our way out of again. We were eight days in coming hither from Lyons, the four last in crossing the Alps. Such uncouth rocks and such uncomely inhabitants, my dear West, I hope I shall never see them again. At the foot of Mount Cenis we were obliged to quit our chaise, which was taken all to pieces and loaded on mules; and we were carried in low arm-chairs, on poles, swathed in beaver bonnets, beaver gloves, beaver stockings, muffs, and bear-skins. When we came to the top beheld the snows fallen; and such quantities, and conducted by such heavy clouds that hung glouting, that I thought we never could have waded through them. The descent is two leagues, but steep, and rough as O—— father's face, over which, you know, the devil walked with hob-nails in his shoes."—Walpole's *Works*, vol. iv. p. 431.

flock about him, and think him very odd for not doing so too. He falls plump into Italy.

XII.

Arrives at Turin; goes to Genoa, and from thence to Placentia; crosses the river Tribia: the ghost of Hannibal appears to him; and what it, and he, say upon the occasion. Locked out of Parma in a cold winter's night; the Author by an ingenious stratagem, gains admittance. Despises that city, and proceeds through Reggio to Modena. How the Duke, and Duchess lie over their own stables, and go every night to a vile Italian comedy; despises them, and it; and proceeds to Bologna.

XIII.

Enters into the dominions of the Pope o' Rome. Meets the devil, and what he says on the occasion. Very publick, and scandalous doings between the vines and the elm-trees, and how the olive-trees are shocked thereupon. Author longs for Bologna sausages, and hams; and how he grows as fat as a hog.

XIV.

Observations on antiquities. The Author proves that Bologna was the ancient Tarentum; that the battle of Salamis, contrary to the vulgar opinion, was fought by land, and that not far from Ravenna. That the Romans were a colony of the Jews, and that Eneas was the same with Ehud.

XV.

Arrival at Florence. Is of opinion, that the Venus of Medicis is a modern performance, and that a very indifferent one, and much inferior to the K. Charles at Charing Cross. Account of the city, and manners of the inhabitants. A learned Dissertation on the true situation of Gomorrah. . . .

And here will end the first part of these instructive and entertaining voyages. The Subscribers are to pay twenty guineas; nineteen down, and the remainder upon delivery of the book. *N.B.*—A few are printed on the softest royal brown paper for the use of the curious.

MY DEAR, DEAR WHARTON[1]—(Which is a dear more than I give anybody else. It is very odd to begin with a parenthesis, but) You may think me a beast for not haveing sooner wrote to you, and to be sure a beast I am. Now, when one owns it, I don't see what you have left to say. I take this opportunity to inform you (an opportunity I have had every week this twelvemonth) that I am arrived safe at Calais, and am at present at—

[1] Thomas Wharton, M.D. (1717-1794), of Old-Park, near Durham. With this gentleman Mr. Gray contracted an acquaintance very early; and though they were not educated together at Eton, yet afterwards at Cambridge, when the Doctor was Fellow of Pembroke Hall, they became intimate friends, and continued so to the time of Mr. Gray's death.—[*Mason.*]

Florence, a city in Italy in I don't know how many degrees N. latitude. Under the line I am sure it is not, for I am at this instant expiring with cold. You must know, that not being certain what circumstances of my history would particularly suit your curiosity, and knowing that all I had to say to you would overflow the narrow limits of many a good quire of paper, I have taken this method of laying before you the contents, that you may pitch upon what you please, and give me your orders accordingly to expatiate thereupon: for I conclude you will write to me; won't you? oh! yes, when you know, that in a week I set out for Rome, and that the Pope is dead, and that I shall be (I should say, God willing; and if nothing extraordinary intervene; and if I'm alive, and well; and in all human probability) at the coronation of a new one. Now as you have no other correspondent there, and as if you do not, I certainly shall not write again (observe my impudence), I take it to be your interest to send me a vast letter, full of all sorts of news, and bawdy, and politics, and such other ingredients, as to you shall seem convenient with all decent expedition. Only do not be too severe upon the Pretender; and if you like my style, pray say so. This is à la Françoise; and if you think it a little too foolish, and impertinent, you shall be treated alla Toscana with a thousand Signoria Illustrissimas, in the meantime I have the honour to remain Your lofing frind tell deth, T. GRAY.

Florence, March 12, N. S. [1740].

P.S.—This is à l'Angloise. I don't know where you are; if at Cambridge, pray let me know all how, and about it; and if my old friends, Thompson, or Clarke fall in your way, say I am extremely theirs. But if you are in town, I entreat you to make my best compliments to Mrs. Wharton. Adieu.—Yours sincerely a second time.

XXVIII.—TO MRS. DOROTHY GRAY.

Florence, March 19, 1740.

THE Pope[1] is at last dead, and we are to set out for Rome on Monday next. The conclave is still sitting there, and likely to continue so some time longer, as the two French Cardinals are but just arrived, and the German ones are still expected. It agrees mighty ill with those that remain inclosed: Ottoboni[2] is already dead of an apoplexy; Altieri[3] and several others are said to be dying, or very bad: yet it is not expected to break up till after Easter. We shall lie at Sienna the first night, spend a day there, and in two more get to Rome. One begins to see in this country the first promises of an Italian spring,

[1] Clement XII. (Lorenzo Corsini). He had been elected in July 1730, and died Feb. 6, 1740.—[*Ed.*]

[2] Cardinal Pietro Ottoboni (1667-1740) had died on the 28th of February. He was a very wealthy patron of art and letters. —[*Ed.*]

[3] Three of the Altieri family were Cardinals at this time. The one Gray mentions was Giambattista Altieri (1663-1740), Archbishop of Tyre, who died on the 12th of March.—[*Ed.*]

clear unclouded skies, and warm suns, such as are not often felt in England; yet, for your sake, I hope at present you have your proportion of them, and that all your frosts, and snows, and short breaths are, by this time, utterly vanished. I have nothing new or particular to inform you of; and, if you see things at home go on much in their old course, you must not imagine them more various abroad. The diversions of a Florentine Lent are composed of a sermon in the morning, full of hell and the devil; a dinner at noon, full of fish and meagre diet; and in the evening, what is called a Conversazione, a sort of assembly at the principal people's houses, full of I cannot tell what. Besides this, there is twice a week a very grand concert. . . .

XXIX.—TO MRS. DOROTHY GRAY.

Rome, April 2, N. S., 1740.

THIS is the third day since we came to Rome, but the first hour I have had to write to you in. The journey from Florence cost us four days, one of which was spent at Sienna, an agreeable, clean, old city, of no great magnificence or extent; but in a fine situation, and good air. What it has most considerable is its cathedral, a huge pile of marble, black and white laid alternately, and laboured with a Gothic niceness and delicacy in the old-fashioned way. Within too are some paintings and sculpture of considerable hands. The sight of this, and some collections that were shewed us in private houses, were a sufficient employment for the little time we were to pass there: and the next morning we set forward on our journey through a country very oddly composed; for some miles you have a continual scene of little mountains cultivated from top to bottom with rows of olive-trees, or else elms, each of which has its vine twining about it, and mixing with the branches; and corn sown between all the ranks. This diversified with numerous small houses and convents, makes the most agreeable prospect in the world. But, all of a sudden, it alters to black barren hills, as far as the eye can reach, that seem never to have been capable of culture, and are as ugly as useless. Such is the country for some time before one comes to Mount Radicofani, a terrible black hill, on the top of which we were to lodge that night. It is very high, and difficult of ascent; and at the foot of it we were much embarrassed by the fall of one of the poor horses that drew us. This accident obliged another chaise, which was coming down, to stop also; and out of it peeped a figure in a red cloak, with a handkerchief tied round its head, which, by its voice and mien, seemed a fat old woman: but upon its getting out, appeared to be Senesino,[1] who was returning from Naples to Sienna, the place of his birth and residence. On the highest

[1] Certain nicknames were borne by Italian singers in succession, and this is evidently not the famous Senesino (Ferdinando Tenducci), the sopranist, for he was only a boy at the time. Perhaps Francesco Bernardi is intended.—[*Ed.*]

part of the mountain is an old fortress, and near it a house built by one of the Grand Dukes for a hunting-seat, but now converted into an inn. It is the shell of a large fabric, but such an inside, such chambers, and accommodations, that your cellar is a palace in comparison; and your cat sups and lies much better than we did; for, it being a saint's eve, there was nothing but eggs. We devoured our meagre fare; and, after stopping up the windows with the quilts, were obliged to lie upon the straw beds in our clothes. Such are the conveniences in a road, that is, as it were, the great thoroughfare of all the world. Just on the other side of this mountain, at Ponte-Centino, one enters the patrimony of the church; a most delicious country, but thinly inhabited. That night brought us to Viterbo, a city of a more lively appearance than any we had lately met with; the houses have glass windows, which is not very usual here; and most of the streets are terminated by a handsome fountain. Here we had the pleasure of breaking our fast on the leg of an old hare and some broiled crows. Next morning, in descending Mount Viterbo, we first discovered (though at near thirty miles' distance) the cupola of St. Peter's, and a little after began to enter on an old Roman pavement, with now and then a ruined tower, or a sepulchre on each hand. We now had a clear view of the city, though not to the best advantage, as coming along a plain quite upon a level with it; however it appeared very vast, and surrounded with magnificent villas and gardens. We soon after crossed the Tiber, a river that ancient Rome made more considerable than any merit of its own could have done. However, it is not contemptibly small, but a good handsome stream; very deep, yet somewhat of a muddy complexion. The first entrance of Rome is prodigiously striking. It is by a noble gate, designed by Michael Angelo, and adorned with statues; this brings you into a large square, in the midst of which is a vast obelisk of granite, and in front you have at one view two churches of a handsome architecture, and so much alike that they are called the twins; with three streets, the middlemost of which is one of the longest in Rome. As high as my expectation was raised, I confess, the magnificence of this city infinitely surpasses it. You cannot pass along a street but you have views of some palace, or church, or square, or fountain, the most picturesque and noble one can imagine. We have not yet set about considering its beauties, ancient and modern, with attention; but have already taken a slight transient view of some of the most remarkable. St. Peter's I saw the day after we arrived, and was struck dumb with wonder. I there saw the Cardinal d'Auvergne, one of the French ones, who upon coming off his journey, immediately repaired hither to offer up his vows at the high altar, and went directly into the Conclave; the doors of which we saw opened to him, and all the other immured Cardinals came thither to receive him. Upon his entrance they were closed again directly. It is supposed they will not come to an agreement about a Pope till after Easter, though the confinement is very disagreeable. I have hardly philosophy enough to see the infinity of fine things, that are here daily in the power of anybody that has money, without regretting the want of it; but custom has the power of making things easy to one. I have not yet seen his majesty of Great Britain, etc., though I have the two boys in the gardens of the Villa Borgese, where they go a-shooting almost every day; it was at a distance, indeed, for we did not choose to meet them, as you may imagine. This letter (like all those the English send or receive) will pass through the hands of that family, before it comes to those it was intended for. They do it more honour than it deserves; and all they will learn from thence will be, that I desire you to give my duty to my father, and wherever else it is due, and that I am, etc.

XXX.—TO MRS. DOROTHY GRAY.

Rome, April 15, 1740. Good-Friday.

To-day I am just come from paying my adoration at St. Peter's to three extraordinary relics, which are exposed to public view only on these two days in the whole year, at which time all the confraternities in the city come in procession to see them. It was something extremely novel to see that vast church, and the most magnificent in the world, undoubtedly, illuminated (for it was night) by thousands of little crystal lamps, disposed in the figure of a huge cross at the high altar, and seeming to hang alone in the air. All the light proceeded from this, and had the most singular effect imaginable as one entered the great door. Soon after came one after another, I believe, thirty processions, all dressed in linen frocks, and girt with a cord, their heads covered with a cowl all over, only two holes to see through left. Some of them were all black, others red, others white, others party-coloured; these were continually coming and going with their tapers and crucifixes before them; and to each company, as they arrived and knelt before the great altar, were shewn from a balcony at a great height, the three wonders, which are, you must know, the head of the spear that wounded Christ; St. Veronica's handkerchief, with the miraculous impression of his face upon it; and a piece of the true cross, on the sight of which the people thump their breasts, and kiss the pavement with vast devotion. The tragical part of the ceremony is half a dozen wretched creatures, who with their faces covered, but naked to the waist, are in a side chapel disciplining themselves with scourges full of iron prickles; but really in earnest, as our eyes can testify, which saw their backs and arms so raw we should have taken it for a red satin doublet torn, and shewing the skin through, had we not been convinced of the contrary by the blood which was plentifully sprinkled about them. It is late; I give you joy of Port-Bello,[1] and many other things, which I hope are all true. . . . .

XXXI.—TO RICHARD WEST.

Rome, April 16, N. S., 1740.

NOT so delicate;[2] nor, indeed, would his conscience suffer him to write to you, till he received de vos nouvelles, if he had not the tail of another person's letter to use by way of evasion. I sha'n't describe, as being in the only place in the world that deserves it, which may seem an odd reason—but they say as how it's fulsome, and everybody does it (and, I suppose, everybody says the same thing), else I should tell you a vast deal about the Coliseum, and the Conclave, and the Capitol, and these matters. A-propos du Colisée, if you don't know what it is, the Prince Borghese will be very capable of giving you some account of it, who told an Englishman that asked what it was built for—"They say 'twas for Christians to fight tigers in."

We are just come from adoring a great piece of the true cross, St. Longinus's spear, and St. Veronica's handkerchief; all which have been this evening exposed to view in St. Peter's. In the same place, and on the same occasion, last night, Walpole saw a poor

[1] The capitulation of Porto Bello to Admiral Vernon, with a fleet of six ships.—[*Ed.*]

[2] This was appended to a letter from Walpole to West, in which Walpole said: "I am in a violent hurry and have no more time; so Gray finishes this delicately."—[*Ed.*]

creature naked to the waist, discipline himself with a scourge filled with iron prickles, till he had made himself a raw doublet, that he took for red satin torn, and shewing the skin through. I should tell you that he fainted away three times at the sight, and I twice and a half at the repetition of it. All this is performed by the light of a vast fiery cross, composed of hundreds of little crystal lamps, which appear through the great altar under the grand tribunal, as if hanging by itself in the air.

All the confraternities of the city resort thither in solemn procession, habited in linen frocks, girt with a cord, and their heads covered with a cowl all over, that has only two holes before to see through. Some of these are all black, others parti-coloured and white; and with these masqueraders that vast church is filled, who are seen thumping their breasts, and kissing the pavement with extreme devotion. But methinks I am describing—'tis an ill habit, but this, like everything else, will wear off. We have sent you our compliments by a friend of yours, and correspondent in a corner, who seems a very agreeable man; one Mr. Williams. I am sorry he staid so little a while in Rome. I forget Porto Bello all this while; pray let us know where it is, and whether you or Asheton had any hand in the taking of it. Duty to the Admiral. Adieu!—Ever yours,

T. GRAY.

XXXII.—TO RICHARD WEST.

Tivoli, May 20, 1740.

THIS day being in the palace of his Highness the Duke of Modena, he laid his most serene commands upon me to write to Mr. West, and said he thought it for his glory, that I should draw up an inventory of all his most serene possessions for the said West's perusal.—Imprimis, a house, being in circumference a quarter of a mile, two feet and an inch; the said house containing the following particulars, to wit, a great room. Item, another great room; item, a bigger room; item, another room; item, a vast room; item, a sixth of the same; a seventh ditto; an eighth as before; a ninth as above-said; a tenth (see No. 1); item, ten more such, besides twenty besides, which, not to be too particular, we shall pass over. The said rooms contain nine chairs, two tables, five stools and a cricket. From whence we shall proceed to the garden, containing two millions of superfine laurel hedges, a clump of cypress-trees, and half the river Teverone, that pisses into two thousand several chamberpots. Finis.—Dame Nature desired me to put in a list of her little goods and chattels, and, as they were small, to be very minute about them. She has built here three or four little mountains, and laid them out in an irregular semicircle; from certain others behind, at a greater distance, she has drawn a canal, into which she has put a little river of hers, called Anio; she has cut a huge cleft between the two innermost of her four hills, and there she has left it to its own disposal; which she has no sooner done, but, like a heedless chit, it tumbles headlong down a declivity fifty feet perpendicular, breaks itself all to shatters, and is converted into a shower of rain, where the sun forms many a bow, red, green, blue, and yellow. To get out of our metaphors without any further trouble, it is the most noble sight in the world. The weight of that quantity of waters, and the force they fall with, have worn the rocks they throw themselves among into a thousand irregular craggs, and to a vast depth. In this channel it goes boiling along with a mighty noise till it comes to another steep, where you see it a second time come roaring down (but first you must walk two miles farther) a greater height than before, but not with that quantity of waters; for by this time it has divided itself, being crossed and opposed by the rocks, into four several streams, each of which, in emulation of the great one, will tumble down too; and it does tumble down, but not from an equally elevated place; so that you have at one view all these cascades intermixed with groves of olive and little woods, the mountains rising behind them, and on the top of one (that which forms the extremity of one of the half-circle's horns), is seated the town itself. At the very extremity of that extremity, on the brink of the precipice, stands the Sybils' temple, the remains of a little rotunda, surrounded with its portico, above half of whose beautiful Corinthian pillars are still standing and entire; all this on one hand. On the other, the open Campagna of Rome, here and there a little castle on a hillock, and the city itself on the very brink of the horizon, indistinctly seen (being 18 miles off), except the dome of St. Peter's; which, if you look out of your window, wherever you are, I suppose, you can see. I did not tell you that a little below the first fall, on the side of the rock, and hanging over that torrent, are little ruins which they shew you for Horace's house, a curious situation to observe the

> —præceps Anio, ac Tiburni lucus, et uda
> Mobilibus pomaria rivis.

Mæcenas did not care for such a noise, it seems, and built him a house (which they also carry one to see) so situated that it sees nothing at all of the matter, and for anything he knew there might be no such river in the world. Horace had another house on the other side of the Teverone, opposite to Mæcenas's; and they told us there was a bridge of communication, by which "andava il detto Signor per trastullarsi coll istesso Orazio." In coming hither we crossed the Aquæ Albulæ, a vile little brook that stinks like a fury, and they say it has stunk so these thousand years. I forgot the Piscina of Quintilius Varus, where he used to keep certain little fishes. This is very entire, and there is a piece of the aqueduct that supplied it too; in the garden below is old Rome, built in little, just as it was, they say. There are seven temples in it, and no houses at all; they say there were none.

May 21.

We have had the pleasure of going twelve miles out of our way to Palestrina. It has rained all day as if heaven and us were coming together. See my honesty, I do not mention a syllable of the temple of Fortune, because I really did not see it; which, I think, is pretty well for an old traveller. So we returned along the Via Prænestina, saw the Lacus Gabinus and Regillus, where, you know, Castor and Pollux appeared upon a certain occasion. And many a good old tomb we left on each hand, and many an aqueduct,

> Dumb are whose fountains, and their channels dry.

There are, indeed, two whole modern ones, works of Popes, that run about thirty miles a-piece in length; one of them conveys still the famous Aqua Virgo to Rome, and adds vast beauty to the prospect. So we came to Rome again, where waited for us a splendidissimo regalo of letters; in one of which came You, with your huge characters and wide intervals, staring. I would have you to know, I expect you should take a handsome crow-quill[1] when

[1] This was, as Mr. Gray wrote himself, small, neat, and terse. I have several of his letters to me. But as to spectacles, though he could joke about them when he had no occasion for them, yet thirty years after, when he really wanted them and could not read well without them, his delicacy was such, and

you write to me, and not leave room for a pin's point in four sides of a sheet of royal. Do you but find matter, I will find spectacles.

I have more time than I thought, and I will employ it in telling you about a ball that we were at the other evening. Figure to yourself a Roman villa; all its little apartments thrown open, and lighted up to the best advantage. At the upper end of the gallery, a fine concert, in which La Diamantina,[1] a famous virtuosa, played on the violin divinely, and sung angelically; Giovannino and Pasqualini (great names in musical story) also performed miraculously. On each side were ranged all the secular grand monde of Rome, the Ambassadors, Princesses, and all that. Among the rest Il Serenissimo Pretendente[2] (as the Mantova gazette calls him) displayed his rueful length of person, with his two young ones, and all his ministry around him. "Poi nacque un grazioso ballo," where the world danced, and I sat in a corner regaling myself with iced fruits, and other pleasant rinfrescatives.

his dislike of appearing old, that he only made use of an hand glass to help him to read with. I often told him of the comfort of spectacles, yet he deferred the use of them.—[*Cole.*]

[1] A violinist who called herself La Diamantina, in imitation of the great Italian actress, Patricia Adami, who had borne that title.—[*Ed.*]

[2] James Edward, Chevalier de St. George (1688-1765), called the Pretender.

XXXIII.—TO RICHARD WEST.

Rome, May 1740.

I AM to-day just returned from Alba, a good deal fatigued; for you know the Appian[1] is somewhat tiresome.[2] We dined at Pompey's; he indeed was gone for a few days to his Tusculan, but, by the care of his Villicus, we made an admirable meal. We had the dugs of a pregnant sow, a peacock, a dish of thrushes, a noble scarus just fresh from the Tyrrhene, and some conchylia of the Lake with garum sauce. For my part I never eat better at Lucullus's table. We drank half a dozen cyathi a-piece of ancient Alban to Pholoë's health; and, after bathing, and playing an hour at ball, we mounted our essedum again, and proceeded up the mount to the temple. The priests there entertained us with an account of a wonderful shower of birds' eggs, that had fallen two days before, which had no sooner touched the ground, but they were converted into gudgeons; as also that the night past, a dreadful voice had been heard out of the Adytum, which spoke Greek during

[1] "Appia *longarum* teritur regina viarum."
Statii Silv., ii. 2, 12.—[*Mit.*]

[2] However whimsical this humour may appear to some readers, I chose to insert it, as it gives me an opportunity of remarking that Mr. Gray was extremely skilled in the customs of the ancient Romans; and has catalogued, in his common place book, their various eatables, wines, perfumes, clothes, medicines, etc., with great precision, referring under every article to passages in the Poets and Historians where their names are mentioned.—[*Mason.*]

a full half-hour, but nobody understood it. But quitting my Romanities, to your great joy and mine, let me tell you in plain English, that we come from Albano. The present town lies within the inclosure of Pompey's Villa in ruins. The Appian way runs through it, by the side of which, a little farther, is a large old tomb, with five pyramids upon it, which the learned suppose to be the burying-place of the family, because they do not know whose it can be else. But the vulgar assure you it is the sepulchre of the Curiatii, and by that name (such is their power) it goes. One drives to Castel Gondolfo, a house of the Pope's, situated on the top of one of the Collinette, that forms a brim to the basin, commonly called the Alban lake. It is seven miles round; and directly opposite to you, on the other side, rises the Mons Albanus, much taller than the rest, along whose side are still discoverable (not to common eyes) certain little ruins of the old Alba longa. They had need be very little, as having been nothing but ruins ever since the days of Tullus Hostilius. On its top is a house of the Constable Colonna's, where stood the temple of Jupiter Latialis. At the foot of the hill Gondolfo, are the famous outlets of the lake, built with hewn stone, a mile and a half under ground. Livy, you know, amply informs us of the foolish occasion of this expence, and gives me this opportunity of displaying all my erudition, that I may appear considerable in your eyes. This is the prospect from one window of the palace. From another you have the whole Campagna, the City, Antium, and the Tyrrhene sea (twelve miles distant) so distinguishable, that you may see the vessels sailing upon it. All this is charming. Mr. Walpole says, our memory sees more than our eyes in this country. Which is extremely true; since, for realities, Windsor, or Richmond hill, is infinitely preferable to Albano or Frescati. I am now at home, and going to the window to tell you it is the most beautiful of Italian nights, which, in truth, are but just begun (so backward has the spring been here, and everywhere else, they say). There is a moon! there are stars for you! Do not you hear the fountain? Do not you smell the orange flowers? That building yonder is the convent of S. Isidore; and that eminence, with the cypress-trees and pines upon it, the top of M. Quirinal. This is all true, and yet my prospect is not two hundred yards in length. We send you some Roman inscriptions to entertain you. The first two are modern, transcribed from the Vatican library by Mr. Walpole.

Pontifices olim quem fundavere priores,
  Præcipuâ Sixtus perficit arte tholum;[1]
Et Sixti tantum se gloria tollit in altum,
  Quantum se Sixti nobile tollit opus:
Magnus honos magni fundamina ponere templi,
  Sed finem cæptis ponere major honos.

---

[1] Sixtus V. built the dome of St. Peter's.—[*Mason.*] St. Peter's was begun by Nicholas V. in 1450; the Cupola was completed in 1590; in 1612-14, the Church and Vestibule were finished: in 1667 the Colonnade. Up to 1694 it is computed that forty-seven millions of Scudi, upwards of ten million and a half sterling, have been expended upon it.—[*Mit.*]

Saxa agit Amphion, Thebana ut mænia condat:
Sixtus & immensæ pondera molis agit.[1]
Saxa trahunt ambo longè diversa : sed arte
Hæc trahit Amphion ; Sixtus & arte trahit.
At tantum exsuperat Dircæum Amphiona Sixtus,
Quantum hic exsuperat cætera saxa lapis.[2]

Mine is ancient, and I think not less curious. It is exactly transcribed from a sepulchral marble at the villa Giustiniani. I put stops to it, when I understand it.

Dis Manibus
Claudiæ, Pistes
Primus Conjugi
Optumae, Sanctae,
Et Piae, Benemeritate.

Non æquos, Parcae, statuistis stamina vitæ.
Tam bene compositos potuistis sede tenere.
Amissa est conjux. cur ego & ipse moror?
Si · bella · esse · mî · iste · mea · vivere · debuit ·
Tristia contigerunt qui amissâ conjuge vivo.
Nil est tam miserum, quam totam perdere vitam.
Nec vita enasci dura peregistis crudelia pensa, sorores,
Ruptaque deficiunt in primo munere fusi.
O nimis injustæ ter denos dare munus in annos,
Deceptus · grautus · fatum · sic · pressit · egestas ·
Dum vitam tulero, Primus Pistes lugea conjugium.

XXXIV.—TO MRS. DOROTHY GRAY.

Naples, June 17, 1740.

OUR journey hither was through the most beautiful part of the finest country in the world; and every

[1] He raised the obelisk in the great area.—[*Mit.*]

[2] Mitford printed these two inscriptions as if they formed one. They, and the succeeding text also, are in a hopeless state of error and confusion.—[*Ed.*]

spot of it on some account or other, famous for these three thousand years past.[1] The season has hitherto been just as warm as one would wish it; no unwholesome airs, or violent heats, yet heard of: the people call it a backward year, and are in pain about their corn, wine, and oil; but we, who are neither corn, wine, nor oil, find it very agreeable. Our road was through Velletri, Cisterna, Terracina, Capua, and Aversa, and so to Naples. The minute one leaves his Holiness's dominions, the face of things begins to change from wide uncultivated plains to olive groves and well-tilled fields of corn, intermixed with ranks of elms, every one of which has its vine twining about it, and hanging in festoons between the rows from one tree to another. The great old fig-trees, the oranges in full bloom, and myrtles in every hedge, make one of the delightfullest scenes you can conceive; besides that, the roads are wide, well-kept, and full of passengers, a sight I have not beheld this long time. My wonder still increased upon entering the city, which I think for number of people, outdoes both Paris and London. The streets are one continued market, and thronged with populace so much

[1] Mr. Gray wrote a minute description of everything he saw in this tour from Rome to Naples; as also of the environs of Rome, Florence, etc. But as these papers are apparently only memorandums for his own use, I do not think it necessary to print them, although they abound with many uncommon remarks, and pertinent classical quotations. The reader will please to observe throughout this section, that it is not my intention to give Mr. Gray's Travels, but only extracts from the Letters which he writ during his travels.—[*Mason.*]

that a coach can hardly pass. The common sort are a jolly lively kind of animals, more industrious than Italians usually are; they work till evening; then take their lute or guitar (for they all play) and walk about the city, or upon the sea-shore with it, to enjoy the fresco. One sees their little brown children jumping about stark-naked, and the bigger ones dancing with castanets, while others play on the cymbal to them. Your maps will show you the situation of Naples; it is on the most lovely bay in the world, and one of the calmest seas: it has many other beauties besides those of nature. We have spent two days in visiting the remarkable places in the country round it, such as the bay of Baiæ, and its remains of antiquity; the lake Avernus, and the Solfatara, Charon's grotto, etc. We have been in the Sybil's cave and many other strange holes under ground (I only name them because you may consult Sandy's *Travels*); but the strangest hole I ever was in, has been to-day at a place called Portici, where his Sicilian Majesty has a country-seat. About a year ago, as they were digging, they discovered some parts of ancient buildings above thirty feet deep in the ground: curiosity led them on, and they have been digging ever since; the passage they have made, with all its turnings and windings, is now more than a mile long. As you walk you see parts of an amphitheatre, many houses adorned with marble columns, and incrusted with the same; the front of a temple, several arched vaults of rooms painted in fresco.

Some pieces of painting have been taken out from hence finer than anything of the kind before discovered, and with these the king has adorned his palace; also a number of statues, medals, and gems; and more are dug out every day. This is known to be a Roman town,[1] that in the emperor Titus's time was overwhelmed by a furious eruption of Mount Vesuvius, which is hard by. The wood and beams remain so perfect that you may see the grain! but burnt to a coal, and dropping into dust upon the least touch. We were to-day at the foot of that mountain, which at present smokes only a little, where we saw the materials that fed the stream of fire, which about four years since ran down its side. We have but a few days longer to stay here; too little in conscience for such a place. . . .

XXXV.—TO PHILIP GRAY.

Florence, July 16, 1740.

AT my return to this city, the day before yesterday, I had the pleasure of finding yours dated June the 9th. The period of our voyages, at least towards the South, is come as you wish. We have been at Naples, spent nine or ten days there, and returned to Rome,

[1] It should seem by the omission of its name, that it was not then discovered to be Herculaneum.—[*Mason.*] This was not the case; see a letter from Walpole to West on this subject (Walpole's *Works*, vol. iv. p. 448), dated Naples, June 14, 1740, where he calls the town by the name of Herculaneum.—[*Mit.*]

where finding no likelihood of a Pope yet these three months, and quite wearied with the formal assemblies and little society of that great city, Mr. Walpole determined to return hither to spend the summer, where he imagines he shall pass his time more agreeably than in the tedious expectation of what, when it happens, will only be a great show. For my own part, I give up the thoughts of all that with but little regret; but the city itself I do not part with so easily, which alone has amusements for whole years. However, I have passed through all that most people do, both ancient and modern; what that is you may see better than I can tell you, in a thousand books. The Conclave we left in greater uncertainty than ever; the more than ordinary liberty they enjoy there, and the unusual coolness of the season, makes the confinement less disagreeable to them than common, and, consequently maintains them in their irresolution. There have been very high words, one or two (it is said) have come even to blows; two more are dead within this last month, Cenci and Portia; the latter died distracted: and we left another (Altieri) at the extremity: yet nobody dreams of an election till the latter end of September. All this gives great scandal to all good catholics, and everybody talks very freely on the subject. The Pretender (whom you desire an account of) I have had frequent opportunities of seeing at church, at the corso, and other places; but more particularly, and that for a whole night, at a great ball given by Count Patrizii to the Prince and Princess Craon[1] (who were come to Rome at that time, that he might receive from the hands of the Emperor's minister there, the order of the golden fleece) at which he and his two sons were present. They are good fine boys, especially the younger, who has the more spirit of the two, and both danced incessantly all night long. For him, he is a thin ill-made man, extremely tall and awkward, of a most unpromising countenance, a good deal resembling King James the Second, and has extremely the air and look of an idiot, particularly when he laughs or prays. The first he does not often, the latter continually. He lives private enough with his little court about him, consisting of Lord Dunbar, who manages everything, and two or three of the Preston Scotch Lords, who would be very glad to make their peace at home.

We happened to be at Naples on Corpus Christi Day, the greatest feast in the year, so had an opportunity of seeing their Sicilian Majesties to advantage. The King walked in the grand procession, and the Queen (being big with child) sat in a balcony. He followed the Host to the church of St. Clara, where high mass was celebrated to a glorious concert of music. They are as ugly a little pair as one can see; she a pale girl, marked with the small-pox; and he

[1] See them mentioned in Walpole's letters to H. Mann repeatedly. Madame de Mirepoix, the French Ambassadress in England, was their daughter, and Prince Beauvau, a marshall of France, their son. The Princess had been mistress of Leopold the Duke of Lorraine.—[*Mit.*]

a brown boy with a thin face, a huge nose, and as ungain as possible.

We are settled here with Mr. Mann in a charming apartment; the river Arno runs under our windows, which we can fish out of. The sky is so serene, and the air so temperate, that one continues in the open air all night long in a slight nightgown without any danger; and the marble bridge is the resort of everybody, where they hear music, eat iced fruits, and sup by moonlight; though as yet (the season being extremely backward everywhere) these amusements are not begun. You see we are now coming northward again, though in no great haste; the Venetian and Milanese territories, and either Germany or the South of France (according to the turn the war may take), are all that remain for us, that we have not yet seen; as to Loretto, and that part of Italy, we have given over all thoughts of it.

XXXVI.—TO RICHARD WEST.

Florence, July 16, 1740.

You do yourself and me justice, in imagining that you merit, and that I am capable of sincerity. I have not a thought, or even a weakness, I desire to conceal from you; and consequently on my side deserve to be treated with the same openness of heart. My vanity perhaps might make me more reserved towards you, if you were one of the heroic race, superior to all human failings; but as mutual wants are the ties of general society, so are mutual weaknesses of private friendships, supposing them mixt with some proportion of good qualities; for where one may not sometimes blame, one does not much care ever to praise. All this has the air of an introduction designed to soften a very harsh reproof that is to follow; but it is no such matter: I only meant to ask, Why did you change your lodging? Was the air bad, or the situation melancholy? If so, you are quite in the right. Only, is it not putting yourself a little out of the way of a people, with whom it seems necessary to keep up some sort of intercourse and conversation, though but little for your pleasure or entertainment (yet there are, I believe, such among them as might give you both), at least for your information in that study, which, when I left you, you thought of applying to? for that there is a certain study necessary to be followed, if we mean to be of any use in the world, I take for granted; disagreeable enough (as most necessities are) but, I am afraid, unavoidable. Into how many branches these studies are divided in England, everybody knows; and between that which you and I had pitched upon and the other two, it was impossible to balance long. Examples shew one that it is not absolutely necessary to be a blockhead to succeed in this profession. The labour is long, and the elements dry and unentertaining; nor was ever anybody (especially those that afterwards made a figure in it) amused or even not disgusted in the beginning; yet upon a further acquaintance, there is surely matter for curiosity and reflection. It is strange if, among all that huge mass of words, there be not somewhat intermixed for thought. Laws have been the result of long deliberation, and that not of dull men, but the contrary; and have so close a connection with history, nay, with philosophy itself, that they must partake a little of what they are related to so nearly. Besides, tell me, have you ever made the attempt? Was not you frighted merely with the distant prospect? Had the Gothic character and bulkiness of those volumes (a tenth part of which perhaps it will be no further necessary to consult, than as one does a dictionary) no ill effect upon your eye? Are you sure, if Coke had been printed by Elzevir, and bound in twenty neat pocket volumes, instead of one folio, you should never have taken him for an hour, as you would a Tully, or drank your tea over him? I know how great an obstacle ill spirits are to resolution. Do you really think, if you rid ten miles every morning, in a week's time you should not entertain much stronger hopes of the Chancellorship, and think it a much more probable thing than you do at present? The advantages you mention are not nothing; our inclinations are more than we imagine in our own power; reason and resolution determine them, and support under many difficulties. To me there hardly appears to be any medium between a public life and a private one; he who prefers the first, must put himself in a way of being serviceable to the rest of mankind, if he has a mind to be of any consequence among them. Nay, he must not refuse being in a certain degree even dependent upon some men who are so already. If he has the good fortune to light on such as will make no ill use of his humility, there is no shame in this: if not, his ambition ought to give place to a reasonable pride, and he should apply to the cultivation of his own mind those abilities which he has not been permitted to use for others' service. Such a private happiness (supposing a small competence of fortune) is almost always in every one's power, and the proper enjoyment of age, as the other is the employment of youth. You are yet young, have some advantages and opportunities, and an undoubted capacity, which you have never yet put to the trial. Set apart a few hours, see how the first year will agree with you, at the end of it you are still the master; if you change your mind, you will only have got the knowledge of a little somewhat that can do no hurt, or give you cause of repentance. If your inclination be not fixed upon anything else, it is a symptom that you are not absolutely determined against this, and warns you not to mistake mere indolence for inability. I am sensible there is nothing stronger against what I would persuade you to, than my own practice; which may make you imagine I think not as I speak. Alas! it is not so; but I do not act what I think, and I had rather be the object of your pity, than you should be that of mine; and be assured, the advantage that I may receive from it, does not diminish my concern in hearing you want somebody to converse with freely, whose advice might be of more weight, and always at hand. We have some time since come to the southern period of our voyages; we spent about nine days at Naples. It is the largest and most populous city, as its environs are the most deliciously fertile country, of all Italy. We sailed in the bay of Baiæ, sweated in the Solfatara, and died in the grotto del Cane, as all strangers do; saw the Corpus Christi procession, and the King and the Queen, and the city underground (which is a wonder I reserve to tell you of another time), and so returned to Rome for another fortnight; left it (left Rome!) and came hither for the summer. You have seen[1] an Epistle to Mr. Ashton, that seems to me full of spirit and thought, and a good deal of poetic fire. I would know your opinion. Now I talk of verses, Mr. Walpole and I have frequently wondered you should never mention a certain imitation of Spenser,[2] published last year by a namesake of yours, with which we are all enraptured and enmarvailed.

XXXVII.—TO RICHARD WEST.

Florence, July 31, N. S. 1740.

THOUGH[3] far unworthy to enter into so learned and political a correspondence, I am employed pour bar-

[1] The reader will find this in Dodsley's *Miscellany*, and also amongst Mr. Walpole's *Fugitive Pieces*.—[*Mason.*]

[2] "On the Abuse of Travelling," by Gilbert West (1705-1756).—[*Ed.*]

[3] Appended to a letter by Horace Walpole to West.—[*Ed.*]

bouiller une page de sept pouces et demie en hauteur, et cinq en largeur; and to inform you that we are at Florence, a city of Italy, and the capital of Tuscany; the latitude I cannot justly tell, but it is governed by a Prince called Great Duke; an excellent place to employ all one's animal sensations in, but utterly contrary to one's rational powers. I have struck a medal upon myself: the device is thus, O, and the motto *Nihilissimo*, which I take in the most concise manner to contain a full account of my person, sentiments, occupations, and late glorious successes. If you choose to be annihilated too, you cannot do better than undertake this journey. Here you shall get up at twelve o'clock, breakfast till three, dine till five, sleep till six, drink cooling liquors till eight, go to the bridge till ten, sup till two, and so sleep till twelve again.

> Labore fessi venimus ad larem nostrum
> Desideratoque acquiescimus lecto:
> Hoc est, quod unum est, pro laboribus tantis.
> O quid solutis est beatius curis?[1]

We shall never come home again; a universal war is just upon the point of breaking out; all out-lets will be shut up. I shall be secure in my nothingness, while you that will be so absurd as to exist, will envy me. You don't tell me what proficiency you make in the noble science of defence. Don't you start still at the sound of a gun? Have you learned to say Ha!

[1] See *Catulli Carm.*, XXXI. v. 7. The order of the lines is somewhat transposed in the quotation in Gray's Letter.—[*Mit.*]

ha! and is your neck clothed with thunder? Are your whiskers of a tolerable length? And have you got drunk yet with brandy and gunpowder? Adieu, noble Captain! T. GRAY.

XXXVIII.—TO MRS. DOROTHY GRAY.

Florence, August 21, N. S., 1740.

IT is some time since I have had the pleasure of writing to you, having been upon a little excursion cross the mountains to Bologna. We set out from hence at sunset, passed the Appennines by moonlight, travelling incessantly till we came to Bologna at four in the afternoon next day. There we spent a week agreeably enough, and returned as we came. The day before yesterday arrived the news of a Pope; and I have the mortification of being within four days' journey of Rome, and not seeing his coronation, the heats being violent, and the infectious air now at its height. We had an instance, the other day, that it is not only fancy. Two country fellows, strong men, and used to the country about Rome, having occasion to come from thence hither, and travelling on foot, as common with them, one died suddenly on the road; the other got hither, but extremely weak, and in a manner stupid; he was carried to the hospital, but died in two days. So, between fear and laziness, we remain here, and must be satisfied with the accounts other people give us of the matter.

The new Pope is called Benedict XIV.[1] being created Cardinal by Benedict XIII. the last Pope but one. His name is Lambertini, a noble Bolognese, and Archbishop of that city. When I was first there I remember to have seen him two or three times; he is a short, fat man, about sixty-five years of age, of a hearty, merry countenance, and likely to live some years. He bears a good character for generosity, affability, and other virtues; and, they say, wants neither knowledge nor capacity. The worst side of him is, that he has a nephew or two; besides a certain young favourite, called Melara, who is said to have had, for some time, the arbitrary disposal of his purse and family. He is reported to have made a little speech to the Cardinals in the Conclave, while they were undetermined about an election, as follows: "Most eminent Lords, here are three Bolognese of different characters, but all equally proper for the Popedom. If it be your pleasures to pitch upon a Saint, there is Cardinal Gotti;[2] if upon a Politician, there is Aldrovandi;[3] if upon a Booby, here am I." The Italian is much more expressive, and, indeed, not to be translated; wherefore, if you meet with anybody that understands it, you may shew them what he said in the language he spoke it. "Emin^{ssimi}.

[1] Prospero Lambertini. He died in 1758.—[*Ed.*]

[2] Vincenzo Luigi Gotti (1664-1742), made a Cardinal by Benedict XIII. in 1728. He was very nearly elected Pope by the Conclave which Gray is describing.—[*Ed.*]

[3] Pompeo Aldovrandi (not Aldrovandi), Bishop of Montefiascone (1668-1752).—[*Ed.*]

Sigr[i]. Ci siamo trè, diversi sì, mà tutti idonei al Papato. Si vi piace un Santo, c' è l'Gotti; se volete una testa scaltra, e Politica, c' è l'Aldrovandè; se un Coglione, ecco mi!" Cardinal Coscia [1] is restored to his liberty, and, it is said, will be to all his benefices. Corsini (the late Pope's nephew) as he has had no hand in this election, it is hoped, will be called to account for all his villanous practices. The Pretender, they say, has resigned all his pretensions to his eldest boy, and will accept of the Grand Chancellorship, which is thirty thousand crowns a-year; the pension he has at present is only twenty thousand. I do not affirm the truth of this article; because, if he does, it is necessary he should take the ecclesiastical habit, and it will sound mighty odd to be called his Majesty the Chancellor.—— So ends my Gazette.

XXXIX.—TO RICHARD WEST.

Florence, September 25, N. S., 1740.

WHAT I send you now, as long as it is, is but a piece of a poem. It has the advantage of all fragments, to need neither introduction nor conclusion: besides, if you do not like it, it is but imagining that which went before, and came after to be infinitely better.

[1] Niccolo Coscia (1682-1755), Archbishop of Benevento, had been imprisoned by the Pope since 1731. He soon fell into disgrace again, and died impoverished and obscure a few years later at Naples. His unscrupulous ambition and early success had marked him as a dangerous enemy to Rome.—[*Ed.*]

Look in Sandy's *Travels* for the history of Monte Barbaro, and Monte Nuovo.[1]

[1] To save the reader trouble, I here insert the passage referred to:—"West of Cicero's villa stands the eminent Gaurus, a stony and desolate mountain, in which there are diverse obscure caverns, choked almost with earth, where many have consumed much fruitless industry in searching for treasure. The famous Lucrine Lake extended formerly from Avernus to the aforesaid Gaurus: but is now no other than a little sedgy plash, choked up by the horrible and astonishing eruption of the new mountain: whereof, as oft as I think, I am easy to credit whatsoever is wonderful. For who here knows not, or who elsewhere will believe, that a mountain should arise (partly out of a lake and partly out of the sea) in one day and a night, unto such a height as to contend in altitude with the high mountains adjoining? In the year of our Lord 1538, on the 29th of September, when for certain days foregoing the country hereabout was so vexed with perpetual earthquakes, as no one house was left so entire as not to expect an immediate ruin; after that the sea had retired two hundred paces from the shore (leaving abundance of fish, and springs of fresh water rising in the bottom), this mountain visibly ascended about the second hour of the night, with an hideous roaring, horribly vomiting stones and such store of cinders as overwhelmed all the building thereabout, and the salubrious baths of Tripergula, for so many ages celebrated; consumed the vines to ashes, killing birds and beasts: the fearful inhabitants of Puzzol flying through the dark with their wives and children; naked, defiled, crying out, and detesting their calamities. Manifold mischiefs have they suffered by the barbarous, yet none like this which Nature inflicted.——This new mountain, when newly raised, had a number of issues; at some of them smoking and sometimes flaming; at others disgorging rivulets of hot waters; keeping within a terrible rumbling; and many miserably perished that ventured to descend into the hollowness above. But that hollow on the top is at present an orchard, and the mountain throughout is bereft of its terrors."—Sandy's *Travels*, book IV. pp. 275, 277, and 278.—[*Mason.*]

. . . .

There was a certain little ode [1] set out from Rome in a letter of recommendation to you, but possibly fell into the enemies' hands, for I never heard of its arrival. It is a little impertinent to enquire after its welfare; but you, that are a father, will excuse a parent's foolish fondness. Last post I received a very diminutive letter. It made excuses for its unentertainingness, very little to the purpose; since it assured me, very strongly, of your esteem, which is to me the thing; all the rest appear but as the petits agrémens, the garnishing of the dish. P. Bougeant, in his *Langage des Bêtes*, fancies that your birds, who continually repeat the same note, say only in plain terms, "Je vous aime, ma chère; ma chère, je vous aime;" and that those of greater genius indeed, with various trills, run divisions upon the subject; but that the *fond*, from whence it all proceeds, is "toujours je vous aime." Now you may, as you find yourself dull or in humour, either take me for a chaffinch or nightingale; sing your plain song, or show your skill in music, but in the bottom let there be, toujours de l'Amitié.

As to what you call my serious letter; be assured, that your future state is to me entirely indifferent. Do not be angry, but hear me; I mean with respect to myself. For whether you be at the top of Fame, or entirely unknown to mankind; at the Council-table, or at Dick's coffee-house; sick and simple, or

[1] The Alcaic Ode.

well and wise; whatever alteration mere accident works in you (supposing it utterly impossible for it to make any change in your sincerity and honesty, since these are conditions sine quâ non), I do not see any likelihood of my not being yours ever.

XL.—TO PHILIP GRAY.

Florence, October 9, 1740.

THE beginning of next spring is the time determined for our return at furthest; possibly it may be before that time. How the interim will be employed, or what route we shall take is not so certain. If we remain friends with France, upon leaving this country we shall cross over to Venice, and so return through the cities north of the Po to Genoa; from thence take a felucca to Marseilles, and come back through Paris. If the contrary fall out, which seems not unlikely, we must take the Milanese, and those parts of Italy, in our way to Venice; from thence pass through the Tirol into Germany, and come home by the Low Countries. As for Florence, it has been gayer than ordinary for this last month, being one round of balls and entertainments, occasioned by the arrival of a great Milanese Lady; for the only thing the Italians shine in, is their reception of strangers. At such times everything is magnificence: the more remarkable, as in their ordinary course of life they are parsimonious, even to a degree of nastiness. I saw in one of the vastest palaces in Rome (that of Prince Pamfilio) the apartment which he himself inhabited, a bed that most servants in England would disdain to lie in, and furniture much like that of a soph at Cambridge, for convenience and neatness. This man is worth £30,000 sterling a year. As for eating, there are not two Cardinals in Rome that allow more than six paoli, which is three shillings a day, for the expence of their table: and you may imagine they are still less extravagant here than there. But when they receive a visit from any friend, their houses and persons are set out to the greatest advantage, and appear in all their splendour; it is, indeed, from a motive of vanity, and with the hopes of having it repaid them with interest, whenever they have occasion to return the visit. I call visits going from one city of Italy to another; for it is not so among acquaintance of the same place on common occasions. The new Pope has retrenched the charges of his own table to a sequin (ten shillings) a meal. The applause which all he says and does meets with, is enough to encourage him really to deserve fame. They say he is an able and honest man; he is reckoned a wit too. The other day, when the Senator of Rome came to wait upon him, at the first compliments he made him, the Pope pulled off his cap: his Master of the Ceremonies, who stood by his side, touched him softly, as to warn him that such a condescension was too great in him, and out of all manner of rule. Upon which he turned to him and said, "Oh! I cry you mercy, good Master, it is true, I am but a Novice of a Pope; I have not yet so much as learned ill manners." . . .

XLI.—TO PHILIP GRAY.

Florence,[1] January 12, 1741.

WE still continue constant at Florence, at present one of the dullest cities in Italy. Though it is the middle of the Carnival there are no public diversions; nor is masquerading permitted as yet. The Emperor's obsequies are to be celebrated publicly the 16th of this month; and after that, it is imagined everything will go on in its usual course. In the meantime, to employ the minds of the populace, the Government has thought fit to bring into the city in a solemn manner, and at a great expence, a famous statue of the Virgin called the Madonna dell'Impruneta, from the place of her residence, which is upon a mountain seven miles off. It never has been practised but at times of public calamity; and was done at present to avert the ill effects of a late great inundation, which it was feared might cause some epidemical distemper. It was introduced a fortnight ago in procession, attended by the Council of Regency, the Senate, the Nobility, and all the Religious Orders, on foot and bare-headed, and so carried to the great church, where it was frequented by an infinite concourse of people from all the country round. Among the rest I paid

[1] Between the date of this and the foregoing letter the reader will perceive an interval of full three months: as Mr. Gray saw no new places during this period, his letters were chiefly of news and common occurrences, and are therefore omitted.—[*Mason.*]

my devotions almost every day, and saw numbers of people possessed with the devil who were brought to be exorcised. It was indeed in the evening, and the church-doors were always shut before the ceremonies were finished, so that I could not be eye-witness of the event; but that they were all cured is certain, for one never heard any more of them the next morning. I am to-night just returned from seeing our Lady make her exit with the same solemnities she entered. The show had a finer effect than before; for it was dark; and everybody (even those of the mob that could afford it) bore a white wax flambeau. I believe there were at least five thousand of them, and the march was near three hours in passing before the window. The subject of all this devotion is supposed to be a large Tile with a rude figure in bas-relief upon it. I say supposed, because since the time it was found (for it was found in the earth in ploughing) only two people have seen it; the one was, by good luck, a saint; the other was struck blind for his presumption. Ever since she has been covered with seven veils; nevertheless, those who approach her tabernacle cast their eyes down, for fear they should spy her through all her veils. Such is the history, as I had it from the Lady of the house where I stood to see her pass; with many other circumstances; all which she firmly believes, and ten thousand besides.

We shall go to Venice in about six weeks, or sooner. A number of German troops are upon their march into this State, in case the King of Naples thinks proper to attack it. It is certain he has asked the Pope's leave for his troops to pass through his country. The Tuscans in general are much discontented, and foolish enough to wish for a Spanish government, or any rather than this. . . .

XLII.—TO RICHARD WEST.

Florence, April 21, 1741.

I KNOW not what degree of satisfaction it will give you to be told that we shall set out from hence the 24th of this month, and not stop above a fortnight at any place in our way. This I feel, that you are the principal pleasure I have to hope for in my own country. Try at least to make me imagine myself not indifferent to you; for I must own I have the vanity of desiring to be esteemed by somebody, and would choose that somebody should be one whom I esteem as much as I do you. As I am recommending myself to your love, methinks I ought to send you my picture (for I am no more what I was, some circumstances excepted, which I hope I need not particularise to you); you must add then, to your former idea, two years of age, a reasonable quantity of dulness, a great deal of silence, and something that rather resembles, than is, thinking; a confused notion of many strange and fine things that have swum before my eyes for some time, a want of love for general society, indeed an inability to it. On the good side you may add a sensibility for what others feel, and indulgence for their faults and weaknesses, a love of truth, and detestation of everything else. Then you are to deduct a little impertinence, a little laughter, a great deal of pride, and some spirits. These are all the alterations I know of, you perhaps may find more. Think not that I have been obliged for this reformation of manners to reason or reflection, but to a severer school-mistress, Experience. One has little merit in learning her lessons, for one cannot well help it; but they are more useful than others, and imprint themselves in the very heart. I find I have been haranguing in the style of the Son of Sirach, so shall finish here, and tell you that our route is settled as follows: First to Bologna for a few days, to hear the Viscontina sing; next to Reggio, where is a Fair. Now, you must know, a Fair here is not a place where one eats gingerbread or rides upon hobby-horses; here are no musical clocks, nor tall Leicestershire women; one has nothing but masquing, gaming, and singing. If you love operas, there will be the most splendid in Italy, four tip-top voices, a new theatre, the Duke and Duchess in all their pomps and vanities. Does not this sound magnificent? Yet is the city of Reggio but one step above Old Brentford. Well; next to Venice by the 11th of May, there to see the old Doge wed the Adriatic Whore. Then to Verona, so to Milan, so to Marseilles, so to Lyons, so to Paris, so to West, etc., in sæcula sæculorum. Amen.

Eleven months, at different times, have I passed at Florence; and yet (God help me) know not either people or language. Yet the place and the charming prospects demand a poetical farewell, and here it is.[1]

. . . .

I will send you, too, a pretty little Sonnet of a Sig^r^. Abbate Buondelmonte,[2] with my imitation of it.

"Spesso Amor sotto la forma
D'amistà ride, e s'asconde:
Poi si mischia, e si confonde
Con lo sdegno, e col rancor.
In Pietade ei si trasforma;
Par trastullo, e par dispetto;
Mà nel suo diverso aspetto
Sempr' egli, è l' istesso Amor."

Lusit amicitiæ interdum velatus amictu,
Et benè compositâ veste fefellit Amor.
Mox iræ assumpsit cultus, faciemque minantem,
Inque odium versus, versus et in lacrymas:
Ludentem fuge, nec lacrymanti, aut crede furenti;
Idem est dissimili semper in ore Deus.

Here comes a letter from you.—I must defer giving my opinion of *Pausanias*[3] till I can see the whole, and only have said what I did in obedience to your commands. I have spoken with such freedom

[1] It has already been printed in this edition, vol. i. p. 181. —[*Ed.*]

[2] Giuseppe Maria Buondelmonti (1713-1757), a littérateur of Tuscany, a very erudite and estimable man, and a long while Commander of the Order of Malta.—[*Ed.*]

[3] Some part of a Tragedy under that title, which Mr. West had begun; but I do not find amongst Mr. Gray's papers either the sketch itself, or Mr. Gray's free critique upon it, which he here mentions.—[*Mason.*]

on this head, that it seems but just you should have your revenge; and therefore I send you the beginning not of an Epic Poem, but of a Metaphysic one.[1] Poems and Metaphysics (say you, with your spectacles on) are inconsistent things. A metaphysical poem is a contradiction in terms. It is true, but I will go on. It is Latin too to increase the absurdity. It will, I suppose, put you in mind of the man who wrote a treatise of Canon Law in Hexameters. Pray help me to the description of a mixt mode, and a little Episode about Space.

XLIII.—TO RICHARD WEST.

I TRUST to the country, and that easy indolence you say you enjoy there, to restore you your health and spirits; and doubt not but, when the sun grows warm enough to tempt you from your fireside, you will (like all other things) be the better for his influence. He is my old friend, and an excellent nurse, I assure you. Had it not been for him, life had often been to me intolerable. Pray do not imagine that Tacitus, of all authors in the world, can be tedious. An annalist, you know, is by no means master of his subject; and I think one may venture to say, that if those Pannonian affairs are tedious in his hands, in another's they would have been insupportable. However, fear

[1] The beginning of the first book of a didactic Poem, *De Principiis Cogitandi.* The fragment which he now sent contained the first 53 lines.—[*Mason.*]

not, they will soon be over, and he will make ample amends. A man, who could join the *brilliant* of wit and concise sententiousness peculiar to that age, with the truth and gravity of better times, and the deep reflection and good sense of the best moderns, cannot choose but have something to strike you. Yet what I admire in him above all this, is his detestation of tyranny, and the high spirit of liberty that every now and then breaks out, as it were, whether he would or no. I remember a sentence in his Agricola that (concise as it is) I always admired for saying much in a little compass. He speaks of Domitian, who upon seeing the last will of that General, where he had made him Coheir with his Wife and Daughter, "Satis constabat lætatum eum, velut honore, judicioque: tam cæca & corrupta mens assiduis adulationibus erat, ut nesciret a bono patre non scribi hæredem, nisi malum principem."

As to the *Dunciad*,[1] it is greatly admired; the Genii of Operas and Schools, with their attendants, the pleas of the Virtuosos and Florists, and the yawn of dulness in the end, are as fine as anything he has written. The Metaphysicians' part is to me the worst; and here and there a few ill-expressed lines, and some hardly intelligible.

I take the liberty of sending you a long speech of

[1] This was the *New Dunciad*, as it was called, The Fourth Book, "found merely by accident, in taking a survey of the library of a late eminent nobleman," and published in 1742. In 1743 it was appended to a complete edition.—[*Ed.*]

Agrippina;[1] much too long, but I could be glad you would retrench it. Aceronia, you may remember, had been giving quiet counsels. I fancy, if it ever be finished, it will be in the nature of Nat. Lee's Bedlam Tragedy, which had twenty-five acts and some odd scenes.

XLIV.—TO RICHARD WEST.

London, April, Thursday.

You are the first who ever made a Muse of a Cough;[2] to me it seems a much more easy task to versify in one's sleep (that indeed you were of old famous for[3]), than for want of it. Not the wakeful nightingale (when she had a cough), ever sung so sweetly. I give you thanks for your warble, and wish you could sing yourself to rest. These wicked remains of your illness will sure give way to warm weather and gentle exercise; which I hope you will not omit as the season advances. Whatever low spirits and indolence, the effect of them, may advise to the contrary, I pray you add five steps to your walk daily for my sake; by the help of which, in a month's time, I propose to set you on horseback.

[1] Gray's first original production in English verse, of which he wrote only one complete scene and a few odd lines. May, the translator of Lucan and, of course, Racine, had dramatised the same story before him.—[*Ed.*]

[2] West, who was now very near his end, had sent Gray, on the 4th of April, some hexameters about his own "importunissima tussis," the cough which Gray here refers to.—[*Ed.*]

[3] I suppose at Eton School.—[*Mason.*]

I talked of the *Dunciad* as concluding you had seen it; if you have not, do you choose I should get and send it you? I have myself, upon your recommendation, been reading *Joseph Andrews*.[1] The incidents are ill laid and without invention; but the characters have a great deal of nature, which always pleases even in her lowest shapes. Parson Adams is perfectly well; so is Mrs. Slipslop, and the story of Wilson; and throughout he shows himself well read in Stage-Coaches, Country Squires, Inns, and Inns of Court. His reflections upon high people and low people, and misses and masters, are very good. However the exaltedness of some minds (or rather as I shrewdly suspect their insipidity and want of feeling or observation), may make them insensible to these light things (I mean such as characterise and paint nature), yet surely they are as weighty and much more useful than your grave discourses upon the mind,[2] the passions, and what not. Now as the paradisaical pleasures of the Mahometans consist in playing upon the flute and lying with Houris, be mine to read eternal new romances of Marivaux and Crebillon.

You are very good in giving yourself the trouble

[1] Fielding's *Joseph Andrews*, published in February of that year. Perhaps the famous commendation of the French romances of the day, which immediately follows, had been suggested by Fielding's remarks on the *Paysan Parvenu*, and *Marianne* in his novel.—[*Ed.*]

[2] He seems here to glance at Hutcheson, the disciple of Shaftsbury; of whom he had not a much better opinion than of his master.—[*Mason.*]

to read and find fault with my long harangues. Your freedom (as you call it), has so little need of apologies, that I should scarce excuse your treating me any otherwise; which, whatever compliment it might be to my vanity, would be making a very ill one to my understanding. As to matter of stile, I have this to say: the language of the age is never the language of poetry; except among the French, whose verse, where the thought or image does not support it, differs in nothing from prose. Our poetry, on the contrary, has a language peculiar to itself; to which almost every one, that has written, has added something by enriching it with foreign idioms and derivatives: nay sometimes words of their own composition or invention. Shakespear and Milton have been great creators this way; and no one more licentious than Pope or Dryden, who perpetually borrow expressions from the former. Let me give you some instances from Dryden, whom everybody reckons a great master of our poetical tongue.——Full of *museful mopeings*—unlike the *trim* of love—a pleasant *beverage*—a *roundelay* of love—stood silent in his *mood*—with knots and *knares* deformed—his *ireful mood*—in proud *array*—his *boon* was granted—and *disarray* and shameful rout—*wayward* but wise—*furbished* for the field—the *foiled dodderd* oaks—*disherited*—*smouldering* flames—*retchless* of laws—*crones* old and ugly—the *beldam* at his side—the *grandam-hag*—*villanise* his Father's fame.——But they are infinite: and our language not being a settled thing (like the French) has an undoubted right to words of an hundred years old, provided antiquity have not rendered them unintelligible. In truth, Shakespear's language is one of his principal beauties; and he has no less advantage over your Addisons and Rowes in this, than in those other great excellences you mention. Every word in him is a picture. Pray put me the following lines into the tongue of our modern dramatics :-

> "But I, that am not shaped for sportive tricks,
> Nor made to court an amorous looking-glass :
> I, that am rudely stampt, and want love's majesty
> To strut before a wanton ambling nymph :
> I, that am curtail'd of this fair proportion,
> Cheated of feature by dissembling nature,
> Deform'd, unfinish'd, sent before my time
> Into this breathing world, scarce half made up—"

And what follows. To me they appear untranslatable; and if this be the case, our language is greatly degenerated. However, the affectation of imitating Shakespear may doubtless be carried too far; and is no sort of excuse for sentiments ill-suited, or speeches ill-timed, which I believe is a little the case with me. I guess the most faulty expressions may be these—*silken* son of *dalliance*—*drowsier* pretensions—wrinkled *beldams*—*arched* the hearer's brow and *riveted* his eyes in *fearful extasie*. These are easily altered or omitted; and indeed if the thoughts be wrong or superfluous, there is nothing easier than to leave out the whole. The first ten or twelve lines are, I believe, the best; and as for the rest, I was betrayed into a good deal of it by Tacitus; only what he has said in five words, I imagine I have said in fifty lines. Such is the misfortune of imitating the inimitable. Now, if you are of my opinion, una litura may do the business better than a dozen; and you need not fear unravelling my web. I am a sort of spider; and have little else to do but spin it over again, or creep to some other place and spin there. Alas! for one who has nothing to do but amuse himself, I believe my amusements are as little amusing as most folks. But no matter; it makes the hours pass; and is better than ἐν ἀμαθίᾳ καὶ ἀμουσίᾳ καταβιῶναι. Adieu.

XLV.—TO RICHARD WEST.

London, April 1742.

I SHOULD not have failed to answer your letter immediately, but I went out of town for a little while, which hindered me. Its length (besides the pleasure naturally accompanying a long letter from you) affords me a new one, when I think it is a symptom of the recovery of your health, and flatter myself that your bodily strength returns in proportion. Pray do not forget to mention the progress you make continually. As to *Agrippina*, I begin to be of your opinion; and find myself (as women are of their children) less enamoured of my productions the older they grow. She[1] is laid up to sleep till next summer;

[1] He never after awakened her; and I believe this was occasioned by the strictures which his friend had made on his dra-

so bid her good-night. I think you have translated Tacitus very justly, that is, freely; and accommodated his thoughts to the turn and genius of our language; which, though I commend your judgment, is no commendation of the English tongue, which is too diffuse, and daily grows more and more enervate. One shall never be more sensible of this, than in turning an Author like Tacitus. I have been trying it in some parts of Thucydides (who has a little resemblance of him in his conciseness) and endeavoured to do it closely, but found it produced mere nonsense. If you have any inclination to see what figure Tacitus makes in Italian, I have a Tuscan translation of Davanzati, much esteemed in Italy; and will send you the same speech you sent me; that is, if you care for it. In the meantime accept of *Propertius*.[1] . . .

matic style; which (though he did not think them well founded, as they certainly were not) had an effect which Mr. West, we may believe, did not intend them to have. I remember some years after I was also the innocent cause of his delaying to finish his fine ode on the "Progress of Poetry." I told him on reading the part he showed me, that "though I admired it greatly, and thought that it breathed the very spirit of Pindar, yet I suspected it would by no means hit the public taste." Finding afterwards that he did not proceed in finishing it, I often expostulated with him on the subject; but he always replied, "No, you have thrown cold water upon it." I mention this little anecdote to show how much the opinion of a friend, even when it did not convince his judgment, affected his inclination. —[*Mason.*]

[1] A translation of the first elegy of the second book into English rhyme; omitted by Mason. It is published in this edition, vol. i. p. 153.—[*Ed.*]

XLVI.—TO RICHARD WEST.

London, May 8, 1742.

I REJOICE to see you putting up your prayers to the May.[1] She cannot choose but come at such a call. It is as light and genteel as herself. You bid me find fault; I am afraid I cannot; however I will try. The first stanza (if what you say to me in it did not make me think it the best) I should call the worst of the five (except the fourth line). The two next are very picturesque, Miltonic, and musical; her bed is so soft and so snug that I long to lie with her. But those two lines "Great nature" are my favourites. The exclamation of the flowers is a little step too far. The last stanza is full as good as the second and third; the last line bold, but I think not too bold. Now, as to myself and my translation, pray do not call names. I never saw Broukhusius in my life. It is Scaliger who attempted to range *Propertius* in order; who was, and still is, in sad condition.[2] . . . You see, by what I sent you, that I converse as usual with none but the dead: they are my old friends, and almost make me long to be with them. You will not wonder, therefore, that I, who live only in times past, am able to tell you no news of the present. I have finished the Peloponnesian war much to my

[1] West had obliged his friend with a very pretty "Ode on May," in which he addressed himself to

"Dear Gray that always in my heart
Possessest far the better part."—[*Ed.*]

[2] Here some criticism on West's Elegy is omitted.—[*Mason.*]

honour, and a tight conflict it was, I promise you. I have drank and sung with Anacreon for the last fortnight, and am now feeding sheep with Theocritus. Besides, to quit my figure (because it is foolish) I have run over Pliny's Epistles and Martial ἐκ παρέργου; not to mention Petrarch, who, by the way, is sometimes very tender and natural. I must needs tell you three lines in Anacreon, where the expression seems to me inimitable. He is describing hair as he would have it painted.

"Ἕλικας δ' ἐλευθέρους μοι
Πλοκάμων ἄτακτα συνθεὶς
Ἄφες ὡς θέλωσι κεῖσθαι."

Guess, too, where this is about a dimple.[1]

" Sigilla in mento impressa Amoris digitulo
Vestigio demonstrat mollitudinem."

XLVII.—TO RICHARD WEST.[2]

London, May 27, 1742.

MINE, you are to know, is a white Melancholy, or rather Leucocholy for the most part; which, though

[1] West replied that the fragment about a dimple was in Aulus Gellius. Upon which Mitford has a note to say that this is wrong, and that it is in Mori Marcellus. But there is no such writer. The lines are quoted in the *De Honestis Veterum Dictis* of Marcellus Nonius, a grammarian of the third century.—[*Ed.*]

[2] West died five days after this letter was written, and was buried in the chancel of Hatfield Church before Gray even knew that his decease was imminent. In a note hitherto unpublished Dyce says that Mitford told him "that West's death was hastened by mental anguish, there having been good reason to suspect that *his mother poisoned his father.*"—[*Ed.*]

it seldom laughs or dances, nor ever amounts to what one calls Joy or Pleasure, yet is a good easy sort of a state, and *ça ne laisse que de s'amuser.* The only fault of its insipidity; which is apt now and then to give a sort of *Ennui,* which makes one form certain little wishes that signify nothing. But there is another sort, black indeed, which I have now and then felt, that has somewhat in it like Tertullian's rule of faith, *Credo quia impossibile est;* for it believes, nay, is sure of everything that is unlikely, so it be but frightful; and on the other hand excludes and shuts its eyes to the most possible hopes, and everything that is pleasurable; from this the Lord deliver us! for none but he and sunshiny weather can do it. In hopes of enjoying this kind of weather, I am going into the country for a few weeks, but shall be never the nearer any society; so, if you have any charity, you will continue to write. My life is like Harry the Fourth's[1] supper of Hens, "Poulets à la broche, Poulets en Ragôut, Poulets en Hâchis, Poulets en Fricasées." Reading here, Reading there; nothing but books with different sauces. Do not let me lose my desert then; for though that be Reading too, yet it has a very different flavour. The May seems to be come since your invitation; and I propose to bask in her beams and dress me in her roses.

Et caput in vernâ semper habere rosâ.[2]

---

[1] Francis the First's supper of Hens, v. Boccaccio.—[*Rogers.*]
[2] *Propert.*, iii. 3, 44.

I shall see Mr. * * and his Wife, nay, and his Child too, for he has got a Boy. Is it not odd to consider one's Cotemporaries in the grave light of Husband and Father? There is my Lords [Sandwich] and [Halifax], they are Statesmen: do not you remember them dirty boys playing at cricket? As for me, I am never a bit the older, nor the bigger, nor the wiser than I was then: no, not for having been beyond sea. Pray how are you?

I send you an inscription for a wood joining to a park of mine (it is on the confines of Mount Cithœron, on the left hand, as you go to Thebes); you know I am no friend to hunters, and hate to be disturbed by their noise.

'Αζόμενος πολύθηρον ἑκηβόλου ἄλσος ἀνάσσας,
 Τᾶς δεινᾶς τεμένη λεῖπε κυναγὲ θεᾶς,
Μοῦνοι ἄρ' ἔνθα κυνῶν ζαθέων κλαγγεῦσιν ὑλαγμοι,
 'Ανταχεῖς Νυμφᾶν ἀγροτέραν κελάδῳ.

Here follows also the beginning of an Heroic Epistle; but you must give me leave to tell my own story first, because Historians differ. Massinissa was the son of Gala, King of the Massyli; and, when very young at the head of his father's army, gave a most signal overthrow to Syphax, King of the Masæsylians, then an ally of the Romans. Soon after Asdrubal, son of Gisgo the Carthaginian General, gave the beautiful Sophonisba, his daughter, in marriage to the young prince. But this marriage was not consummated on account of Massinissa's being obliged to hasten into Spain, there to command his father's troops, who were auxiliaries of the Carthaginians. Their affairs at this time began to be in a bad condition; and they thought it might be greatly for their interest, if they could bring over Syphax to themselves. This in time they actually effected; and to strengthen their new alliance, commanded Asdrubal to give his daughter to Syphax. (It is probable their ingratitude to Massinissa arose from the great change of affairs, which had happened among the Massylians during his absence; for his father and uncle were dead, and a distant relation of the royal family had usurped the throne.) Sophonisba was accordingly married to Syphax; and Massinissa, enraged at the affront, became a friend to the Romans. They drove the Carthaginians before them out of Spain, and carried the war into Africa, defeated Syphax, and took him prisoner; upon which Cirtha (his capital) opened her gates to Lælius and Massinissa. The rest of the affair, the marriage, and the sending of poison, everybody knows. This is partly taken from Livy, and partly from Appian.

. . . .

XLVIII.—TO THOMAS WHARTON.

My dear Wharton—It is a long time, since I ought to have returned you my thanks for the pleasure of your letter; I should say, the prodigy of your letter, for such a thing has not happened above twice within this last age to mortal man, and no one here can conceive what it may portend. Mr. Trollope, I suppose, has told you, how I was employed a part of the time; how by my own indefatigable application for these ten years past, and by the care and vigilance of that worthy magistrate, the Man-in-Blew[1] (who, I'll assure you, has not spared his labour, nor could have done more for his own son), I am got half-way to the Top[2] of Jurisprudence, and bid as fair as another body to open a case of impotency with all decency and circumspection. You see my ambition: I do not doubt, but some thirty years hence I shall convince the world and you, that I am a very pretty young fellow, and may come to shine in a profession perhaps the noblest in the world, next to man-midwifery. As for yours; if your distemper and you can but agree about going to London, I may reasonably expect in a much shorter time to see you in your three-cornered villa, doing the honours of a well-furnished table with as much dignity, as rich a mien, and as capacious a belly as Dr. Mead.[3] Methinks I see Dr. Askew at the lower end of it, lost in admiration of your goodly person and parts, cramming down his envy (for it will rise) with the wing of a pheasant, and drowning it in neat Burgundy. But not to tempt your asthma too much with such a prospect, I should think you might be almost as happy as, and as great as, this, even in the

[1] Servant of the Vice-Chancellor's for the time being, usually known by the name of Blue-coat, whose business it is to attend Acts for Degrees.—[*Mason.*]

[2] *i.e.* Bachelor of Civil Law.—[*Mason.*]

[3] Dr. Richard Mead (1673-1754), the famous physician.—[*Ed.*]

country. But you know best; and I should be sorry to say anything, that might stop you in the career of glory. Far be it from me to hamper the wheels of your gilded chariot. Go on, Sr Thomas; and when you die (for even physicians must die) may the faculty in Warwick Lane erect your statue in Sr John Cutler's own niche.

As to Cambridge it is, as it was, for all the world; and the people are, as they were; and Mr. Trollope is as he was, that is, half-ill, half-well. I wish with all my heart they were all better, but what can one do? There is no news, only I think I heard a whisper, as if the Vice-Chancellor should be with child (but I beg you not to mention this, for I may come into trouble about it); there is some suspicion, that the Professor of Mathematics had a hand in the thing. Dr. Dickens says the University will be obliged to keep it, as it was got in Magistratu.

I was going to tell you how sorry I am for your illness, but, I hope, it is too late to be sorry now. I can only say, that I really *was* very sorry. May you live a hundred Christmases, and eat as many collars of brawn stuck with rosemary. Adieu, I am sincerely yours, T. G[RAY].

Dec. 27 [1742]. Wont you come to the jubilee? Dr. Long[1] is to dance a saraband and hornpipe of

[1] See Life of Dr. Long, in Nichols' Ed. of *J. Taylor's Tracts*, p. liv.–lviii. there is a copy of verses by R. Long, Master of Pembroke, on the death of Fred., P. of Wales, the last in the

his own invention, without lifting either foot once from the ground.

XLIX.—TO THOMAS WHARTON.

YOU write so feelingly to little Mr. Brown, and represent your abandoned condition in terms so touching, that, what gratitude could not effect in several months, compassion has brought about in a few days, and broke that strong attachment, or rather allegiance, w[ch] I and all here owe to our sovereign lady and mistress, the president of presidents, and head of heads (if I may be permitted to pronounce her name, that ineffable Octogrammaton) the power of *Laziness.* You must know she had been pleased to appoint me (in preference to so many old servants of hers, who had spent their whole lives in qualifying themselves for the office) grand picker of straws, and push-pin player in ordinary to her Supinity (for that is her title), the first is much in the nature of lord president

volume. The English Poems collected from the Oxford and Cambridge verses on the death of Fred., P. of Wales., Edinb., 1751, beginning,

> "Yes! I will weep for thy untimely fate,
> Oh! much lov'd Prince! that part I can perform.
> To take my portion of the general grief,
> Although by seventy winters' freezing blasts,
> All chill'd my blood, and damp'd poetic fire."

In this volume, among the *Oxford* contributors, are S. Spence, J. Musgrave, J. Heskin, B. Kennicott, R. Louth; among the *Cambridge*, F. Neville, Erasm. Darwin, R. Cumberland, and R. Long.—[*Mit.*]

of the council, and the other, like the groom-porter, only without the profit. But as they are both things of very great honour in this country, I considered with myself the load of envy attending such great charges, and besides (between you and I) I found myself unable to support the fatigue of keeping up the appearance, that persons of such dignity must do, so I thought proper to decline it, and excused myself as well as I could: however as you see such an affair must take up a good deal of time, and it has always been the policy of this court to proceed slowly, like the Imperial, and that of Spain, in the dispatch of business; so that you will the easier forgive me, if I have not answered your letter before.

You desire to know, it seems, what character the Poem of your young friend[1] bears here. I wonder to hear you ask the opinion of a nation, where those who pretend to judge, don't judge at all; and the rest (the wiser part) wait to catch the judgment of the world immediately above them, that is, Dick's coffee-house, and the Rainbow; so that the readier way would be to ask Mrs. This and Mrs. T'other, that keeps the bar there. However, to shew you I'm a judge, as well as my countrymen, tho' I have rather

[1] "Pleasures of the Imagination:" from the posthumous publication of Dr. Akenside's *Poems*, it should seem that the Author had very much the same opinion afterwards of his own Work, which Mr. Gray here expresses: since he undertook a reform of it which must have given him, had he concluded it, as much trouble as if he had written it entirely new.—[*Mason.*] Akenside's *Poems* appeared anonymously in January 1744.—[*Ed.*]

turned it over, than read it (but no matter: no more have they), it seems to me above the middleing, and now and then (but for a little while) rises even to the best, particularly in description. It is often obscure, and even unintelligible, and too much infected with the Hutchinson-jargon; in short its great fault is that it was published at least nine years too early; and so methinks in a few words, à la mode du temple, I have very pertly dispatched what perhaps may for several years have employed a very ingenious man worth fifty of myself. Here is a small poem, called the "Enthusiast,"[1] which is all pure description, and as they tell me by the same hand. Is it so, or not? Item, a more bulky one upon "Health,"[2] wrote by a physician: do you know him? Master Tommy Lucretius[3] (since you are so good to enquire after the child) is but a puleing chitt yet, not a bit grown to speak of, I believe, poor thing! it has got the worms, that will carry it off at last. Oh Lord! I forgot to tell you, that Mr. Trollope and I are in a course of tar-water, he for his present, and I for my future dis-

[1] "The Enthusiast, or the Lover of Nature," by Joseph Warton.

[2] "The Art of preserving Health," a Didactic Poem, by John Armstrong, 1744.

[3] Master Tommy Lucretius seems to be the Author's more familiar name for the Poem, "De Principiis Cogitandi." The reader is requested to compare all the latter part of this Letter, with that, which is intended to represent it in Mason's Edition. The passage about Socrates is so altered by Mason, as to be but little short of perfect nonsense.—[*Mit.*] Mitford misdated this Letter 1746.—[*Ed.*]

tempers; if you think it will kill me, send away a man and horse directly, for I drink like a fish. I should be glad to know how your —— goes on, and give you joy of it.

You are much in the right to have a taste for Socrates, he was a divine man. I must tell you, by way of the news of the place, that the other day, Mr. Traigneau (entering upon his Professorship) made an apology for him an hour long in the schools, and all the world, except Trinity College, brought in Socrates guilty. Adieu, Dr Sir, and believe me your Friend and Servant, T. G.

Cambridge, Thursday, April 26 [endorsed 1744].

L.—TO THOMAS WHARTON.

My dear Wharton—This is only to entreat you would order *mes gens* to clean out the apartments, spread the carpets, air the beds, put up the tapestry, unpaper the frames, etc.; fit to receive a great potentate, who comes down in the flying coach, drawn by green dragons on Friday, the 10th instant. As the ways are bad, and the dragons a little out of repair (for they don't actually fly; but only go, like a lame ostrich, something between a hop and a trot) it will probably be late when he lands, so he would not choose to be known, and desires there may be no bells, nor bonfires. But as persons incog. love to be seen, he will slip into the coffee-house. Is Mr. Trollope among you? good lack! he will pull off my head for never writing to him, oh Conscience, Conscience!

Fragment.

London, October 8 [44 or 45].

LI.—TO THOMAS WHARTON.

I AM not lost; here am I at Stoke, whither I came on Tuesday, and shall be again in town on Saturday, and at Cambridge on Wednesday or Thursday, you may be anxious to know what has past. I wrote a note the night I came, and immediately received a very civil answer. I went the following evening to see the *party* (as Mrs. Foible says), was something abashed at his confidence: he came to meet me, kissed me on both sides with all the ease of one, who receives an acquaintance just come out of the country, squatted me into a Fauteuil, begun to talk of the town and this and that and t'other, and continued with little interruption for three hours, when I took my leave very indifferently pleased, but treated with wondrous good breeding. I supped with him next night (as he desired) Ashton[1] was there, whose formalities tickled me inwardly, for he I found was to be angry about the letter I had wrote him. However in going home together our hackney-coach jumbled us into a sort of reconciliation: he hammered out somewhat like an excuse; and I received it very readily, because I cared not twopence, whether it were true or not. So we

[1] See Walpole's *Letter to Mann*, vol. ii. p. 371.—[*Ed.*]

grew the best acquaintance imaginable, and I sat with him on Sunday some hours alone, when he informed me of abundance of anecdotes much to my satisfaction, and in short opened (I really believe) his heart to me with that sincerity, that I found I had still less reason to have a good opinion of him, than (if possible) I ever had before. Next morning I breakfasted alone with Mr. W[alpole]; when we had all the eclaircissement[1] I ever expected, and I left him far better satisfied, than I had been hitherto. When I return, I shall see him again. Such is the epitome of my four days. Mr. and Mrs. Simms and Mad^lle. Nanny have done the honours of Leaden Hall to a miracle, and all join in a compliment to the Doctor. Your brother is well, the books are in good condition. Mad^me. Chenevix has frightened me with Ecritoires she asks three

[1] It appears by this Letter, that the reconciliation which is mentioned as having taken place between Gray and Walpole, was (as far at least as the former was concerned) rather an act of civility and good manners, than the re-establishment of a cordial and sincere attachment. I am now, by the kindness of a gentleman, to whom I have been more than once obliged, enabled to lay before the public the real cause of their separation, on the authority of the late Mr. Isaac Reed; in whose handwriting, in Wakefield's *Life of Gray*, is the following note: "Mr. Roberts, of the Pell-office, who was likely to be well informed, told me at Mr. Deacon's, 19th April 1799. That the quarrel between Gray and Walpole was occasioned by a suspicion Mr. Walpole entertained, that Mr. Gray had spoken ill of him to some friends in England. To ascertain this, he clandestinely opened a letter, and resealed it, which Mr. Gray, with great propriety, resented; there seems to have been but little cordiality afterwards between them."—[*Mit.*]

guineas for, that are not worth three half-pence: I have been in several shops and found nothing pretty. I fear it must be bespoke at last.

The day after I went you received a little letter directed to me, that seems wrote with a skewer, please to open it, and you 'll find a receipt of Dan. Adcock for ten pound, wch I will beg you to receive of Gillham for me. If the letter miscarried, pray take care the money is paid to no one else. I expect to have a letter from you when I come to town, at your lodgings. Adieu, S$^{r.}$ I am sincerely yours,

T. G.

Stoke, Thursday, [post-mark 16th Nov.]
[endorsement 1744 or 1745.]

LII.—TO JOHN CHUTE—FRAGMENT.

. . . Jews-harp, ask Mr. Whithed, whither when he goes to Heaven, he does not expect to see all his favourite Hens, all his dear little *Pouls*, untimely victims of the pot and the spit, come pipping and gobling in a melodious voice about him; I know he does; there's nothing so natural. Poor Conti! is he going to be a Cherub? I remember here (but he was not ripe then) he had a very promising squeak with him, and that his mouth, when open, made an exact square. I have never been at Ranelagh Gardens since they were opened (for what does it signify to me), but they do not succeed, people see it once, or twice, and so they go to Vauxhall; well, but is not it a very great design, very new, finely lighted, well, yes, ay, very fine truly, so they yawn and go to Vauxhall, and then it's too hot, and then it's too cold, and here's a wind, and there's a damp, and so the women go to bed, and the men to a —— House. You are to take notice, that in our Country, Delicacy and Indelicacy amount to much the same thing. The first will not be pleased with anything, and the other cannot. However, to do us justice, I think we are a reasonable, but by no means a pleasurable people; and to mend us we must have a dash of the French and Italian; yet I don't know how. Travelling does not produce its right effect.—I find I am talking, but you are to attribute it to my having at last found a Pen that writes.

You are so good, 'tis a shame to scold at you, but you never till now certified me, that you were at Casa Ambrosio. I did not know in what light to consider you. I had an Idea, but did not know where to put it, for an Idea must have a place per campeggiar bene. You were an Intaglia unset, a Picture without a frame, but now all is well; tho' I am not very sure yet, whether you are above stairs, or on the ground-floor, but by your mentioning the Terrazino, it must be the latter. Do the Frogs of Arno sing as sweetly as they did in my days? do you sup al fresco? Have you a Mugherino tree, and a *Nanny?* I fear, I don't spell this last word right, pray ask Mr. M. Oh! dear! I fear I was a blunderer about Hyacynths, for to be sure they cannot be taken out of the ground, till they have done blooming, and they are perhaps just now in flower. That you may know my *Place*, I am just going into the country, for one easy fortnight, and then in earnest intend to go to Cambridge, to Trinity Hall: my sole reason (as you know) is to look, as if——and when I feel it go against my stomach, I remember it was your Prescription, and so it goes down. Look upon me, then, my dear Sir, in my proper light, and consider how necessary it is to me, to hear from you as often as you can bestow an hour upon me. I flatter myself, your kindness will try to get the better of your indolence, when you reflect how cruelly alone I must be in the midst of that crowd!

The remainder of this page I hope you will pardon me, if I dedicate to my good dear Mr. Mann. Sir, I had the pleasure of receiving your good dear letter, and only deferred thanking you till now, that I might be able to execute your little commission first, the contents of which I send to your Brother, along with this letter. But first let me enquire how you do? alas! Sir, you may call 'em Benevoli, or whatever soft names you please, but I much fear they don't understand their business, like our people with a thousand consonants. I perfectly believe Dr. Cocchis' good intentions, but he is not the executioner himself, and here it is not sufficient to wish well. If it were, I'm certain my wishes are fervent enough to be felt even at Florence, in spite of all the lands, and seas, and enemies that lie betwixt us. They are daily employed for your happiness, and will, I hope, be of more use to you, than they have been to myself. The Books I send you are the *Etat de la France*, 3 vol. fol. upon my word, an excellent book. He is a sensible, knowing Englishman, only had the misfortune to be born in France. *Life of Mahomet* by the same author, it is famous, you are desired to make no reflections, nor draw consequences, when you read it. Ld. Burleigh's *Papers* seem very curious, and well enough chose: by the way, they have lately published Thurlow's *Papers* here, in 7 vol. folio, out of which it would be hard to collect a Pocket volume worth having. Dr. Middleton's *Cicero*, 2 vol. and a letter on the Catholic religion worth your reading. *Philip de Commines*, 5 vol. the Louvre edition is much more splendid, but wants the supplement and notes, which are here. *W*ⁿ· *on the M*ˢ·[1] a very impudent fellow, his dedications will make you laugh. Ludlow's *Memoirs*, 3 vol. as unorthodox in Politics, as the other in Religion. *2 lyttel Bookys tocheing Kyng James the Fyrst;* very rare. *Le Sopha*,[2] de Crebillon—Collect. of Plays, 10 vol. There are none of Shakspear, because you had better have all his works together, they come to about £7. 18s. 6d. the whole cargo. You will find among them 3 Parts of *Marianne*[3] for Mr. Chute; if he has them already, how can I help it? why would he make no mention of Mad. de Thevire to one?

[1] Warburton's *Reflections on the Miraculous Powers.*—[*Ed.*]
[2] The well-known satirical romance, published in 1740.
[3] The novel by Marivaux.

And now let me congratulate you as no longer a Min: but for del mondo veramente un Ministrone, and King of the Mediterranean. Pray your Majesty, give orders to your men of war, if they touch at Naples, to take care of ma collection, and be sure don't let them bombard Genoa. If you can bully the Pope out of the Apollo Belvidere, well and good: I'm not against it. I'm enchanted with your good sister the Queen of Hungary; as old as I am, I could almost fight for her myself. See what it is to be happy. Everybody will fight for those that have no occasion for them. Pray take care to continue so, but whether you do, or not, I am truly yours,

T. G.

July [1745], London.

The Parliament's up, and all the world are made Lords, and Secretaries, and Commissioners.

LIII.—TO HORACE WALPOLE.

Cambridge, February 3, 1746.

DEAR SIR—You are so good to enquire after my usual time of coming to town: it is a season when even you, the perpetual friend of London, will, I fear, hardly be in it—the middle of June: and I commonly return hither in September; a month when I may more probably find you at home.

Our defeat[1] to be sure is a rueful affair for the

[1] Defeat at Falkirk, under General Hawley. See *Jacobite Memoirs*, or Forbes' *Papers*, p. 89.—[*Mit.*]

honour of the troops; but the Duke is gone it seems with the rapidity of a cannon-bullet to undefeat us again.[1] The common people in town at least know how to be afraid: but we are such uncommon people here as to have no more sense of danger than if the battle had been fought when and where the battle of Cannæ was.

The perception of these calamities, and of their consequences, that we are supposed to get from books, is so faintly impressed, that we talk of war, famine, and pestilence, with no more apprehension than of a broken head, or of a coach overturned between York and Edinburgh.

I heard three people, sensible middle-aged men (when the Scotch were said to be at Stamford, and actually were at Derby), talking of hiring a chaise to go to Caxton (a place in the high road) to see the Pretender and the Highlanders as they passed.

I can say no more for Mr. Pope (for what you keep in reserve may be worse than all the rest).[2] It is natural to wish the finest writer, one of them, we ever had, should be an honest man. It is for the interest even of that virtue, whose friend he professed himself, and whose beauties he sung, that he should not be found a dirty animal. But, however,

1 "The Duke is gone post to Edinburgh, where he hoped to arrive to-night, if possible to relieve Stirling." V. H. Walpole's *Let. to Mann*, vol. ii. p. 121.—[*Mit.*]

2 This is probably a reference to the scandals about Atossa and the *Patriot King*. Pope had died on the 30th of May 1744.—[*Ed.*]

this is Mr. Warburton's business, not mine, who may scribble his pen to the stumps and all in vain, if these facts are so. It is not from what he told me about himself that I thought well of him, but from a humanity and goodness of heart, ay, and greatness of mind, that runs through his private correspondence, not less apparent than are a thousand little vanities and weaknesses mixed with those good qualities, for nobody ever took him for a philosopher. If you know anything of Mr. Mann's state of health and happiness, or the motions of Mr. Chute homewards, it will be a particular favour to inform me of them, as I have not heard this half-year from them.—I am sincerely yours, T. GRAY.

LIV.—TO JOHN CHUTE.

MY DEAR SIR—Three days ago as I was in the Coffee-House very deep in advertisements, a servant came in and waked me (as I thought) with the name of Mr. Chute; for half a minute I was not sure, but that it was you transported into England, by some strange chance, the Lord knows how, till he brought me to a coach that seem'd to have lost its way, by looking for a needle in a bottle of hay. In it was a lady who said she was not you, but only a near relation, and was so good to give me a letter, with which I return'd to my den, in order to prey upon it. I had wrote to you but a few days ago, and am glad of so good an excuse to do it again, which I may the better do, as my last was all out, and nothing to the purpose, being design'd for a certain Mr. Chute at Rome, and not him at Florence.

I learn from it that I have been somewhat smarter than I ought, but (to shew you with how little malice) I protest I have not the least idea what it was. My memory would be better, did I read my own letters so often as I do yours: you must attribute it to a sort of kittenish disposition that scratches, where it means to caress. However, I repent neither, if 'tis that has made you write. I know, I need not ask pardon, for you have forgiven me: nay, I have a good mind, to complain myself—How could you say, that I designed to hurt you, because I knew you could feel. I hate the thoughts of it, and would not for the world wound anything that was sensible. 'Tis true, I should be glad to scratch the careless, or the foolish; but no armour is so impenetrable as indifference, and stupidity, and so I may keep my claws to myself. For another instance of the shortness of my memory, would you believe, I have so little knowledge of the Florentine History, as not to guess who the Lady Errant is, you mention? sure it can't be the R$^{di.}$ and her faithful swain, or may be M. G$^{di.}$ and the little abbé; what you do there so long I have no conception; if you stay at other places in proportion, I despair of ever seeing you again. 'Tis true indeed Mr. Mann is not everywhere; I am shock'd to think of his sufferings, but he of all men was born to suffer with a good grace. He is a Stoick without knowing it, and seems to think pain a pleasure. I am very sorry to compliment him upon such an occasion, and wish with all my heart, he were not so pleased. I much fear his books are gone already; but if not, to be sure he shall have *Middleton* and the *Sofa*;[1] it seems most people here are not such admirers of it as I was: but I wont give up an inch of it, for all that. Did I tell you about Mr. Garrick, that the town are horn-mad after: there are a dozen Dukes of a night at Goodmansfields sometimes, and yet I am stiff in the opposition. Our fifth Opera was the *Olympiade*, in which they retained most of Pergolesi's songs, and yet 'tis gone already, as if it had been a poor thing of Galuppis'.[2] Two nights did I enjoy it all alone, snug in a nook of the gallery, but found no one in those regions had ever heard of Pergolesi,[3] nay, I heard several affirm it was a composition of Pescetti's.[4] Now there is a 6th sprung up, by the name of *Cephalo and Procri*. My Lady of Queensbury is come out against my Lady of Marlborough, and she has her spirit too, and her originality, but more of the woman, I think, than t'other. As to the facts, it don't signify two pence who's in the right; the manner of fighting, and character of the combatants is all: 'tis hoped old Sarah

[1] The *Sofa* of Crebillon, see p. 128.—[*Ed.*]

[2] Baldassaro Galuppi (1706-1785).

[3] Giambattista Pergolesé (1710-1736).

[4] Giambattista Pescetti, died in 1758, a composer of facile operas, then popular, now entirely forgotten.—[*Ed.*]

will at her again. A play of Mr. Glover's[1] I am told, is preparing for the stage, call'd *Boadicea;* it is a fine subject, but I have not an extreme opinion of him. The invalides at Chelsea intend to present Ranelagh Gardens, as a nuisance, for breaking their first sleep with the sound of fiddles; it opens, I think, to-night. Messieurs the Commons are to ballot for 7 persons to-morrow, commission'd to state the public accounts, and they are to be such, who have no places, nor are any ways dependent on the King. The Committee have petitioned for all papers relating to the Convention. A bill has pass'd the lower house, for indemnifying all who might subject themselves to penalties, by revealing any transaction with regard to the conduct of my Lord Orford, and to-morrow the Lords are summon'd about it. The wit of the times consists in Satyrical Prints; I believe there have been some hundreds within this month. If you have any hopeful young designer of caricaturas, that has a political turn, he may pick up a pretty subsistence here: let him pass thro' Holland to improve his taste by the way. We are all very sorry for poor Queen Hungary: but we know of a second battle (which perhaps you may never hear of, but from me), as how Prince Lobbycock came up in the nick of time, and cut 120,000 of them all to pieces; and how the King

[1] Richard Glover (1712-1785), a merchant and Whig M.P., who wrote the once-famous epic of *Leonidas.* His tragedy of *Boadicea* awakened great expectations, but was a failure on the stage. It was not brought out until 1753.—[*Ed.*]

of Prussia narrowly escap'd aboard a ship, and so got down the Dannub to Wolf-in-Bottle, where Mr. Mallyboyce lay encamped; and how the Hannoverians, with Prince Hissy-Castle, at their head, fell upon the French Mounseers, and took him away with all his treasure, among which is Pitt's diamond, and the great cistern—all this is firmly believed here, and a vast deal more: upon the strength of which we intend to declare war with France.

You are so obliging as to put me in mind of our last year's little expeditions; alas! Sir, they are past, and how many years will it be, at the rate you go on, before we can possibly renew them in this country: in all probability I shall be gone first on a long expedition to that undiscover'd country, from whose bourn no traveller returns: however (if I can), I will think of you, as I sail down the *River of Eternity.* I can't help thinking, that I should find no difference almost between this world, and t'other (for I converse with none but the dead here), only indeed I should receive nor write no more letters (for the Post is not very well regulated). If you see the King of Naples, pray talk with him on this subject, for I see he is upon settling one between his country and Constantinople, and I take this to be but a little more difficult.

My dab of Musick, and Prints, you are very good to think of sending with your own, to which I will add a farther trouble, by desireing you to send me some of the roots of a certain Flower, which I have seen at Florence. It is a huge white Hyacynth tinged with pink (Mr. M. knows what I mean, by the same token that they grow sometimes in the fat Gerina's *Boosom*), I mean if they bear a reasonable price, which you will judge of for me: but don't give yourself any pains about it, for if they are not easily had, and at an easy rate, I am not at all eager for them. Do you talk of *Strumming?* ohi me! who have not seen the face of a *Haspical*, since I came home; no! I have hang'd up my Harp on the Willows: however, I look at my musick now and then, that I may not forget it; for when you return, I intend to sing a song of thanksgiving, and praise the Lord with a cheerful noise of many-stringed instruments. Adieu! dear Sir, I am sincerely yours,

T. G.

O. S. London. Not forgetting my kiss-hands to Mr. Whithed.

M . . 1 . [1746?] [torn.]

LV.—TO JOHN CHUTE.

My dear Sir—What do you choose I should think of a whole year's silence; have you absolutely forgot me, or do you not reflect, that it is from yourself alone I can have any information concerning you. I do not find myself inclined to forget you, the same regard for your Person, the same desire of seeing you again I felt when we parted, still continues with me as fresh as ever; don't wonder then if in spite of appearances, I try to flatter myself with the hopes of finding sentiments something of the same kind, however, buried in some dark corner of your heart; and perhaps more than half extinguished by long absence and various cares of a different nature. I will not alarm your indolence with a long letter, my demands are only three, and may be answer'd in as many words,—how you do? where you are? and when you return? if you choose to add anything farther, it will be a work of superer—— I will not write so long a word entire, least I fatigue your delicacy, and you may think it incumbent on you to answer it by another of equal dimensions. You believe me, I hope, with great sincerity, yours,

T. G.

P.S.—For ought I know you may be in England. My very true compliments (not such as People make to one another) wait upon Mr. Whithed. He will be the most travelled Gentleman in Hampshire.

October 25, Cambridge.

LVI.—TO THOMAS WHARTON.

MY DEAR WHARTON—I am just returned hither from town, where I have past better than a fortnight (including an excursion that I made to Hampton Court, Richmond, Greenwich, and other places), and am happily met by a letter from you, one from Tuthill, and another from Trollope. As I only run over Dr. Andrew's Answers hastily in a Coffee-house, all I could judge was that they seemed very unfavourable on the whole to our cause, and threw everything into the hands of a visitour, for which reason I thought they might have been concealed, till the Attorney-General's opinion arrived, which will perhaps raise the spirits of such, as the other may have damped a little; or leave room at least to doubt, whether the matter be so clear on the Master's side as Andrew would have it. You can't suppose that I was in the least uneasy about Mr. Brown's[1] fortitude, who wants nothing but a foot in height and his own hair, to make him a little old Roman: with two dozen such I should not hesitate to face an army of heads, though they were all as tall as Dr. Adams. I only wish everybody may continue in as good a disposition as they were; and imagine, if possible, Roger[2] will be fool enough to keep them so. I saw Trollope for about an hour in London; and imagining he could not be left in the dark as to your consultations, I mentioned, that I had cast an eye over Andrew's paper, and that it was not so favourable as we hoped. He spoke however with horrour of going to law; with great passion of the master; and with pleasure of

[1] The Rev. James Brown, in 1770 elected Master of Pembroke College, and joint executor with Mason of Gray's will. He died in 1784.

[2] Dr. Roger Long, Master of Pembroke College, Cambridge.

himself for quitting a place, where he had not found a minute's ease in I know not how long: yet I perceive his thoughts run on nothing else; he trembled while he spoke. He writes to me here on the same subject; and after abusing Roger, he adds, Whartoni rubro hæc subscribe libello.

My evenings have been chiefly spent at Ranelagh and Vauxhall, several of my mornings, or rather noons, in Arlington Street,[1] and the rest at the tryal of the Lords. The first day I was not there, and only saw the Lord High Steward's parade in going; the second and third [. . . Peers were all in their robes . . . by their wearing bag-wigs and hats instead of coronets. My Lord High-Steward][2] was the least part of the shew, as he wore only his baron's robe, and was always asking the heralds what he should do next, and bowing or smileing about to his acquaintance. As to his speech, you see it; people hold it very cheap, tho' several incorrectnesses have been altered in the printed copy. Kilmarnock[3] spoke in mitigation of his crime near half an hour, with a decent courage, and in a strong, but pathetic, voice. His figure would prejudice people in his favour, being

[1] At Mr. Walpole's.

[2] All words after "third" to "was the least part" have been lost from the bottom of the MS.; but some person has stated on the top of the MS. page that some of the words were what are here given.—[*Ed.*]

[3] William Boyd, fourth Earl of Kilmarnock in Scotland, beheaded on Tower Hill, August 18, 1746.

"Pitied by gentle minds Kilmarnock died."—*Johnson*.—[*Mit.*]

tall and genteel; he is upwards of forty, but to the eye not above thirty-five years of age. What he said appears to less advantage, when read. Cromartie[1] (who is about the same age, a man of lower stature, but much like a gentleman), was sinking into the earth with grief and dejection. With eyes cast down, and a voice so low, that no one heard a syllable, that did not sit close to the bar; he made a short speech to raise compassion. It is now, I see printed; and is reckoned extremely fine. I believe, you will think it touching and well expressed: if there be any meanness in it, it is lost in that sorrow he gives us for so numerous and helpless a family. Lady Cromartie[2] (who is said to have drawn her husband into these circumstances) was at Leicester House on Wednesday, with four of her children; the Princess saw her, and made no other answer than by bringing in her own children and placing them by her; which (if true) is one of the prettiest things I ever heard. She was also at the Duke's, who refused to admit her: but she waited till he came to his coach, and threw herself at his knees, while her children hung upon him, till he promised her all his interest could do; and before on several occasions he has been heard to speak very mildly of Cromartie, and very severely of Kilmarnock.

[1] George Mackenzie, third Earl of Cromartie.

[2] Lady Cromartie was Isabel, daughter of Sir William Gordon, of Invergordon, Bart. "Lady Cromartie went down incog. to Woolwich to see her son pass by without the power of speaking to him. I never heard a more melancholy instance of affection."—Walpole's *Letters to Mann*, vol. ii. p. 156.—[*Mit.*]

So if any be spared, it will probably be the former, though he had a pension of £600 a-year from the government, and the order for giving quarter to no Englishman was found in his pocket. As to Balmerino,[1] he never had any hopes from the beginning. He is an old soldier-like man, of a vulgar manner and aspect, speaks the broadest Scotch, and shews an intrepidity, that some ascribe to real courage, and some to brandy. You have heard perhaps, that the first day (while the Peers were adjourned to consider of his plea, and he left alone for an hour and a half in the bar) he diverted himself with the axe, that stood by him, played with its tassels, and tryed the edge with his finger: and some lord, as he passed by him, saying he was surprised to hear him alledge anything so frivolous, and that could not possibly do him the least service; he answered, that as there were so many ladies present, he thought it would be uncivil to give them no amusement. The Duke of Argyle, telling him, how sorry and how astonished he was to see him engaged in such a cause. My Lord (says he) for the two Kings and their rights I cared not a farthing, which prevailed; but I was starving; and by God if Mahomet had set up his standard in the Highlands, I had been a good Mussulman for bread, and stuck close to the party, for I must eat. The Solicitor-General came up to speak to him too, and he

[1] Arthur Elphinstone, sixth and last Lord Balmerino in Scotland. He was beheaded at the same time and place with Lord Kilmarnock.

turns about to old Williamson. Who is that Lawyer, that talks to me? My Lord, it is Mr. Murray. Ha! Mr. Murray, my good Friend (says he, and shook him by the hand) and how does your good mother? oh! she was of admirable service to us; we should have done nothing without her in Perthshire. He recommends (he says) his Peggy[1] ('tis uncertain[2] . . . the favour of the Government, for she has. . . .

I have been diverted with an account of Lord Lovat[3] in his confinement at Edinburgh. There was a Captain Maggett, that is obliged to lie in the room every night with him. When first he was introduced to him, he made him come to his bed-side where he lay in a hundred flannel waistcoats and a furred night-gown, took him in his arms, and gave him a long embrace, that absolutely suffocated him. He will speak nothing but French; insists upon it, that Maggett is a Frenchman and calls him, mon cher Capitaine Magot (you know *Magot* is a monkey); at

[1] Margaret, Lady Balmerino, daughter of Captain Chalmers.

[2] The MS. has here been torn.—[*Ed.*]

[3] Simon Fraser, Lord Lovat, beheaded on Tower Hill the 9th of April 1747. Thus mentioned in one of Walpole's Letters, April 16, 1747. "You have heard that old Lovat's Tragedy is over. . . . I must tell you an excessive good thing of George Selwyn. Some women were scolding him for going to see the execution, and asked him how he could be such a barbarian, to see the head cut off? 'Nay (says he), if that was such a crime, I am sure I have made amends, for I went to see it sewed on again.' When he was at the undertaker's, as soon as they had stitched him together, and were going to put the body into the coffin, George, in my Lord Chancellor's voice, said,—'My Lord Lovat, your lordship may rise.'"—[*Mit.*]

his head lie two Highland women at his feet two Highland men. By his bed-side is a close-stool to which he rises two or three times in a night, and always says,—Ah, mon cher Capitaine Magot! vous m'excuserez, mais la Nature demande que je chie! He is to be impeached by the House of Commons, because not being actually in arms, it would otherwise be necessary, that the jury of Inverness should find a Bill of Indictment against him, which it is very sure they would not do. When the Duke returned to Edinburgh they refused to admit Kingston's Light Horse and talked of their privileges. But they came in sword in hand, and replied, that when the Pretender was at their gates, they had said nothing of their privileges. The Duke rested some hours there, but refused to see the magistracy.

I believe you may think it full time, that I close my budget of stories: Mr. W[alpole] I have seen a good deal, and shall do a good deal more, I suppose, for he is looking for a house somewhere about Windsor[1] during the Summer. All is mighty free, and even friendly more than one could expect. You remember a paper in the Museum on Message-Cards which he told me was Fielding's, and asked my opinion about: it was his own, and so was the Advertisement on Good Breeding, that made us laugh so.

[1] See Walpole's *Letters to Mann*, vol. ii. p. 172. I have taken a pretty house at Windsor, and am going there for the remainder of the Summer. I have taken a small house here within the Castle!—[*Mit.*]

Mr. A[shton] I have had several conversations with, and do really believe he shews himself to me such as he really is: I don't tell you, I like him ever the better for it; but that may be my fault, not his. The Pelhams lie very hard at his stomach: he is not 40 yet, but he is 31, he says, and thinks it his duty to be married. One thing of that kind is just broke off; she had [£]12,000 in her own hands. This is a profound secret, but I not conceiving that he told it m[e as][1] such, happened to tell it to Stonhewer, who told it to Lyne, who told it Asht[on]: again, all i[n the][1] space of three hours whereby I incurred a scolding; so pray don't let me fall under [a][1] second, and lose all my hopes of rising in the church. He is still, as I said, resolute to m[arry][1] out of hand; only two things he is terrified at, lest she should not breed, and lest she should love him: I comforted him by saying, there was no danger of either.

The Muse, I doubt, is gone, and has left me in far worse company: if she returns, you will hear of her. You see I have left no room for a catalogue, which is a sort of policy, for it's hardly possible my memory should supply one: I will try by next time, which will be soon, if I hear from you. If your curiosity require any more circumstances of these tryals[2] . . . will see . . . find some gre . . . . My best compliments

[1] The words in brackets have been supplied by Mitford, a piece being torn from the edge of the MS.—[*Ed.*]

[2] After "tryals" three-quarters of a line is lost, and "will see" are only the first words of the next line, and "find some gre" of the next following.—[*Ed.*]

to the little man of the world. Adieu, my dear Wharton.—Believe me very truly yours,

T. GRAY.

Stoke, Sunday [post-mark 13th August]
[endorsement 1746].

LVII.—TO THOMAS WHARTON.

MY DEAR WHARTON—What can one say to these things? if it had been in the power of lawyers to interpret into common sense statutes made by old monks, or monk-directed old women, we might have hoped for a more favourable answer to our queries? as it is, I fear they may have done more hurt than good: all I know, is this, that I should rejoice poor T[uthill] had some place to rest the sole of his foot in; and I flatter myself you will never omit anything in your power to support his little interest among a people, with whom you first raised it. I would gladly know the time of your audit, for I would be at Cambridge by that time, if I could. Mr. W[alpole] has taken a house in Windsor and I see him usually once a week; but I think, that will hardly detain me beyond the time I proposed to myself. He is at present gone to town to perform the disagreeable task of presenting and introducing about a young Florentine, the Marquis Rinuccini,[1] who comes recommended to him. The D[uke][2] is

[1] A young "cub," the son of an elder Marquis of the same name, who had been Tuscan Envoy in England.—[*Ed.*]

[2] The Duke of Cumberland.

here at his lodge with three whores, and three Aid-de-camps; and the country swarms with people. He goes to races, and they make a ring about him, as at a bear-baiting; and no wonder, for they do the same at Vauxhall and Ranelagh. At this last, somebody was telling me they heard a man lamenting to some women of his acquaintance, and saying, how he had been up close to him, and he never repented of anything so much in his life, as that he did not touch him.

I am not altogether of your opinion, as to your Historical consolation in time of trouble. A calm melancholy it may produce, a stiller sort of despair, (and that only in some circumstances and on some constitutions) but I doubt no real content or comfort can ever arise in the human mind, but from Hope. Old Balmerino when he had read his paper to the people, pulled off his spectacles, spit upon his handkerchief, and wiped them clean for the use of his posterity; and that is the last page of his history. Have you seen Hogarth's print of Lord Lovat? it is admirable.

I cannot help thinking if I had been near you, I should have represented the horror of the thing in such a light, as that you should never have become a prey to Mr. Davie. I know, that he'll get you up in a corner some day, and pick your bones and John will find nothing of you, but such a little heap, as a cat that is a good mouser leaves, the head and the tail piled together. My concern for you produced a vision, not such a one as you read in the *Spectators*, but actually a dream. I thought I was in t'other world and confined in a little apartment much like a cellar, enlightened by one rush candle that burned blue. On each side of me sate (for my sins) Mr. Davie, and my friend Mr. A[shton]; they bowed continually and smiled in my face, and while one filled me out very bitter tea, the other sweetened it with a vast deal of brown sugar: altogether it much resembled Syrup of Buckthorn. In the corner sat Tuthill[1] very melancholy, in expectation of the tea-leaves.

I take it very ill you should have been in the twentieth year of the War,[2] and yet say nothing of the Retreat from before Syracuse: is it, or is it not the finest thing you ever read in your life? and how does Xenophon, or Plutarch agree with you? for my part I read Aristotle; his Poetics, Politics, and Morals, though I don't well know which is which. In the first place he is the hardest Author by far I ever meddled with. Then he has a dry conciseness, that makes one imagine one is perusing a table of contents rather than a book; it tastes for all the world like chopped hay, or rather like chopped logick; for he has a violent affection to that art, being in some sort his own invention; so that he often loses himself in little trifling distinctions and verbal niceties, and what is worse leaves you to extricate yourself as you can.

[1] This name has been deleted, but is probably correct.—[*Ed.*]

[2] Thucydides, *Lib.* vii.—[*Mason.*]

Thirdly, he has suffered vastly by the Transcribblers, as all Authors of great brevity necessarily must. Fourthly and lastly he has abundance of fine uncommon things, which make him well worth the pains he gives one. You see what you have to expect. This and a few Autumnal verses are my entertainments during the fall of the leaf. Nothwithstanding which my time lies heavy on my hands, and I want to be at home again.

I have just received a visit from A[shton], he tells me we have certainly a peace with Spain very far advanced, which 'tis likely will produce a general one and that the king, when he has finished it, is determined to pass the rest of his days at Windsor, which to me is strange, however it comes from the Pelhamites. I send you here a page of books: enough I imagine to chuse out of, considering the state of your Coll. Finances. The best Editions of ancient authors should be the first things, I reckon, in a library: but if you think otherwise, I will send a page of a different kind. Pray write soon, and think me very faithfully yours, T. G.

September 11, 1746, Stoke.

Say many good things to Mr. Brown from me.

ANCIENTS.

1. Artistophanes, Kusteri. Amst. fol. 1710.
2. Aristotelis Opera, ed. Du Val. 4 v. fol. Paris, 1654. Gr. Lat. (Fabricius likewise recom-

mends the Edition of Sylburgius, all Greek, 1587. 5 v. 4to. apud Wechelios).

3. Arrian, Jac. Gronovii. Lugd. Bat. 1704.
4. Apollonius Rhodius, Hoelzlinii. Elzev. 1641. 8vo.
5. Arati, atq. Eratosthenis Fragmenta. Oxon. 8vo. 1672.
6. Aristidis Opera, ed. S. Jebb. 2 v. 4to. Oxon. 1722-30.
7. M. Aurelius, Gatakeri. Ultraject. fol. 1698.
8. Ammianus Marcellinus. H. Valesii. Par. 1681. fol.
9. Ausonius, Tollii. Amst. Blaeu, 1761. 8vo.
10. Antonini Itinerarium. Varior. Wesselingii. 4to. 1735.
11. Bertii Theatrum Geographicum. fol. Amst. 1618. Elzev. (it contains the best edition of Ptolemy, by M. Servetus).
12. Boethius. Varior. Basil, 1650. fol.
13. Corpus Oratorum. Græc. H. Stephani. fol. 1575.
14. Q. Curtius. Snakenburgi. 1724. 4to.
15. Cassiodori Opera. Garetii. Rothomagi, 1679. 2 vol. fol.
16. Diodorus Siculus, the last new edition in 2 vol. fol.
17. Dionysius Halicarn. Hudsoni. 2 vol. fol. Oxon, 1704.
18. Dio Prusæensis. Morelli. Paris, 1604. fol.
19. Dicæarchi Fragmenta. H. Steph. Genevæ. 1589. 8vo.
20. Dion Cassius. Hanoviæ. 1606. fol.
21. Epistolæ Græc. Antiquæ a Caldorina Societate. fol. Aurel. Allobrogum, 1606.

22. Ennii. Fragmenta. Hesselii. 4to. 1707. Amst.
23. Festus. de Verborum Significatione, Dacerii, in Us. Delphini 4to. Paris, 1618.
24. Florus. Varior. 1692. 8vo.
25. Geoponica, Cassiani Bassi. ed. P. Needham. Cantab. 1704. 8vo.
26. Aulus Gellius. Oiselii, etc. 1706. 4to.
27. Gemistius Pletho. fol. 1540. Basil.
28. Himerius & Polemo. H. Stephani. 4to. 1567.
29. Hesiodus Grævii. Amst. 8vo. 1667.
30. Historiæ Augustæ Scriptores. Varior. ap. Hackios, 2 v. 8vo. 1670-1.
31. Hierocles. Mer. Casauboni. 8vo. Lond. 1665.
32. Hist. Byzantinæ Scriptores. Par. & Romæ from 1645 to 1702. (I think, including Banduri's Antiquities, there are 30 vol. fol.)
33. Harpocration, Jac. Gronovii. 1696. Lug. Bat. 4to.
34. Isocrates. H. Wolfii. ap. H. Steph. 1693. fol.
35. Josephus, Hudsoni. 2 vol. 1726. Amst. fol.
36. Libanius. Morelli. 2 vol. fol. Paris, 1606-27.
37. Libanii Epistolæ. fol. 1738. Amst.
38. Lycophron, Potteri. Oxon. fol. 1697.
39. Livius. Creverii. 6 vol. 4to. Par.
40. Lucanus, Oudendorpii. 2 vol. 4to. 1728.
41. Macrobius. J. F. Gronovii. 1670. 8vo. Lug. Bat. (unfinished).
42. Nicander. G. Morelli. Par. 4to. 1557.
43. Oppian. Ritterhusii. Lug. Bat. 1597.
44. Pausanias. Kuhnii. Lipsiæ. 1696. fol.

45. Pomponius Mela. Jac. Gronovii. 8vo. 1722.
46. Plinii Hist. Naturalis, Harduini. Par. 5 vol. 4to. 1685. and republished ib. 3 vol. fol. 1723.
47. Polybius. Varior. 3 vol. 8vo. 1670. Amst.
48. Philostratorum Opera. Olearii. Lips. fol. 1709.
49. Philo Judæus, ed. Mangey. 2 vol. fol. Lond. 1742.
50. Pollucis Onomasticon. Varior. fol. 2 vol. 1706.
51. Prudentius. N. Heinsii. Amst. Elzev. 1667. 12mo.
52. Palladius, de Brachmanibus. Ed. Bisse. 4to. 1665. Lond.
53. Plautus. 2 vol. Gronovii, etc. 8vo. 1684. Amst.
54. Panegyrici Veteres. in Us. Delphini, 4to. 1677. Par.
55. Poetæ Minores. ed. P. Burmanni. 2 vol. 4to. 1731. Lug. Bat.
56. Plinii Epistolæ, Cortii & Var. 1734. 4to. Amst.
57. Excerpta ex Polybio, etc. H. Valesii. 4to. 1634. Par.
58. Rutilii Itinerarium. Grævii. 1687. 8vo. Amst.
59. Sophocles, P. Stephani. 4to. 1603.
60. Suetonius, Grævii. 1691. 4to. & 1703. Pitisci 2 vol. 4to. Leov$^{\text{diæ.}}$ 1714. (I don't know, which is the best Edition.)
61. Stephanus Byzantinus, Ab. Berkelii. 1688. fol. L. Bat.—Lucæ Holstenii Notæ. Amst. fol.
62. Sidonius, Sirmondi. 1652. Par. 4to. & cum Operibus Sirmondi.
63. Synesius. Petavii. Par. 1640. fol.
64. Symmachus. J. Parei. Neap. Nemetum. 1617. 8vo.
65. Silius Italicus, Drakenburgi. Ultraj. 1717. 4to.

66. Senecæ Tragediæ, Schroderi. 4to. Delf. 1728.
67. Themistius. Harduini. Par. fol. 1684.
68. Theocritus. Varior. 1604. 4to. apud Commelin.
69. Thucydides, Dukeri, fol.
70. Valerius Flaccus Burmanni. L. Bat. 1724. 4to.
71. Aurelius Victor. Arntzenii. 1733. 4to.
72. Valerius Maximus. Torrentii. 4to L. Bat. 1726.
73. Xenophon, Leunclavii, fol. 1625. Par and the three vol. that Hutchinson has published, 4to. Oxon.

ANTIQUARIES, GRAMMARIANS, ETC.

Bonanni, delle Antiche Syracuse. 2 vol. Palermo. 1717.

Boissard, Antiquitates Urb. Romanæ. 3 vol. fol. Francof.

Bergier, Hist. des grands Chemins de L'Emp. Romaine. 2 vol. 4to. Brux. 1728.

Bellori. Vet. Philosophorum, etc. Imagines, 1685. fol. Romæ.

Du Cange, Glossarium Latinitatis mediæ, vel infimæ, 3 vol. fol.

——— Græcum, ejusd. ætatis. 3 vol. fol. 1678. Par. both republished in 1733.

Ang. Caninius de Hellenismo, ed. a T. Crenio. 1700. L. Bat. 8vo.

Dodwell, de Vet. Græc. & Rom. Cyclo. cum Annal. Thucydideis. Xenophenteis. Oxon. 4to. 1701.

——— Annales Statiani. Velleiani. Quintilianei.

——— Prælectiones, in Schol. Camdenianâ. Ox. 1692. 8vo.

——— Exercitationes, de Ætate Phalaridis & Pythagoræ. 1709.

Fabretti Inscriptiones. 1691. Romæ. fol.

Fabricii Bibl. Græca, vol. 14. 4to. 1708. (This I believe you have.)

——— Latina. 3 vol. 8vo. 1721.

——— Antiquaria. 4to. 1713.

Fabretti, de Aquæductibus. Rom. 4to. 1680. Romæ.

——— de Columnâ Trajani, etc. 1685. fol. Romæ.

Gruteri Inscriptiones, ed. Grævii. 4 vol. fol. 1708.

Salengre, Thesaurus Antiq. Romanarum. 3 vol. 1716. fol. Hagæ.

Muratori, Thesaurus Antiq. 2 vol. fol. 173. . .

Gyraldi (Lilii) Opera. ed. Jensii. fol. 1696. L. Bat.

Goldasti Epistolæ Philologicæ. 8vo. Lipsiæ.

Heineccii Antiq^uum.^ Romanæ Jurisprudentiæ Syntagma. 2 vol. 8vo. 1724.

Hankius de Byzantin. Scriptoribus. 1677. Lips. 4to.

Heindreich, de Carthagin. Republicâ. Francof. ad Oderum.

Loydii, Series Olympiadum, etc. fol. Oxon. 1700.

Martinii Lexicon Philologicum. ed. Grævii. 2 vol. fol. 1701. Amst.

Montfaucon Paleographia Græca. 1708. fol. Par.

Notitia Dignitatum utriusq. Imperio, a P. Labbæo. 1651. Par. 8vo. (This may perhaps be in the Byzantine collection.)

Palmerii Græcia Antiqua. 1678. 4to. L. Bat. (unfinished).

Petavius, de Doctrinâ Temporum. 2 vol. 1703. fol.

Streinnius de Rom. Familiarum Stemmatibus. fol. 1659 Par.

Ursinus, Vel. Imagines & Elogia. 1570. fol. Romæ.
——— de Familiis Romanis 1577. ibid.
Vaillant Ptolemæorum Hist. 1701. fol. Amst. Seleucidarum. 4to. Par. 1681. Arsacidarum.

LVIII.—TO THOMAS WHARTON.

My dear Wharton—I would make you an excuse (as indeed I ought) if they were a sort of thing I ever gave credit to myself in these cases, but I know they are never true. Nothing so silly as indolence, when it hopes to disguise itself: every one knows it by its saunter; as they do his Majesty (God bless him), at a masquerade by the firmness of his tread, and the elevation of his chin. However, somewhat I had to say, that has a little shadow of reason in it. I have been in town (I suppose you know) flaunting about at public places of all kinds with my two Italianised friends. The world itself has some attractions in it to a solitary of six years' standing; and agreeable well-meaning people of sense (thank Heaven there are so few of them) are my peculiar magnet. It is no wōnder then, if I felt some reluctance at parting with them, so soon; or if my spirits, when I returned back to my cell, should sink for a time, not indeed to storm and tempest, but a good deal below changeable. Besides Seneca says (and my pitch of philosophy does not pretend to be much above Seneca) Nunquam mores, quos extuli, refero aliquid ex eo, quod composui, turbatur: aliquid ex his, quæ fugavi, redit. And it will happen to such as we, mere imps of science. Well it may, when Wisdom herself is forced often—

> ———— "In sweet retired solitude
> To plume her feathers, and let grow her wings,
> That in the various bustle of resort
> Were all too ruffled and sometimes impaired." [1]

It is a foolish thing that one can't only not live as one pleases, but where and with whom one pleases, without money. Swift somewhere says, that money is liberty; and I fear money is friendship too, and society, and almost every external blessing. It is a great tho' ill-natured, comfort to see most of those, who have it in plenty, without pleasure, without liberty, and without friends.

Mr. Brown (who I assure you holds up his head and his spirits very notably) will give you an account of your college proceedings, if they may be so called, where nothing proceeds at all. Only the last week Roger was so wise to declare ex motu proprio, that he took Mr. Delaval[1] (who is now a Fell.-Commoner), into his own tuition. This raised the dirty spirit of his friend, Mr. May (now tutor in Francis's room) against him, and even gentle Mr. Peele (who never acts but in conjunction), together with Mr. Brown (who pretended to be mighty angry, though in reality heartily glad), and they all came to an eclaircissement

[1] Milton's *Comus*, v. 376.

[2] Edward Delaval of Pembroke College, known as "Marcello."—[*Ed.*]

in the parlour. They abused him pretty reasonably, and it ended in threatening them as usual with a visitor. In short, they are all as rude as may be, leave him at table by himself, never go into the parlour, till he comes out; or if he enters, when they are there, continue sitting even in his own magisterial chair. May bickers with him publicly about twenty paltry matters, and Roger t'other day told him he was impertinent. What would you have more? you see they do as one would wish. If you were here, all would be right. I am surprised not to hear you mention, when that will be; pray give an account of yourself.—I am very sincerely yours,

T. G.

P.S.—When I went to town part of my errand was to sell a little stock I had, to pay off Birkett's old debt now at Xmas, but it was so low, I should have lost near 12 per cent, and so it continues. If you think of being here near that time, and find it not inconvenient to you to lend me £40, you will save me the money I mention (as I remember you once offered). But if any inconvenience attend it you must imagine I don't by any means desire it; and you need not be at the trouble of any excuse, as I well know, nothing but the not being able would hinder your doing it immediately. Let me know, because otherwise I have another journey to make to town.

December 11 [endorsed 1746], Cambridge.

LIX.—TO THOMAS WHARTON.

My dear Wharton.—I have received your bill, and am in confusion to hear you have got in debt yourself in order to bring me out of it. I did not think to be obliged to you so much, nor on such terms: but imagined you would be here, and might easily spare it. The money shall be repaid as soon as ever it is wanted, and sooner if the stocks rise a little higher.

My note you will find at the end of my letter, which you ought to have, *ἐάν τι κατὰ τὸ ἀνθρώπινον συμβαίνῃ*. The rest of my acknowledgements, are upon record; where they ought to be, with the rest of your kindnesses. The bill was paid me here. I suppose there is no likelihood of its being stopped in town.

It surprises me to hear you talk of so much business, and the uncertainty of your return; and what not? Sure you will find time to give me an account of your transactions, and your intentions. For your ears, don't let 'em think of marrying you! for I know if you marry at all, you will be *married.* I mean, passively. And then (besides repenting of what you were not guilty of) you will never go abroad, never read anything more, but farriery-books, and justice-books; and so either die of a consumption; or live on and grow fat, which is worse. For me, and my retirement (for you are in the right to despise my dissipation de quinze jours), we are in the midst of

Diog. Lærtius and his philosophers, as a proœmium to the series of their works, and those of all the poets and orators that lived before Philip of Macedon's death; and we have made a great Chronological Table[1] with our own hands, the wonder and amazement of Mr. Brown; not so much for public events, though these too have a column assigned them, but rather, in a literary way, to compare the times of all great men, their writings and transactions. It begins at the 30th Olympiad, and is already brought down to the 113th; that is, 332 years. Our only modern assistants, are Marsham, Dodwell, and Bentley. Tuthill continues quiet in his Læta Pupertas, and by this time (were not his friends of it), would have forgot there was any such place as Pembroke in the world. All things there are just in statu quo; only the fellows, as I told you, are grown pretty rudish to their sovereign in general, for Francis is now departed. Poor dear Mr. Delaval indeed has had a little misfortune. Intelligence was brought, that he had with him a certain gentlewoman, properly called Nell Burnet, but whose Nom de Guerre was Captain Hargraves), in an officer's habit, whom he had carried all about

[1] This laborious work was formed much in the manner of the President Hénault's *Histoire de France.* Every page consisted of nine columns: one for the Olympiad, the next for the Archons, the third for the public affairs of Greece, the three next for the Philosophers, and the three last for Poets, Historians, and Orators. I do not find it carried farther than the date above-mentioned.—[*Mason.*]

to see chapels and libraries, and make visits in the face of day. The master raised his Posse comitatus in order to search his chambers, and after long feeling and snuffling about the bed, he declared they had certainly been there; which was very true, and the Captain was then locked up in a cupboard there, while his lover stood below in order to convey him out at window when all was over. However they took care not to discover her, though the master affirmed; had he but caught her, he would soon have known, whether it was a man, or a woman. Upon this Mr. Delaval was desired to cut out his name, and did so. Next day Dr. L[ong] repented, and wrote a paper to testify he never knew any hurt of him; which he brought to Dr. Whaley, who would have directly admitted him here, if Stuart had not absolutely refused. He was offered about at several colleges, but in vain. Then Dr. L. called two meetings to get him re-admitted there, but every one was inexorable, and so he has lost his pupil, who is gone, I suppose, to lie with his aunt Price. Trollope continues in Dev'reux Court. All our hopes are now in the Commencement.

Have you seen the works of two young authors, a Mr. Warton[1] and a Mr. Collins,[2] both writers of

[1] This was the *Poems* of Joseph Warton (1722-1800), published December 1746. It had been originally proposed that Collins and Warton should appear in the same volume.—[*Ed.*]

[2] On the 20th of December 1746 was published *Odes on Several Descriptive and Allegoric Subjects*, by William Collins, a celebrated little volume, the rare worth of which Gray,

Odes? it is odd enough, but each is the half of a considerable man, and one the counterpart of the other. The first has but little invention, very poetical choice of expression, and a good ear. The second, a fine fancy, modelled upon the antique, a bad ear, great variety of words, and images with no choice at all. They both deserve to last some years, but will not. Adieu! dear S^r.—I am very sincerely yours,

T. G.

December 27, [1746].

I was thirty year old yesterday. What is it o'clock by you?

LX.—TO THOMAS WHARTON.

MY DEAR WHARTON—You ask me, what I would answer in case any one should ask me a certain question concerning you. In my conscience, I should say, yes; and the readier as I have had a revelation about it: 'twas in a dream, that told me you had taken a fancy to one of the four last letters in the alphabet. I think it can't be X, nor Z (for I know of no female Zeno, or Xenophon) it may be Y perhaps, but I have somehow a secret partiality for W, am I near it, or no? by this time I suppose, 'tis almost a done thing. There is no struggling with Destiny, so I acquiesce.

oddly enough, never seems to have perceived. Warton's venture was instantly successful, Collins' a decided failure, and the greater poet, in a fit of irritation, burned the remainder of his edition.—[*Ed.*]

Thus far only I should be glad to know with certainty, whether it be likely [MS. torn] should continue in statu quo, till the Commencement (which I don't conceive) for [MS. torn] I should think it rather better for T[uthill] to give up his pretensions with a good grace, than to wait the pleasure of those dirty cubs, who will infallibly prefer the first that offers of their own people. But I submit this to your judgment, who (as you first made him a competitor) ought to determine at what time he may most decently withdraw. I have some uneasiness too on Brown's account, who has sacrificed all his interests with so much frankness, and is still so resolute to do everything for us without reserve, that I should see him with great concern under the paw of a fell visitor, and exposed to the insolence of that old rascal, the master. Tr[ollo]pe (if you remember) would engage himself no longer than the end of this year: 'tis true he has never said anything since, tending that way; but he is not unlikely to remember it at a proper time. And as to Sm[art]:[1] he must necessarily be abîmé, in a very short time. His debts daily increase (you remember the state they were in, when you left us). Addison, I know, wrote smartly to him last week; but it has had no effect, that signifies only I observe he takes hartshorn from morning to night lately: in the

[1] Christopher Smart (1722-1770), the poet, admitted to Pembroke College October 30, 1739, elected a fellow of the College in 1745. He was liable to fits of insanity, during one of which he wrote his famous *Song to David.* He was an imitator of Gray's Odes.—[*Ed.*]

meantime he is amusing himself with a Comedy[1] of his own writing, which he makes all the boys of his acquaintance act, and intends to borrow the Zodiack room, and have it performed publickly. Our friend Lawman, the mad attorney, is his copyist; and truly the author himself is to the full as mad as he. His piece (he says) is inimitable, true sterling wit, and humour by God; and he can't hear the Prologue without being ready to die with laughter. He acts five parts himself, and is only sorry, he can't do all the rest. He has also advertised a collection of Odes; and for his Vanity and Faculty of Lying, they are come to their full maturity. All this, you see, must come to a Jayl, or Bedlam, and that without any help, almost without pity. By the way, now I talk of a Jayl, please to let me know, when and where you would have me pay my own debts.

Chapman[2] (I suppose you know) is warm in his mastership. Soon after his accession I was to see him: there was a very brilliant (Cambridge) assembly,

[1] Called a *Trip to Cambridge, or the grateful Fair*. Which was acted in Pembroke College Hall, the parlour of which made the green-room. No remains of this play have been found, but a few of the Songs, and the "Soliloquy of the Princess Periwinkle sola, attended by fourteen Maids of great Honour," containing the well-known simile of the Collier, Barber, and the Brickdust man. "Thus when a Barber and a Collier fight," etc.—[*Mit.*]

[2] Dr. Thomas Chapman, "the conceited and overbearing Master of Magdalen," who died 1760. He was Prebendary of Durham, and Master of Magdalen College from 1746 to his death.—[*Ed.*]

Middleton, Rutherforth,[1] Heberden,[2] Robinson, Coventry, and various others. He did the honours with a great deal of comical dignity, assisted by a Bedmaker in greasy leather breeches and a livery, and now he is gone to town to get preferment. But what you'll wonder at and what delights me, Coventry is his particular confident (tho' very disagreeably to himself) he can't open his door, but he finds the master there, who comes to set with him at all hours, and brings his works with him, for he is writing a great book on the Roman Constitution.[3] Well, upon the strength of this I too am grown very great with Coventry, and to say the truth (bating his nose, and another circumstance, which is nothing to me) he is the best sort of man in this place. M[iddleto]n has published a small octavo on the Roman Senate, well enough, but nothing of very great consequence, and is now gone to be inducted into a Sinc-cure (not £100 a year) that Sir J. Frederick gave him. What's worse, for the sake of this little nasty thing (I am told) he is determined to[4] suppress a work, that

[1] Thomas Rutherford, Regius Professor of Divinity from 1756 to 1771, a leading mathematician of the time.—[*Ed.*]

[2] William Heberden of St. John's, at that time Lecturer on the Materia Medica.—[*Ed.*]

[3] An "Essay on the Roman Senate," by Thomas Chapman, D.D., Master of Magdalen College in Cambridge, and Chaplain in Ordinary to his Majesty, 1750, 8vo. A Review of this Book, as well as of Middleton's and other writers on the same subject, was published by Hooke, 4to, 1758.—[*Mit.*]

[4] Gray was happily misinformed. Conyers Middleton was not bribed to withdraw his famous *Free Inquiry into the Miracu-*

would have made a great noise, or publish it all mangled and disfigured, and this when he has (I am assured) near £700 a year of his own already, and might live independent, and easy, and speak his mind in the face of the whole world Clerical and Laïcal. Such a passion have some men to lick the dust, and be trampled upon. The Fellow-Commoners (the bucks) are run mad, they set women upon their heads in the streets at noon-day, break open shops, game in the coffee-houses on Sundays, and in short act after my [MS. torn] heart.

My works are not so considerable as you imagine. I have read *Pausanias* and *Athenæus* all through, and *Æschylus* again. I am now in *Pindar* and *Lysias:* for I take Verse and Prose together, like bread and cheese. The Chronology is growing daily. The most noble of my performances latterly is a Pôme on the uncommon death of Mr. W[alpole]'s Cat, which being of a proper size and subject for a gentleman in your condition to peruse (besides that I flatter myself Miss —— will give her judgment upon it too), I herewith send you. It won't detain you long.[1]—Adieu, my dear Sir, I am ever yours, T. G.

Cambridge, March [endorsed 1747], Tuesday Night.

Trollope is in town still at his lodgings, and has

lous Powers which are supposed to have existed in the Christian Church. It appeared in full in 1748, having been proceeded by an "Introductory Discourse," published very soon after this letter was written.—[*Ed.*]

1 Here the *Ode on the Death of Mr. Walpole's Cat* is inserted. —[*Ed.*]

been very ill. Brown wrote a month ago to Hayes and Christopher, but has had no answer, whether or no, they shall be here at the Commencement. Can you tell? Morley is going to be married to a grave and stayed Maiden of 30 years old with much pelf, and his own relation. Poor Soul!

LXI.—TO HORACE WALPOLE.

Cambridge, March 1, 1747.

As one ought to be particularly careful to avoid blunders in a compliment of condolence, it would be a sensible satisfaction to me (before I testify my sorrow, and the sincere part I take in your misfortune) to know for certain, who it is I lament. I knew Zara and Selima (Selima was it? or Fatima?), or rather I knew them both together; for I cannot justly say which was which. Then as to your handsome Cat, the name you distinguish her by, I am no less at a loss, as well knowing one's handsome cat is always the cat one likes best; or if one be alive and the other dead, it is usually the latter that is the handsomest. Besides, if the point were never so clear, I hope you do not think me so ill-bred or so imprudent as to forfeit all my interest in the survivor; oh no! I would rather seem to mistake, and imagine to be sure it must be the tabby one that had met with this sad accident. Till this affair is a little better determined, you will excuse me if I do not begin to cry:

"Tempus inane peto, requiem, spatiumque doloris."

Which interval is the more convenient, as it gives time to rejoice with you on your new honours.[1] This is only a beginning; I reckon next week we shall hear you are a free-Mason, or a Gormogon[2] at least. —Heigh ho! I feel (as you to be sure have done long since) that I have very little to say, at least in prose. Somebody will be the better for it; I do not mean you, but your Cat, feuë Mademoiselle Selime, whom I am about to immortalise for one week or fortnight, as follows . . .

. . . .

There's a poem for you, it is rather too long for an Epitaph.

LXII.—TO HORACE WALPOLE.

January 1747.

It is doubtless an encouragement to continue writing to you, when you tell me you answer me with pleasure. I have another reason which would make me very copious, had I anything to say: it is, that I write to you with equal pleasure, though not with equal spirits, nor with like plenty of materials. Please to subtract

[1] Mr. Walpole was about this time elected a Fellow of the Royal Society.—[*Mason.*]

[2] See some account of the "Gormogons" in Nicholls' *Life of Hogarth*, p. 424. There is a Print of Hogarth's with the title—"The Mystery of Masonry brought to light by the Gormogons." There is also a Poem, by Harry Carey, called, "The Moderator between the Free Masons and Gormogons;" see also Pope's *Dunciad*, Book iv. ver. 576.—[*Mit.*]

then, so much for spirit, and so much for matter; and you will find me, I hope, neither so slow, nor so short, as I might otherwise seem. Besides, I had a mind to send you the remainder of *Agrippina*, that was lost in a wilderness of papers. Certainly you do her too much honour; she seemed to me to talk like an old boy, all in figures and mere poetry, instead of nature and the language of real passion. Do you remember "Approchez vous, Néron?"[1] Who would not rather have thought of that half line, than all Mr. Rowe's flowers of eloquence? However, you will find the remainder here at the end in an outrageous long speech: it was begun above four years ago (it is a misfortune you know my age, else I might have added), when I was very young. Poor West put a stop to that tragic torrent he saw breaking in upon him:—have a care, I warn you, not to set open the flood-gate again, lest it should drown you and me, and the bishop and all.

I am very sorry to hear you treat philosophy and her followers like a parcel of monks and hermits, and think myself obliged to vindicate a profession I honour, bien que je n'en tienne pas boutique (as Mad. Sevigné says). The first man that ever bore the name, if you remember, used to say, that life was like the Olympic games (the greatest public assembly of his age and country), where some came to shew the strength and agility of their body, as the cham-

[1] The Speech of Agrippina in Racine's *Tragedy of Britannicus*, Act iv. Sc. ii. v. 1.

pions; others, as the musicians, orators, poets, and historians, to shew their excellence in those arts; the traders to get money; and the better sort, to enjoy the spectacle, and judge of all these. They did not then run away from society for fear of its temptations; they passed their days in the midst of it; conversation was their business: they cultivated the arts of persuasion, on purpose to shew men it was their interest, as well as their duty, not to be foolish, and false, and unjust; and that too in many instances with success; which is not very strange, for they shewed by their life, that their lessons were not impracticable; and that pleasures were no temptations, but to such as wanted a clear preception of the pains annexed to them. But I have done preaching à la Grecque. Mr. Ratcliffe,[1] made a shift to behave very rationally without their instructions, at a season which they took a great deal of pains to fortify themselves and others against: one would not desire to lose one's head with a better grace. I am particularly satisfied with the humanity of that last embrace to all the people about him. Sure it must be somewhat embarrassing to die before so much good company!

You need not fear but posterity will be ever glad to know the absurdity of their ancestors: the foolish will be glad to know they were as foolish as they, and the wise will be glad to find themselves wiser.

[1] Brother of the Earl of Derwentwater. He was executed at Tyburn, December 1746, for having been concerned in the rebellion in Scotland.—[*Mit.*]

You will please all the world then; and if you recount miracles you will be believed so much the sooner. We are pleased when we wonder, and we believe because we are pleased. Folly and wisdom, and wonder and pleasure, join with me in desiring you would continue to entertain them: refuse us if you can.—Adieu, dear Sir! T. GRAY.

LXIII.—TO HORACE WALPOLE.

Cambridge 1747.

I HAD been absent from this place a few days, and at my return found Cibber's book[1] upon my table: I return you my thanks for it, and have already run over a considerable part; for who could resist Mrs. Letitia Pilkington's recommendation? (by the way is there any such gentlewoman?[2] or has somebody put on the style of a scribbling woman's panegyric to deceive and laugh at Colley?) He seems to me full as pert and as dull as usual. There are whole pages of common-place stuff, that for stupidity might have been wrote by Dr. Waterland,[3] or any other grave

[1] Colley Cibber's *The Character and Conduct of Cicero, considered from the history of his Life, by Dr. Middleton*, 4to, 1747. —[*Ed.*]

[2] Lætitia Pilkington (1712-1750), a literary adventuress, who traded upon Colley Cibber's good nature. She found herself in the Marshalsea Prison, from which sixteen dukes, she tells us, combined to release her. She obliged the world with some very striking *Memoirs*.—[*Ed.*]

[3] Daniel Waterland (1683-1740), the once famous High Church divine.—[*Ed.*]

divine, did not the flirting saucy phrase give them at a distance an air of youth and gaity. It is very true, he is often in the right with regard to Tully's weaknesses; but was there any one that did not see them? Those, I imagine, that would find a man after God's own heart, are no more likely to trust the Doctor's[1] recommendation than the Player's; and as to Reason and Truth, would they know their own faces, do you think, if they looked in the glass, and saw themselves so bedizened in tattered fringe and tarnished lace, in French jewels, and dirty furbelows, the frippery of a stroller's wardrobe?

Literature, to take it in its most comprehensive sense, and include everything that requires invention or judgment, or barely application and industry, seems indeed drawing apace to its dissolution, and remarkably since the beginning of the war. I remember to have read Mr. Spence's pretty book;[2] though (as he then had not been at Rome for the last time) it must have increased greatly since that in bulk. If you ask me what I read, I protest I do not recollect one syllable; but only in general, that they were the best bred sort of men in the world, just the

[1] Conyers Middleton.—[*Ed.*]

[2] There is probably some confusion of thought here. The famous *Polymetis* of Joseph Spence (1698-1768) was then, in 1747, quite a new book. What Gray remembered to have read was perhaps the *Essay on Pope's Odyssey*, 1736, unless indeed Spence had shown him part of the *Polymetis* in MS. at Florence. This book was an inquiry, in dialogue form, into the agreement between the works of the Roman poets, and the remains of antique art.—[*Ed.*]

kind of *frinds* one would wish to meet in a fine summer's evening, if one wished to meet any at all. The heads and tails of the dialogues, published separate in 16mo, would make the sweetest reading in *natiur* for young gentlemen of family and fortune, that are learning to dance. I rejoice to hear there is such a crowd of dramatical performances coming upon the stage. *Agrippina* can stay very well, she thanks you, and be damned at leisure : I hope in God you have not mentioned, or shewed to anybody that scene (for trusting in its badness, I forgot to caution you concerning it) ; but I heard the other day, that I was writing a Play, and was told the name of it, which nobody here could know, I am sure. The employment you propose to me much better suits my inclination ; but I much fear our joint-stock would hardly compose a small volume ; what I have is less considerable than you would imagine, and of that little we should not be willing to publish all.[1] . . .

[1] What is here omitted was a short catalogue of Mr. West's Poetry then in Mr. Gray's hands ; the reader has seen as much of it in the three foregoing sections as I am persuaded his friend would have published, had he prosecuted the task which Mr. Walpole recommended to him, that of printing his own and Mr. West's poems in the same volume ; and which we also perceive from this letter, he was not averse from doing. This therefore seems to vindicate the Editor's plan in arranging these papers ; as he is enabled by it not only to show what Mr. West would have been, but what Mr. Gray was, I mean not as a poet, for that the world knew before, but as an universal scholar, and (what is still of more consequence) as an excellent moral man.—[*Mason.*]

This is all I can anywhere find. You, I imagine, may have a good deal more. I should not care how unwise the ordinary run of Readers might think my affection for him, provided those few, that ever loved anybody, or judged of anything rightly, might, from such little remains, be moved to consider what he would have been; and to wish that heaven had granted him a longer life and a mind more at ease.

I send you a few lines, though Latin, which you do not like, for the sake of the subject;[1] it makes part of a large design, and is the beginning of the fourth book, which was intended to treat of the passions. Excuse the three first verses; you know vanity, with the Romans, is a poetical licence.

LXIV.—TO HORACE WALPOLE.

Cambridge 1747.

I HAVE abundance of thanks to return you for the entertainment Mr. Spence's book has given me, which I have almost run over already; and I much fear (see what it is to make a figure) the breadth of the margin, and the neatness of the prints, which are better done than one could expect, have prevailed upon me to like it far better than I did in manuscript; for I think it is not the very genteel deportment of Polymetis, nor the lively wit of Mysagetes, that have at all corrupted me.

[1] The admirable apostrophe to Mr. West, with which the fragment of the 4th Book *de Principiis Cogitandi* opens.—[*Mit.*]

There is one fundamental fault, from whence most of the little faults throughout the whole arise. He professes to neglect the Greek writers, who could have given him more instruction on the very heads he professes to treat, than all the others put together; who does not know, that upon the Latin, the Sabine and Hetruscan mythology (which probably might themselves, at a remoter period of time, owe their origin to Greece too) the Romans ingrafted almost the whole religion of Greece to make what is called their own? It would be hard to find any one circumstance that is properly of their invention. In the ruder days of the republic, the picturesque part of their religion (which is the province he has chose, and would be thought to confine himself to) was probably borrowed entirely from the Tuscans, who, as a wealthy and trading people, may be well supposed, and indeed are known, to have had the arts flourishing in a considerable degree among them. What could inform him here, but Dio. Halicarnassus (who expressly treats of those times with great curiosity and industry) and the remains of the first Roman writers? The former he has neglected as a Greek; and the latter, he says, were but little acquainted with the arts, and consequently are but of small authority. In the better ages, when every temple and public building in Rome was peopled with imported deities and heroes, and when all the artists of reputation they made use of were Greeks, what wonder, if their eyes grew familiarised to Grecian forms and habits (especially in a matter of this kind, where so much depends upon the imagination); and if those figures introduced with them a belief of such fables, as first gave them being, and dressed them out in their various attributes, it was natural then, and (I should think) necessary, to go to the source itself, the Greek accounts of their own religion; but to say the truth, I suspect he was a little conversant in those books and that language; for he rarely quotes any but Lucian, an author that falls in everybody's way, and who lived at the very extremity of that period he has set to his enquiries, later than any of the poets he has meddled with, and for that reason ought to have been regarded as but an indifferent authority; especially being a Syrian too. His book (as he says himself) is, I think, rather a beginning than a perfect work; but a beginning at the wrong end: for if anybody should finish it by enquiring into the Greek mythology, as he proposes, it will be necessary to read it backward.

There are several little neglects, that one might have told him of, which I noted in reading it hastily; as page 311, a discourse about orange-trees, occasioned by Virgil's "inter odoratum lauri nemus," where he fancies the Roman Laurus to be our Laurel; though undoubtedly the bay-tree, which is *odoratum*, and (I believe) still called Lauro, or Alloro, at Rome; and that the "Malum Medicum" in the Georgick is the orange;[1] though Theophrastus, whence Virgil bor-

[1] The laurel was imported into Europe by the botanist

rowed it, or even Pliny, whom he himself quotes, might convince him it is the cedrato which he has often tasted at Florence. Page 144 is an account of Domenichino's Cardinal Virtues, and a fling at the Jesuits, neither of which belong to them. The painting is in a church of the Barnabiti, dedicated to St. Carlo Borromeo, whose motto is HUMILITAS. Page 151, in a note, he says, the old Romans did not regard Fortune as a Deity; tho' Servius Tullius (whom she was said to be in love with; nay, there was actually an affair between them) founded her temple in Foro Boario. By the way, her worship was Greek, and this king was educated in the family of Tarquinius Priscus, whose father was a Corinthian; so it is easy to conceive how early the religion of Rome might be mixed with that of Greece, etc. etc.

Dr. Middleton has sent me to-day a book on the Roman Senate,[1] the substance of a dispute between Lord Hervey and him, though it never interrupted *their* friendship, he says, and I dare say not.

LXV.—TO THOMAS WHARTON.

MY DEAR WHARTON—I perceive, that mine did not reach you, till the day after you had wrote your little

Clusius, about the year 1590, from Trebizond. The orange was certainly unknown to Virgil, having been brought from Ispahan at a much later period.—[*Whittaker, MS. note.*]

[1] This was *A Treatise on the Roman Senate*, published by Conyers Middleton in 1747. It principally consisted of letters which had been addressed to Lord Harvey.—[*Ed.*]

letter. If you have time to give the Gentleman (before he goes to town) my note endorsed by you, or will send it to your brother, the money shall be paid in town at the day you mention. The rest of my questions are all sufficiently answered by the news you tell me (not but that I knew it before). What can one say to a person in such circumstances? I need not say, how much happiness I wish you: if that be the way to it, I rejoice to see you with your boots on. It would be cruel to detain you long at present; when you have any leisure, I hope you will let me a little more into the matter. The old maids give you heartily joy, and hug themselves in their virginity. Carlyon is in your room, and I can't well go, and strip him: I reckon he will not remain long here.—Adieu, and think me yours ever, T. G.

March 26 [endorsed 1747], Cambridge.

LXVI.—TO THOMAS WHARTON.

My dear Wharton—I highly approve of your travelling nuptials, and only wonder you don't set forth on Easter day, rather than stay to be dished up there, and put to bed by a whole heap of prurient relations. I don't conceive what one can do with such people, but run away from them. My very letter blushes to think it must speak with you at a time, when there is but one person you can properly have anything to say to.

However, tho' I have not the pleasure of knowing

Mr. Wilkinson, my new relation, much less of knowing how good a Charioteer he is, yet I will readily trust him with my neck to carry to Stilton, or where he pleases. If I arrive there in a shattered condition, I hope the lady you belong to will receive me the more graciously, as a person, that had an ambition to break a limb, or two in her service. But you must desire him (as you say) to invite me.

You shall receive the money as soon as you get to town. My Aunt has it in her hands: when I see you, I shall learn your direction, and she shall come and pay it. I won't trouble you with long letters at present.—Adieu! I am sincerely yours, T. G.

P.S.—My compliments.

[Endorsed March or April 1747]
[Cambridge post mark.]

LXVII.—TO THOMAS WHARTON.

My dear Wharton—I rejoice to hear you are safe arrived, though drawn by *four wild horses*, like people one reads of in the book of martyrs, yet I cannot chuse but lament your condition, so cooped up in the Elvet House with spirits and hobgoblins about you, and pleasure at one entrance quite shut out; you must so much the more set open all the other avenues to admit it, open your folios, open your De L'Isle, and take a prospect of that world, which the cruel architect has hid from your corporeal eyes, and confined 'em to the narrow contemplation of your own *backside,*[1] and kitchen-garden. Mr. Keene has been here, but is now gone to town for a little while, and returns to pass the winter with us. We are tolerably gracious, and he speaks mighty well of you: but when I look upon his countenance and his ways, I can never think of bestowing my poor Tuthill[2] upon him (tho' it were never so advantageous, and they both had a mind to it) and so I have said nothing to either of them. I found, he had no hopes of your petition; and believe you are right in thinking no farther of it. Your mention of Mr. Vane, reminds me of poor Smart (not that I, or any other mortal, pity him) about three weeks ago he was arrested here at the suit of a taylor in London for a debt of about £50 of three years standing. The College had about £28 due to him in their hands, the rest (to hinder him from going to the castle, for he could not raise a shilling) Brown, May, and Peele, lent him upon his note. Upon this he remained confined to his room, lest his creditors here should snap him; and the fellows went round to make out a list of his debts, which amount in Cambridge to above £350; that they might come the readier to some composition, he was advised to go off in the night, and lie hid somewhere or other. He has done so, and this has made the

[1] The old name for the back part of farm-houses where the kitchen and yards were.—[*Mit.*]

[2] Henry Tuthill, of Peterhouse; he was admitted at Pembroke in 1746, admitted a fellow in 1749, and deprived of his fellowship in February 2, 1757. Gray took a great interest in him, and makes frequent allusions to his misfortunes.—[*Ed.*]

creditors agree to an assignment of £50 per annum out of his income, which is above £140, if he lives at Cambridge (not else). But I am apprehensive, if this come to the ears of Mr. Vane he may take away the £40 hitherto allowed him by the Duke of Cleveland; for before all this (last summer) I know they talked of doing so, as Mr. Smart (they said) was settled in the world. If you found an opportunity, possibly you might hinder this (which would totally ruin him now) by representing his absurdity in the best light it will bear: but at the same time they should make this a condition of its continuance; that he live in the College, soberly, and within bounds, for that upon any information to the contrary it shall be absolutely stopped. This would be doing him a real service, though against the grain: yet I must own, if you heard all his lies, impertinence, and ingratitude in this affair, it would perhaps quite set you against him, as it has his only friend (Mr. Addison) totally, and yet one would try to save him, for drunkenness is one great source of all this, and he may change it. I would not tell this matter in the north, were I you, till I found it was known by other means. We have had an opinion from the Attorney General in a manner directly contrary to the former. He does not seem to have been clear then; so that he may possibly not be so now. The King's Bench (he says) can take no cognisance of it; the visitor must do all, and he is the Vice Chancellor by King James's Charter, which is good. This is sad indeed, and the fellows, before they acquiesce in it, seem desirous of consulting Dr. Lee, who is well acquainted with College matters.

Have you seen Lyttleton's Monody[1] on his wife's death? there are parts of it too stiff and poetical; but others truly tender and elegiac, as one would wish. Dodsley is publishing three miscellaneous volumes; some new, many that have been already printed. Lyttleton, Nugent,[2] and G. West[3] have given him several things of theirs. Mr. W[alpole] has given him three odes of mine (which you have seen before) and one of Mr. West's (my friend who is dead) which in spite of the subject is excellent: it is on the late queen's death. There is a Mr. Archibald Bower,[4] a Scotchman bred in Italy, Professor in three Universities there, and of the Inquisition. He was employed by the Court of Rome to write a history of the Popes. As he searched into the materials, his eyes were opened: he came to England, has changed his religion, and continues his work in our language under the patronage of Mr. Pitt, the Yorks, etc. The preface

[1] George Lord Lyttelton (1709-1773) published a Monody on the death, in 1746, of his wife, once Miss Lucy Fortescue, whom he had married in 1741.—[*Ed.*]

[2] Robert Craggs, Earl Nugent (1709-1788.—[*Ed.*]

[3] Gilbert West (1700?-1756), who translated Pindar in 1749, was no connection of Gray's friend R. West.—[*Ed.*]

[4] Archibald Bower (1686-1766), was an impostor who had been a Jesuit, and who described his imaginary adventures in Italy in sympathetic and picturesque colours. He had just (March 25, 1747) put forth proposals for what proved to be a spurious *History of the Popes.*—[*Ed.*]

is come out with the proposals, and promises exceeding well, doubtless there is no part of history more curious, if it be well performed.

My best wishes wait upon Mrs. Wharton, and . . . . My compliments to Miss Wharton, and to King Harry the 8th. Brown will write; he's the . . . little man, and always . . .—Adieu, I am ever yours,[1]

T. G.

November 30, Cambridge [endorsed 1747].

P.S.—I said something to Stonhewer, who (I believe) will do what he can. He is now in London.

LXVIII.—TO THOMAS WHARTON.

My dear Wharton—Though I have been silent so long; do not imagine, I am at all less sensible to your kindness, which (to say the truth) is of a sort, that however obvious and natural it may seem, has never once occurred to any of my good friends in town, where I have been these seven weeks. Their methods of consolation were indeed very extraordinary: they were all so sorry for my loss,[2] that I could not chuse but laugh. One offered me opera tickets, insisted upon carrying me to the grand masquerade, desired me to sit for my picture. Others asked me to their concerts, or dinners and suppers at their houses; or hoped, I would drink chocolate with them, while I stayed in town. All my gratitude (or if you please, my revenge),

[1] The MS. is slightly mutilated here.—[*Ed.*]

[2] The destruction of his house, in Cornhill, by fire.—[*Mit.*]

was to accept of everything they offered me: if it had been but a shilling, I would have taken it. Thank Heaven, I was in good spirits; else I could not have done it. I profited all I was able of their civilities, and am returned into the country loaded with their Bontés and Politesses, but richer still in my own reflections, which I owe in great measure to them too. Suffer a great master to tell them you for me in a better manner.

"Aux sentimens de la Nature,
Aux plaisirs de la Vérité,
Préférant le goût frelaté
Des plaisirs que fait l'Imposture
Ou qu'invente la Vanité ;
Voudrois-je partager ma vie
Entre les jeux de la Folie,
Et l'ennui de l'Oisiveté,
Et trouver la Mélancolie,
Dans le sein de la Volupte?" etc.[1]

Your friendship has interested itself in my affairs so naturally, that I cannot help troubling you with a little detail of them. The house I lost was insured for £500, and with the deduction of three per cent they paid me £485, with which I bought, when Stocks were lower, £525. The rebuilding will cost £590,

[1] These verses are to be found in *La Chartreuse*, 1734, a poetical description of the cell which the poet Gresset occupied in the College Louis le Grand. Jean Baptiste Louis Gresset (1709-1777) exercised a great influence over Gray, who admired him more than any other contemporary verse-writer. His verse was extremely sparkling and light; although his life was so retired as to be almost monastic, he was without a superior in describing the manners of society.—[*Ed.*]

and other expences, that necessarily attend it, will mount that sum to £650. I have an aunt that gives me £100; and another that I hope will lend me what I shall want: but if (contrary to my expectation) I should be forced to have recourse to your assistance; it cannot be for above £50; and that, about Christmas next when the thing is to be finished. And now, my dear Wharton, why must I tell you a thing so contrary to my own wishes, and to yours, I believe? It is impossible for me to see you in the north, or to enjoy any of those agreeable hours I had flattered myself with. I must be in town several times during the Summer, in August particularly, when half the money is to be paid: the relation, that used to do things for me, is from illness now quite incapable; and the good people here would think me the most careless and ruinous of mortals, if I should think of such a journey at this time. The only satisfaction I can pretend to, is that of hearing from you; and particularly about this time, I was bid to expect good news.

Your opinion of Diodorus is doubtless right; but there are things in him very curious, got out of better authors, now lost. Do you remember the Egyptian History, and particularly the account of the gold-mines? My own readings have been cruelly interrupted. What I have been highly pleased with is the new comedy[1]

[1] Gresset's famous comedy of *Le Méchant* was brought out at the Comédie Française on the 27th of April 1745. Villemain says that "Voltaire himself can give you no notion of the eighteenth century if you have not read *Le Méchant*."—[*Ed.*]

from Paris, by Gresset; *Le Méchant*, one of the very best dramas I ever met with. If you have it not, buy his works altogether in two little volumes. They are collected by the Dutch booksellers, and consequently there is some trash; but then there are the Ververt, the epistle to P. Bougeant, the Chartreuse, that to his sister, an ode on his country, and another on Mediocrity; and the *Sidnei*,[1] another comedy, which have great beauties. There is a poem by Thomson, the Castle of Indolence, with some good stanzas. Mr. Mason is my acquaintance: I liked that ode[2] very much, but have found no one else, that did. He has much fancy, little judgment, and a good deal of modesty. I take him for a good and well-meaning creature; but then he is really *in simplicity a child*, and

[1] *Le Sidney* was brought out at the Comédie Française on the 3d of May 1745, six days after the great success of *Le Méchant*.—[*Ed.*]

[2] Ode to a Water Nymph, published about this time in Dodsley's *Miscellany*. On reading what follows, many readers, I suspect, will think me as simple as ever, in forbearing to expunge the paragraph. But as I publish Mr. Gray's sentiments of Authors, as well living as dead, without reserve, I should do them injustice, if I was more scrupulous with respect to myself. My friends, I am sure, will be much amused with this and another passage hereafter of a like sort. My enemies, if they please, may sneer at it; and say (which they will very truly) that twenty-five years have made a very considerable abatement in my general philanthropy. Men of the world will not blame me for writing from so prudent a motive, as that of making my fortune by it; and yet the truth, I believe, at the time was, that I was perfectly well satisfied, if my publications furnished me with a few guineas to see a Play or an Opera.—[*Mason.*]

loves everybody he meets with: he reads little or nothing, writes abundance, and that with a design to make his fortune by it. There is now, I think, no hopes of the Pembroke business coming to anything. My poor Tuthill will be in a manner destitute (even of a curacy) at Midsummer. I need not bid you think of him, if any probable means offer of doing him good: I fear, he was not made to think much for himself. Pray, let me hear from you soon. I am at Mrs. Rogers's of Stoke near Windsor, Bucks.

My thanks, and best compliments to Mrs. Wharton, and your family. Does that name include anybody, that I am not yet acquainted with?—Adieu, I am ever, truly yours, T. GRAY.

June 5, 1748.

LXIX.—TO THOMAS WHARTON.

Stoke, August 19 [inserted 1748.]

MY DEAR WHARTON—After having made my compliments to the god-mothers of the little Doctress, who are to promise and vow for her that she shall understand, and be grateful some twelve or fifteen years hence I congratulate Mrs. Wharton and your family on this occasion, and doubtless desire nothing more than to see you all the next summer, though as to promises, I dare not; lest some unlucky event again come across, and put the performance out of my power. I am not certain whether I shall be obliged to have recourse to your assistance or no about Christmas: but if I am, I will be sure to give you notice in due time.

I am glad you have had any pleasure in Gresset: he seems to me a truly elegant and charming writer. The *Méchant* is the best comedy I ever read. *Edward I*[1] I could scarce get through, it is puerile; though there are good lines; such as this for example:

> "Le jour d'un nouveau règne est le jour des ingrats."

But good lines will make anything rather than a good Play. However you are to consider, this is a collection made by the Dutch booksellers. Many things unfinished or wrote in his youth, or designed not for the world, but to make a few friends laugh, as the *Lutrin Vivant*,[2] etc., there are two noble verses, which as they are in the middle of an ode *to the King*, may perhaps have escaped you:

> "Le cri d'un peuple heureux, est la seule éloquence
> Qui sçait parler des Rois."

which is very true, and should have been a hint to himself not to write odes to the king at all.

My squabble with the Professor I did not think worth mentioning to you. My letter was by no

[1] Gray makes a slip of the pen here. Gresset wrote no *Edward I.* His *Edouard III.* was brought out at the Comédie Française on the 22d of January 1740. It was notable for an innovation up to that time unprecedented on the French stage. In emulation of Shakespeare, one of the characters was killed on the stage itself.—[*Ed.*]

[2] Gresset's *Le Lutrin Vivant*, a tale in verse, was published in the *Poésies* of 1734.—[*Ed.*]

means intended as a composition, and only designed to be shewed to some, who were witnesses to the impertinence, that gave occasion for it: but he was fool enough by way of revenge to make it mighty public.

I don't wonder your Mr. Bolby disapproves Mr. [erased] conduct at Rome: it was indeed very unlike his own. But when everybody there of our nation was base enough either to enter into an actual correspondence with a certain most serene person, or at least to talk carelessly and doubtfully on what was then transacting at home, sure it was the part of a man of spirit to declare his sentiments publicly and warmly. He was so far from making a party, that he and Mr. [erased] were the only persons, that were of that party. As to his ends in it; from his first return to England he has always frequented the Prince's court, and been the open friend of Mr. H. W[alpole]: which could certainly be no way to recommend himself to the ministry: unless you suppose his views were very distant indeed.

I should wish to know (when you can find time for a letter) what you think of my young friend, St[onhewe]r, and what company he is fallen into in the North. I fill up with the beginning of a sort of Essay. What name to give it I know not, but the subject is, the Alliance of Education and Government; I mean to shew that they must necessarily concur to produce great and useful men. .

. . . . . .

I desire your judgment upon so far, before I proceed any farther.—Adieu. I am ever yours,

T. G.

Pray shew it to no one (as it is a fragment) except it be St[onhewe]r, who has seen most of it already I think.

LXX.—TO THOMAS WHARTON.

MY DEAR WHARTON—Shall I be expeditious enough to bring you the news of the peace, before you meet with it in the Papers? not the Peace of Aix la Chapelle, mother of proclamations and of fireworks, that lowers the price of oranges and Malaga-sack, and enhances that of Poor Jack and Barrell'd Cod: no, nor the Peace between Adil-Shah and the Great Mogol; but the Peace of Pembroke signed between the high and mighty Prince Roger, surnamed the Long, Lord of the great Zodiac, the Glass Uranium, and the Chariot that goes without horses, on the one part; and the most noble James Brown, the most serene Theophilus Peele, and the most profound Nehemiah May, etc.: on the other.

In short without farther preliminaries Knowles, Mason, and Tuthill are elected, and the last of them is actually here on the spot, as you will shortly hear from himself. The negotiations, that preceded this wonderful event are inexplicable. The success of the affair was extremely uncertain but the very night before it, and had come to nothing, if Brown fixed and obstinate as a little rock had not resisted the solicitations of Smith, and Smart, almost quarrelled with Peele and May, and given up, as in a huff, the living of Tilney, to which he had that morning been presented. I say, this seemed to them to be done in a huff, but was in reality a thing he had determined to do, be the event of the Election what it would. They were desirous of electing two, as the master proposed, Knowles and Mason, or Mason and Gaskarth, for they were sure he would never admit Tuthill, as he had so often declared it. However, I say, Brown continued stedfast, that all three should come in, or none at all; and when they met next day, he begun by resigning Tilney, and then desired the master would either put an end to their long disputes himself, as they intreated him; or else they would refer the whole to a visitor, and did conjure him to call one in, as soon as possible. The rest did not contradict him, though the proposal was much against their real inclinations. So Roger believing them unanimous (after some few Pribbles and Prabbles), said, well then, if it be for the good of the College—but you intend Knowles shall be senior?—To be sure, master—well then—and so they proceeded to Election, and all was over in a few minutes. I do believe, that Roger despairing now of a visitor to his mind, and advised by all his acquaintance (among whom I reckon Keene, whose acquaintance I have cultivated with the same views you mentioned in your letter to Brown) to finish the matter, had been for some months determined to do so, but not till he made a last effort. He made it indeed, but not having sagacity enough to find out, how near carrying his point he was; being ignorant of the weakness of a part of his College, and they not cunning, or perhaps not dishonest enough, to discover it to him, he thought he had missed his aim, and so gave it up without farther struggling. I hope you will be glad to see so good an end of an affair you gave birth to: Brown is quite happy, and we vastly glad to be obliged to the only man left among them, that one would care to be obliged to. There are two more Fellowships remain to be filled up at the Commencement. By the way Tuthill has been just holding a candle—not to the devil, but to the master, as he was reading some papers in —— Hall: and the boys peep'd in at the screens to see it, and to laugh.

Keene is most sadly *implicated* in the beginning of his reign about an Election, and I am of his Cabinet-council, hitherto for the reasons you wot of, and now because I can't help it. But I am rather tired of College details (as I doubt not, you are) and so I leave this story to be recorded by the Annalists of Peter-house; and let historians of equal dignity tell of the triumphs of Chappy, the installations, the visitations, and other memorable events, that distinguish and adorn his glorious reign.

You ask for some account of books. The principal I can tell you of is a work of the president Montesquieu's, the labour of twenty years. It is called,

L'Esprit des Loix, 2 vols. 4to. printed at Geneva. He lays down the principles on which are founded the three sorts of government, Despotism, the limited Monarchic, and the Republican, and shews how from thence are deducted the laws and customs, by which they are guided and maintained: the education proper to each form, the influences of climate, situation, religion, etc.: on the minds of particular nations, and on their policy. The subject (you see) is as extensive as mankind; the thoughts perfectly new, generally admirable, as they are just, sometimes a little too refined: in short there are faults, but such as an ordinary man could never have committed: the style very lively and concise (consequently sometimes obscure) it is the gravity of Tacitus (whom he admires) tempered with the gayety and fire of a Frenchman.

The time of night will not suffer me to go on, but I will write again in a week. My best compliments to Mrs. Wharton, and your family.—I am ever, most sincerely yours, T. GRAY.

March 9 [1748-9], Thursday, Cambridge.

LXXI.—TO THOMAS WHARTON.

April 25, Cambridge [endorsed 1749.]

MY DEAR WHARTON—I perceive, that second parts are as bad to write, as they can be to read; for this, which you ought to have had a week after the first, has been a full month in coming forth. The spirit of

Lasiness (the spirit of the place), begins to possess even me, that have so long declaimed against it: yet has it not so prevailed, but that I feel that discontent with myself, that *Ennuy*, that ever accompanies it in its beginnings. Time will settle my conscience, time will reconcile me to this languid companion: we shall smoke, we shall tipple, we shall doze together. We shall have our little jokes, like other people, and our long stories; Brandy will finish what Port begun; and a month after the time you will see in some corner of a London *Evening Post*, yesterday, died the Rev$^{rd.}$ Mr. John Grey, Senior-Fellow of Clare-hall, a facetious companion, and well-respected by all that knew him. His death is supposed to have been occasioned by a fit of an apoplexy, being found fallen out of bed with his head in the chamber-pot.

I am half ashamed to write university news to you, but as perhaps you retain some little leven of Pembroke Hall, your nursing mother, I am in hopes you will not be more than half ashamed to read it. Pembroke then is all harmonious and delightful since the pacification: but I wish you would send them up some boys, for they are grown extremely thin from their late long indisposition. Keene's *Implications* have ended queerly, for, contrary to all common sense Peter Nourse and two others have joined Rogers, and brought in a shameful low creature by a majority. The master appeals to the Visitor against their choice, as of a person not qualified. He has received the appeal, and (I suppose) will put in Brocket (Dr. Keene's man) by main force. Chapman is at present in town in waiting; he has just married a Miss Barnwell, niece to one Dr. Barnwell, who was minister of Trompington, with £2000, a plain woman, and about his own age. I hear, that when he went to Leicester-house to know when the Prince would be waited upon with the book of verses on the peace the Prince appointed no day at all; but ordered the verses to be sent, and left there. The design of receiving the University at Newcastle-house is said to be altered; the Duke intending to come hither (I imagine) after the Parliament is risen. Rosse's[1] *Epistles of Tully ad Familiares* will come out in about a week. It is in two handsome 8vo volumes, with an Introduction and Notes in English, but no translation, dedicated to Lord Gower. Now I am come to books, there is a new edition of Montesquieu's Work (which I mentioned to you before) publishing in 2 vols. 8vo. Have you seen old Crebillon's *Catilina*,[2] a Tragedy, which has had a prodigious run at Paris? historical truth is too much perverted in it, which is ridiculous in a story so generally known: but if you can get over this, the sentiments and versification are fine, and most of the characters

[1] John Ross, afterwards Bishop of Exeter (died 1792), issued in 1749 an edition of the *Ad Familiares* of Cicero which roused an angry controversy among scholars.—[*Ed.*]

[2] The *Catalina* of Prosper Jolyot de Crébillon (1674-1762), the tragic poet, was brought out in 1748 by the court-party as a form of annoyance to Voltaire.—[*Ed.*]

(particularly the principal one) painted with great spirit. Observe, if you chuse to send for it, not to have Brindley's edition, which is all false prints, but Vaillant's. There is a Work publishing in Denmark by subscription[1] (4 guineas) *Travels in Egypt* by. Captain Norden. He was once in England (as tutor to a young Count Daniskiold, hereditary Admiral of Denmark) and known to many persons for a man of sense, and that understood drawing extremely well; accordingly it is the plates, that raise it to such a price, and are said to be excellent. The author himself is dead, and his papers are published by the Academy at Copenhagen. Mr. Birch,[2] the indefatigable, has just put out a thick 8vo. of original papers of Queen Elizabeth's time. There are many curious things in it, particularly Letters from Sir Robert Cecil (Salisbury) about his Negotiations with Henry IVth of France; the Earl of Monmouth's odd account of Queen Elizabeth's death, several peculiarities of James Ist, and Prince Henry, etc.; and above all an excellent account of the State of France with characters of the King, his Court and Ministry, by Sir G. Carew, ambassador there. This, I think, is all

[1] This was a *Voyage d' Égypte et de Nubie*, translated from the Danish MS. of Frederik Ludvig Norden (1708-1742), by Des Roches de Parthenay, and edited in 1755, at Copenhagen, as a folio with plates, by the Kongelike Danske Videnskabers Selskab. In 1757 an English version of these famous travels appeared in London, translated from the French by Dr. Templemann of the British Museum.—[*Ed.*]

[2] Thomas Birch, D.D. (1705-1766), the antiquary.—[*Ed.*]

new worth mentioning, that I have seen or heard of, except a Natural History of Peru in Spanish, printed at London by Don —— something, a man of learning, sent thither by that court on purpose.

I shall venture to accept of a part of that kind offer you once made me (for my finances are much disordered this year) by desiring you to lend me twenty guineas. The sooner you can do this, the more convenient it will be to me, and if you can find a method to pay it here; still more so. But if anything should happen, that may defer it, or make this method troublesome: then I will desire you to make it payable in town after the first week in June, when I shall be obliged to go thither.

I want to hear from you, to know of your health and that of your family. My best compliments to Mrs. Wharton, Mr. Brown comes and throws in his *little compliments* too, and we are both very truly yours,

T. G., *i.b.*

LXXII.—TO THOMAS WHARTON.

MY DEAR WHARTON—I promised Dr. Keene long since to give you an account of our magnificences here,[1] but the newspapers and he himself in person have got the start of my indolence, so that by this time you are well acquainted with all the events, that adorned that week of wonders. Thus much I may

[1] The Duke of Newcastle's installation as Chancellor of the University.—[*Mason.*]

venture to tell you, because it is probable nobody else has done it, that our friend Chappy's zeal and eloquence surpassed all power of description. Vesuvio in an eruption was not more violent than his utterancé, nor (since I am at my mountains) Pelion with all its pine-trees in a storm of wind more impetuous than his action. And yet the Senate-house still stands, and (I thank God) we are all safe and well at your service. I was ready to sink for him, and scarce dared to look about me, when I was sure it was all over: but soon found I might have spared my confusion, for all people joined to applaud him: everything was quite right; and I dare swear, not three people here but think him a model of oratory. For all the Duke's little court came with a resolution to be pleased; and when the tone was once given, the University, who ever wait for the judgment of their betters, struck into it with an admirable harmony. For the rest of the performances they were (as usual) very ordinary. Every one, while it lasted, was very gay and very busy in the morning, and very owlish and very tipsey at night. I make no exceptions from the Chancellour to Blew-coat. Mason's Ode was the only entertainment, that had any tolerable elegance; and for my own part, I think it (with some little abatements) uncommonly well on such an occasion. Pray let me know your sentiments, for doubtless you have seen it. The author of it grows apace into my good graces: as I know him more: he is very ingenious with great good nature and simplicity. A little vain, but in so harmless and so comical a way, that it does not offend one at all; a little ambitious, but withal so ignorant in the world and its ways, that this does not hurt him in one's opinion. So sincere and so undisguised, that no mind with a spark of generosity would ever think of hurting him, he lies so open to injury. But so indolent, that if he cannot overcome this habit, all his good qualities will signify nothing at all. After all I like him so well, I could wish you knew him.

Tuthill, who was here at the installation and in high spirits, will come to settle in Cambridge at Michaelmas. And I have hopes, that these two, with Brown's assistance may bring Pembroke into some esteem: but then there is no making bricks without straw. They have no boys at all, and unless you can send us a hamper or two out of the north to begin with, they will be like a few rats straggling about an old deserted mansion-house.

I should be glad (as you will see Keene often) if you could throw in a word, as of your own head merely, about a Fellowship for Stonhewer; he has several times mentioned it himself, as a thing he would try to bring about either at Queen's or Christ's, where he has interest: but I know not how, it has gone off again, and we have heard no more lately about it. I know it is not practicable here at Peterhouse, because of his county; and though at Pembroke we might possibly get a majority, yet Roger is an animal, that might play over again all his old game, and with a better appearance than before. You would therefore oblige me, if you would sound him upon this subject, for it is Stonhewer's wish, and (I think) would be an advantage to him, if he had a reason for continuing here some time longer. If you can get Keene to be explicit about it (but it must seem to be a thought entirely of your own) I will desire you to let me know the result. My best wishes, dear Sir, ever attend on you, and Mrs. Wharton.—I am most sincerely and unalterably yours, T. G.

August 8th [1749], Cambridge.

LXXIII.—TO THOMAS WHARTON.

Stoke, August 9, 1750.

MY DEAR WHARTON—Aristotle says[1] (one may write Greek to you without scandal) that Oἱ [γὰρ] τόποι οὐ διαλύουσι τὴν φιλίαν. ἁπλῶς, ἀλλὰ τὴν ἐνεργείαν. 'Εὰν δὲ χρόνιος ἡ ἀπουσία γένηται, καὶ τῆς φιλίας δοκεῖ λήθην ποιεῖν· ὅθεν εἴρηται,

πολλὰς δὴ φιλίας ἀπροσηγορία διέλυσεν.

But Aristotle may say whatever he pleases, I do not find myself at all the worse for it. I could indeed wish to refresh my ἐνεργεία a little at Durham by a sight of you, but when is there a probability of my being so happy? It concerned me greatly when I

[1] *Vide Aristotelis Ethic. Nicomach.*, Lib. Θ. cap. 5, p. 350, ed. Wilkinson.

heard the other day, that your asthma continued at times to afflict you, and that you were often obliged to go into the country to breathe. You cannot oblige me more than by giving me an account of the state both of your body and mind; I hope the latter is able to keep you cheerful and easy in spite of the frailties of its companion. As to my own, it can do neither one, nor the other; and I have the mortification to find my spiritual part the most infirm thing about me. You have doubtless heard of the loss I have had in Dr. Middleton,[1] whose house was the only easy place one could find to converse in at Cambridge. For my part I find a friend so uncommon a thing, that I cannot help regretting even an old acquaintance, which is an indifferent likeness of it, and though I don't approve the spirit of his books, methinks 'tis pity the world should lose so rare a thing as a good writer.[2] My studies cannot furnish a recommendation of many new books to you; there is a *Defence de l'Esprit des Loix*, by Montesquieu himself. It has some lively things in it, but is very short, and his adversary appears to be so mean a bigot, that he deserved no answer. There are three vols. in 4to. of *Histoire du Cabinet du Roi*, by Messrs. Buffons and D'Aubenton. The

[1] Conyers Middleton (1683-1750), the most able of the deistical writers of the age. His covert assaults upon the orthodox dogmas are submitted to a very able analysis in Mr. Leslie Stephen's *English Thought in the Eighteenth Century*.—[*Ed.*]

[2] Mr. Gray used to say, that good writing not only required great parts, but the very best of those parts.—[*Mason.*]

first is a man of character, but (I am told) has hurt it by his work. It is all a sort of introduction to natural history. The weak part of it is a love of system, which runs through it, the most contrary thing in the world to a science, entirely grounded upon experiments, and that has nothing to do with vivacity of imagination.[1] There are some microscopical observations, that seemed curious to me, on those animalculæ to which we are supposed to owe our origin; and which he has discovered of like figure in females not pregnant, and in almost everything we use for nourishment, even vegetables, particularly in their fruits and seeds. Not that he allows them to be animated bodies, but *molecules organisées.* If you ask what that is, I cannot tell; no more than I can understand a new system of generation which he builds upon it. But what I was going to commend is a general view he gives of the face of the earth, followed by a particular one of all known nations, their peculiar figure and manners, which is the best epitome of Geography I ever met with, and wrote with sense, and elegance: in short these books are well worth turning over. The *Mémoires* of the Abbé de Mongon in five vol., are highly commended, but I have not seen them. He was engaged in several Embassies to Germany, England, etc., during the course of the late war. The Presid.

[1] One cannot therefore help lamenting that Mr. Gray let his imagination lie dormant so frequently, in order to apply himself to this very science.—[*Mason.*]

Henault's[1] *Abrégé Chronologique de l'Hist. de France*, I believe I have before mentioned to you, as a very good book of its kind.

You advised me in your last to be acquainted with Keene, and we are accordingly on very good and civil terms: but to make us love one another (I reckon) you hardly proposed. I always placed the service he did me about Tuthill to your account. This latter has done him some service, about his regulations. If you will give me the pleasure of a letter, while I continue here, it will be a great satisfaction to me. I shall stay a month longer. My best wishes to Mrs. Wharton and your family.—I am ever yours, T. GRAY.

Do not imagine I have forgot my debts, I hope to replace them this year.

LXXIV.—TO THOMAS WHARTON.

MY DEAR WHARTON—A little kind of reproach, that I saw the other day in a letter of yours to Mr. Brown, has made my guilt fly in my face, and given me spirit to be a beast no longer. I desired him to tell you in the beginning of the summer, that I feared my journey into the north would be prevented by the arrival of my cousin, Mrs. Forster (whom you remember by the name of Pattinson) from India. She

[1] Charles Jean François Hénault (1685-1770). The *Abrégé* appeared in 1744.– [*Ed.*]

came in August; and I continued in town with her a month in order to do what little services I could to a person as strange, and as much to seek, as though she had been born in the Mud of the Ganges. After this the year was too far advanced to undertake such an expedition; and the thought of seeing you here in the spring in some measure comforts me for the disappointment; for I depend upon your coming then, when it will be far easier to confer together, and determine about a thing, in which (I fear) I am too much interested to deserve having any great share in the determination[1] . . . . . .

You are aware undoubtedly, that a certain deference, not to say servility, to the heads of colleges is perhaps necessary to a physician, that means to establish himself here: you possibly may find a method to do without it. Another inconvenience your wife, rather than you, will feel, the want of company of her own sex; as the women are few here, squeezy and formal, and little skilled in amusing themselves or other people. All I can say is, she must try to make up for it among the men, who are not over-agreeable neither. I much approve of your settling seriously to your profession; but as your father is old, if you should lose him, what becomes of your interest, and to whom is it then to be transferred? Would you leave London and your practice again to canvass an election for yourself? It seems to me, that, if you execute your

[1] About nineteen lines of the MS. are lost here.—[*Ed.*]

present scheme, you must (in case of Mr. Wharton's death) entirely lay aside all views of that kind. The gradual transition you propose to make through Bath or Cambridge to London is very well judged, and likely enough to succeed. For Bath, I am wholly unacquainted with it, and consequently can say little to the purpose. The way of life there might be more amusing to Mrs. Wharton, than this; but to you, I think, would be less satisfactory. I sincerely congratulate you on the good effects of your new medicine, which is indeed a sufficient recompense for any pains you have taken in that study. But to make a just trial of its efficacy and of your own constitution, you certainly ought to pass a little time at London (a month or so)[1]. . . .

engaged himself to make it up £1000, in case the brothers will not do it, and they have (after some hesitation), refused it. Our good Mr. Brown goes out of his office to-day, of which he is not a little glad. His college, which had much declined for some time, is picking up again: they have had twelve admissions this year; and are just filling up two fellowships with a Mr. Cardell, whom I do not know, but they say, he is a good scholar; and a Mr. Delaval, a Fellow-Commoner (a younger son to old Delaval of Northumberland), who has taken his degree in an exemplary manner, and is very sensible, and knowing. The appeal, which has been so long contended for, will, I believe, at last be yielded to with a good grace, or rather

[1] About sixteen lines of the MS. are lost here.—[*Ed.*]

bestowed, by the advice of the D. of Newcastle, and my Lord Ch$^{r.}$, and will be the best, the most popular thing they can do. But you must not mention it, till it is actually done. I am sorry your friend Chapman will lose all the merit of his pamphlet, which (by the way) has been answered exceedingly well, and with all due contempt. He seems much mortified, and was preparing a reply, but this event, I doubt, will cut him short.

I know of nothing new in the literary way, but the history of Lewis 14th, by Voltaire; not that I have yet seen it, but my expectations are much raised.—Adieu, my dear Wharton, I am ever most truly yours, T. G.

P.S.—I am ready to pay my debts, if you will tell me to whom. My compliments and good wishes to Mrs. Wharton, and the little gentry.

[Endorsed thus:] October 10, 1750.

LXXV.—TO JOHN CHUTE.

My God! Mr. Chute in England? what, and have you seen him, and did he say nothing to you? not a word of me? such was my conversation, when I first heard news so surprising, with a person, that (when I reflect) it is indeed no great wonder you did not much interrogate concerning me, as you knew nothing of what has passed of late.

But let me ask you yourself, have a few years

totally erased me from your memory? you are generous enough perhaps to forget all the obligations I have to you. But is it generosity to forget the person you have obliged too? while I remember myself, I cannot but remember you: and consequently cannot but wonder, when I find nowhere one line, one syllable, to tell me you are arrived. I will venture to say, there is nobody in England, however nearly connected with you, that has seen you with more real joy and affection than I shall. You are, it seems, gone into the country, whither (had I reason to think you wished to see me) I should immediately have followed; as it is, I am returning to Cambridge, but with intention to come back to town again, whenever you do, if you will let me know the time and place.

I readily set Mr. Whd.[1] free from all imputations. He is a fine young personage in a coat all over spangles, just come over from the Tour of Europe to take possession, and be married: and consequently can't be supposed to think of anything, or remember anybody, but you——! however, I don't altogether clear him, he might have said something to one, who remembers him when he was but a Pout. Nevertheless, I desire my hearty gratulations to him, and say I wish him more spangles, and more estates, and more wives.—Adieu! my dear Sir, I am ever yours,

T. Gray.

P.S.—My compliments to Mrs. Chute (who once

[1] Francis Whithead, the nephew of John Chute. Gray and Walpole met these gentlemen in Florence in 1740. Whithead

did me the honour to write to me), and say I give her joy very sincerely of your return.

London, October. To T. G. of Peterhouse, Cambridge.

To John Chute, Esq.
at Mr. Whithead's, of Southwick,
near Farnham, Hampshire.

LXXVI.—TO JOHN CHUTE.

My dear Sir—You have not then forgot me, and I shall see you soon again. It suffices, and there needed no other excuse. I loved you too well not to forgive you, without a reason: but I could not but be sorry for myself.

You are lazy (you say) and listless, and gouty, and old, and vexed, and perplexed: I am all that (the gout excepted) and many things more, that I hope you never will be: so that what you tell me on that head, est trop flateur pour moi. Our imperfections may at least excuse, and perhaps recommend us to one another; methinks I can readily pardon sickness, and age, and vexation, for all the depredations they make within and without, when I think they make us better friends, and better men, which I am persuaded is often the case. I am very sure, I have seen the best tempered, generous, tender young creatures in the world, that would have been very glad to be sorry for people they liked, when under any pain, and

died prematurely, in 1751, of a chill taken in the hunting-field.—[*Ed.*]

could not, merely for want of knowing rightly, what it was themselves.

I find Mr. Walpole then made some mention of me to you; yes, we are together again. It is about a year, I believe, since he wrote to me, to offer it, and there has been (particularly of late), in appearance, the same kindness and confidence almost as of old. What were his motives, I cannot yet guess. What were mine, you will imagine and perhaps blame me. However as yet I neither repent, nor rejoice overmuch, but I am pleased. He is full, I assure you, of your Panegyric. Never anybody had half so much wit, as Mr. Chute (which is saying everything with him, you know) and Mr. Wh$^{d.}$ is the finest young man that ever was imported. I hope to embrace this fine man (if I can), and thank him heartily for being my advocate, tho' in vain. He is a good creature, and I am not sure but I shall be tempted to eat a wing of him with Sellery-Sauce.

I am interrupted. Whenever I know of your time, I will be in town presently. I cannot but make Mrs. Chute my best acknowledgments for taking my part. Heaven keep you all.—I am, my best Mr. Chute, very faithfully yours, T. G.

Cambridge, October 12, Sunday, 1750.

LXXVII.—TO DOROTHY GRAY.

Cambridge, November 7, 1749.

THE unhappy news I have just received from you equally surprises and afflicts me.[1] I have lost a person I loved very much, and have been used to from my infancy; but am much more concerned for your loss, the circumstances of which I forbear to dwell upon, as you must be too sensible of them yourself; and will, I fear, more and more need a consolation that no one can give, except He who has preserved her to you so many years, and at last, when it was His pleasure, has taken her from us to Himself: and perhaps, if we reflect upon what she felt in this life, we may look upon this as an instance of His goodness both to her, and to those that loved her. She might have languished many years before our eyes in a continual increase of pain, and totally helpless; she might have long wished to end her misery without being able to attain it; or perhaps even lost all sense, and yet continued to breathe; a sad spectacle to such as must have felt more for her than she could have done for herself. However you may deplore your own loss, yet think that she is at last easy and happy; and has now more occasion to pity us than we her. I hope, and beg, you will support yourself

[1] The death of his aunt, Mrs. Mary Antrobus, who died the 5th of November, and was buried in a vault in Stoke church-yard near the chancel door, in which also his mother and himself (according to the direction in his will) were afterwards buried.—[*Mason.*]

with that resignation we owe to Him, who gave us our being for our good, and who deprives us of it for the same reason. I would have come to you directly, but you do not say whether you desire I should or not; if you do, I beg I may know it, for there is nothing to hinder me, and I am in very good health.

LXXVIII.—TO HORACE WALPOLE.

Stoke, June 12, 1750.

DEAR SIR—As I live in a place, where even the ordinary tattle of the town arrives not till it is stale, and which produces no events of its own, you will not desire any excuse from me for writing so seldom, especially as of all people living I know you are the least a friend to letters spun out of one's own brains, with all the toil and constraint that accompanies sentimental productions. I have been here at Stoke, a few days (where I shall continue good part of the summer); and having put an end to a thing,[1] whose beginning you have seen long ago, I immediately send it you. You will, I hope, look upon it in the light of a thing with an end to it: a merit that most of my writings have wanted, and are like to want, but which this epistle I am determined shall not want, when it tells you that I am ever yours, T. GRAY.

Not that I have done yet; but who could avoid the temptation of finishing so roundly and so cleverly, in the manner of good Queen Anne's days?

[1] This was the "Elegy in a Country Church-yard."

Now I have talked of writings, I have seen a book which is by this time in the press, against Middleton (though without naming him), by Asheton. As far as I can judge from a very hasty reading, there are things in it new and ingenious, but rather too prolix, and the style here and there savouring too strongly of sermon. I imagine it will do him credit. So much for other people, now to *self* again. You are desired to tell me your opinion, if you can take the pains, of these lines.—I am, once more, ever yours.

LXXIX.—TO HORACE WALPOLE.

Cambridge, February 11, 1751.

As you have brought me into a little sort of distress, you must assist me, I believe, to get out of it as well as I can. Yesterday I had the misfortune of receiving a letter from certain gentlemen (as their bookseller expresses it), who have taken the Magazine of Magazines into their hands. They tell me that an *ingenious* Poem, called reflections in a Country Church-yard, has been communicated to them, which they are printing forthwith; that they are informed that the *excellent* author of it is I by name, and that they beg not only his *indulgence*, but the *honour* of his correspondence, etc. As I am not at all disposed to be either so indulgent, or so correspondent, as they desire, I have but one bad way left to escape the honour they would inflict upon me; and therefore am obliged to desire you would make Dodsley print it immediately (which may be done in less than a week's time) from your copy, but without my name, in what form is most convenient for him, but on his best paper and character; he must correct the press himself, and print it without any interval between the stanzas, because the sense is in some places continued beyond them; and the title must be,—Elegy, written in a Country Church-yard. If he would add a line or two to say it came into his hands by accident, I should like it better. If you behold the Magazine of Magazines in the light that I do, you will not refuse to give yourself this trouble on my account, which you have taken of your own accord before now. If Dodsley do not do this immediately, he may as well let it alone.

LXXX.—TO HORACE WALPOLE.

Ash-Wednesday, Cambridge, 1751.

MY DEAR SIR—You have indeed conducted with great decency my little *misfortune:* you have taken a paternal care of it, and expressed much more kindness than could have been expressed from so near a relation. But we are all frail; and I hope to do as much for you another time.

Nurse Dodsley has given it a pinch or two in the cradle, that (I doubt) it will bear the marks of as long as it lives. But no matter: we have ourselves suffered under her hands before now; and besides, it will only look the more careless and by *accident* as it were. I thank you for your advertisement, which saves my honour, and in a manner *bien flatteuse pour moi*, who should be put to it even to make myself a compliment in good English.

You will take me for a mere poet, and a fetcher and carrier of sing-song, if I tell you that I intend to send you the beginning of a drama,[1] not mine, thank God, as you will believe, when you hear it is finished, but wrote by a person whom I have a very good opinion of. It is (unfortunately) in the manner of the ancient drama, with choruses, which I am to my shame the occasion of; for, as great part of it was at first written in that form, I would not suffer him to change it to a play fit for the stage, and as he intended, because the lyric parts are the best of it, they must have been lost. The story is Saxon, and the language has a tang of Shakespeare, that suits an old-fashioned fable very well. In short I don't do it merely to amuse you, but for the sake of the author, who wants a judge, and so I would lend him *mine*: yet not without your leave, lest you should have us up to dirty our stockings at the bar of your house, for wasting the time and politics of the *nation*. —Adieu, Sir! I am ever yours, T. GRAY.

LXXXI.—TO HORACE WALPOLE.

Cambridge, March 3, 1751.

ELFRIDA (for that is the fair one's name) and her author are now in town together. He has promised

[1] This was the *Elfrida* of Mason.

me, that he will send a part of it to you some morning while he is there; and (if you shall think it worth while to descend to particulars) I should be glad you would tell me very freely your opinion about it; for he shall know nothing of the matter, that is not fit for the ears of a *tender* parent—though, by the way, he has ingenuity and merit enough (whatever his drama may have) to bear hearing his faults very patiently.

I must only beg you not to shew it, much less let it be copied; for it will be published, though not as yet.

I do not expect any more editions;[1] as I have appeared in more magazines than one. The chief errata[2] were *sacred* bower for *secret; hidden* for *kindred* (in spite of dukes and classics); and "*frowning* as in scorn" for *smiling*. I humbly propose, for the benefit of Mr. Dodsley and his matrons, that take *awake*[3] for a verb, that they should read *asleep*, and all will be right. *Gil Blas*[4] is the *Lying Valet* in

[1] Of the "Elegy in a Country Church-yard."

[2] Besides these errors of the text, in the Magazine of Magazines, the following occurred:—"their *harrow* oft the stubborn glebe has broke."—"And read their *destiny* in a nation's eyes."—"With uncouth rhymes and shapeless *culture* decked."—"Slow through the churchway *pass* we saw him borne,"—and many others of less consequence."—[*Ed.*]

[3] "Awake and faithful to her wonted fires."

[4] *Gil Blas* was a comedy by Edward Moore, acted at Drury Lane in 1751. *The Lying Valet* was a farce Garrick had written in 1740.—[*Ed.*]

five acts. The *Fine Lady*[1] has half a dozen good lines dispersed in it. *Pompey* is the hasty production of a Mr. Coventry[2] (cousin to him you knew) a young clergyman; I found it out by three characters, which once made part of a comedy that he shewed me of his own writing. Has that miracle of *tenderness and sensibility* (as she calls it) "Lady Vane" given you any amusement? *Peregrine*,[3] whom she uses as a vehicle, is very poor indeed, with a few exceptions. In the last volume is a character of Mr. Lyttleton, under the name of "Gosling Scrag," and a parody of part of his Monody, under the notion of a Pastoral on the death of his grandmother.—I am ever yours,

T. GRAY.

LXXXII.—TO HORACE WALPOLE.

Cambridge, October 8, 1751.

I SEND you this[4] (as you desire) merely to make up half a dozen; though it will hardly answer your end in furnishing out either a head or a tail-piece. But your own fable[5] may much better supply the place. You have altered it to its advantage; but there is

[1] "The Female Rake, or the Modern Fine Lady" was by Soame Jenyns.—[*Ed.*]

[2] Francis Coventry was the anonymous author of a popular jeu-d'esprit entitled *The History of Pompey the Little; or the Life and Adventures of a Lap-Dog*, first published in 1751.—[*Ed.*]

[3] *Peregrine Pickle*, then just issued.—[*Ed.*]

[4] The "Hymn to Adversity."

[5] The "Entail;" see Walpole's *Works*, vol. i. p. 28.

still something a little embarrassed here and there in the expression. I rejoice to find you apply (pardon the use of so odious a word) to the history of your own times. Speak, and spare not. Be as impartial as you can; and after all, the world will not believe you are so, though you should make as many protestations as bishop Burnet. They will feel in their own breast, and find it very possible to hate fourscore persons, yea, ninety and nine: so you must rest satisfied with the testimony of your own conscience. Somebody has laughed at Mr. Dodsley, or at me, when they talked of the *bat*: I have nothing more either nocturnal or diurnal, to deck his miscellany with. We have a man[1] here that writes a good hand; but he has little failings that hinder my recommending him to you. He is lousy, and he is mad: he sets out this week for Bedlam; but if you insist upon it, I don't doubt he will pay his respects to you. I have seen two of Dr. Middleton's unpublished works. One is about 44 pages in 4to. against Dr. Waterland, who wrote a very orthodox book[2] on the *Importance of the Doctrine of the Trinity*, and insisted that Christians ought to have no communion with such as differ from them in fundamentals. Middleton enters no farther into the doctrine itself than to shew that a mere speculative point can never be called a fundamental: and that

[1] This was apparently the poet Christopher Smart.—[*Ed.*]

[2] Waterland's *Scripture Vindicated* was published in 1731. The *Miscellaneous Works* of Middleton appeared in 1755.—[*Ed.*]

the earlier fathers, on whose concurrent tradition Waterland would build, are so far, when they speak of the three persons from agreeing with the present notion of our church, that they declare for the inferiority of the Son, and seem to have no clear and distinct idea of the Holy Ghost at all. The rest is employed in exposing the folly and cruelty of stiffness and zealotism in religion, and in shewing that the primitive ages of the church, in which tradition had its rise, were (even by the confession of the best scholars and most orthodox writers) *the æra of nonsense and absurdity.* It is finished and very well wrote; but has been mostly incorporated into his other works, particularly the enquiry; and for this reason, I suppose, he has writ upon it, "*This wholly laid aside.*" The second is in Latin, on miracles; to shew, that of the two methods of defending Christianity, one from its intrinsic evidence, the holiness and purity of its doctrines, the other from its external, the miracles said to be wrought confirm it; the first has been little attended to by reason of its difficulty; the second much insisted upon, because it appeared an easier task; but that, in reality, it can prove nothing at all. "Nobilis illa quidem defensio (the first) quam si obtinere potuissent, rem simul omnem expediisse, causamque penitus vicisse viderentur. At causae hujus defendendæ labor cum tantâ argumentandi cavillandique molestiâ conjunctus, ad alteram, quam dixi, defensionis viam, ut commodiorem longè et faciliorem, plerosque adegit——ego verò istiusmodi defensione religionem nostram non modo non confirmari, sed dubiam potiùs suspectamque reddi existimo." He then proceeds to consider miracles in general, and afterwards those of the Pagans compared with those of Christ. I only tell you the plan, for I have not read it out (though it is short); but you will not doubt to what conclusion it tends. There is another thing, I know not what, I am to see. As to the *Treatise on Prayer*, they say it is burnt indeed. —Adieu! I am ever yours, T. GRAY.

LXXXIII.—TO HORACE WALPOLE.

YOUR pen was too rapid to mind the common form of a direction, and so, by omitting the words *near Windsor*, your letter has been diverting itself at another Stoke, near Ailesbury, and came not to my hands till to-day.

The true original chairs were all sold, when the Huntingdons broke; there are nothing now but Halsey chairs, not adapted to the squareness of gothic dowager's rump. And by the way I do not see how the uneasiness and uncomfortableness of a coronation-chair can be any objection with you: every chair that is easy is modern, and unknown to our ancestors. As I remember there were certain low chairs, that looked like ebony, at Esher, and were old and pretty. Why should not Mr. Bentley improve upon them?—I do not wonder at Dodsley. You have talked to him of six *Odes*, for so you are pleased to call everything I write, though it be but a receipt to make apple-dumplings. He has reason to gulp when he finds one of them only a long story. I don't know but I may send him very soon (by your hands) an ode to his own tooth, a high Pindaric upon stilts, which one must be a better scholar than he is to understand a line of, and the very best scholars will understand but a little matter here and there.

It wants but seventeen lines of having an end, I don't say of being finished. As it is so unfortunate to come too late for Mr. Bentley, it may appear in the 4th volume of the *Miscellanies*, provided you don't think it execrable, and suppress it. Pray when the fine book[1] is to be printed, let me revise the press, for you know you can't; and there are a few trifles I could wish altered.

I know not what you mean by hours of love, and cherries, and pine-apples. I neither see nor hear anything here, and am of opinion that is the best way. My compliments to Mr. Bentley, if he be with you. —I am yours ever, T. GRAY.

I desire you would not show that Epigram I repeated to you, as mine. I have heard of it twice already as coming from you.

LXXXIV.—TO HORACE WALPOLE.

I AM obliged to you for Mr. Dodsley's book,[2] and having pretty well looked it over, will (as you desire)

[1] The Edition of his Odes printed at Strawberry-hill.

[2] His collection of Poems.

tell you my opinion of it. He might, methinks, have spared the graces in his frontispiece, if he chose to be economical, and dressed his authors in a little more decent raiment—not in whited-brown paper, and distorted characters, like an old ballad. I am ashamed to see myself; but the company keeps me in countenance: so to begin with Mr. Tickell. This is not only a state-poem (my ancient aversion), but a state-poem on the peace of Utrecht. If Mr. Pope had wrote a panegyric on it, one could hardly have read him with patience: but this is only a poor short-winded imitator of Addison, who had himself not above three or four notes in poetry, sweet enough indeed, like those of a German flute, but such as soon tire and satiate the ear with their frequent return. Tickell has added to this a great poverty of sense, and a string of transitions that hardly become a school-boy. However, I forgive him for the sake of his ballad,[1] which I always thought the prettiest in the world.

All there is of M. Green[2] here, has been printed before; there is a profusion of wit everywhere; reading would have formed his judgment, and harmonised his verse, for even his wood-notes often break out into strains of real poetry and music. The "School Mistress"[3]

[1] "Colin and Lucy," beginning—
"Of Leinster fam'd for maidens fair."

[2] Matthew Green (1696-1737), a poet whom Gray consistently admired, wrote *The Grotto*, 1732, and *The Spleen*, 1737. He was a charming writer of octosyllabic verse, dealing with homely themes in a Dutch spirit of neatness.—[*Ed.*]

[3] By William Shenstone (1714-1763). *The Schoolmistress*, reprinted thus by Dodsley, first appeared in 1741.—[*Ed.*]

is excellent in its kind and masterly; and (I am sorry to differ from you, but) "London"[1] is to me one of those few imitations that have all the ease and all the spirit of an original. The same man's verses[2] on the opening of Garrick's theatre are far from bad. Mr. Dyer[3] (here you will despise me highly) has more of poetry in his imagination than almost any of our number; but rough and injudicious. I should range Mr. Bramston[4] only a step or two above Dr. King, who is as low in my estimation as in yours. Dr. Evans is a furious madman; and pre-existence is nonsense in all her altitudes. Mr. Lyttleton is a gentle elegiac person. Mr. Nugent sure did not write his own Ode.[5] I like Mr. Whitehead's[6] little poems, I mean the Ode on a Tent, the Verses to Garrick, and particularly those to Charles Townsend, better than anything I had seen before of him. I gladly pass over H. Browne and the rest, to come at you. You know I was of the publishing side, and thought your reasons against it none; for though, as Mr. Chute said extremely well, the *still small voice* of Poetry was not made to be heard in a

[1] By Dr. Samuel Johnson, and reprinted from the edition of 1738.—[*Ed.*]

[2] Dr. Samuel Johnson's *Prologue for the opening of Drury Lane Theatre*, 1747.—[*Ed.*]

[3] John Dyer of Aberglasney (1698-1758), author of *Grongar Hill.*—[*Ed.*]

[4] Rev. James Bramston (died 1744), a writer of satire.—[*Ed.*]

[5] Earl Nugent was suspected of paying Mallet to write his best Ode, that addressed to Pulteney, his later and obviously unaided efforts being contemptible.—[*Ed.*]

[6] William Whitehead (1715-1785), the Poet Laureate.—[*Ed.*]

crowd; yet satire will be heard, for all the audience are by nature her friends; especially when she appears in the spirit of Dryden, with his strength, and often with his versification, such as you have caught in those lines on the Royal Unction, on the Papal Dominion, and Convents of both Sexes; on Henry VIII. and Charles II. for these are to me the shining parts of your Epistle.[1] There are many lines I could wish corrected, and some blotted out, but beauties enough to atone for a thousand worse faults than these. The opinion of such as can at all judge, who saw it before in Dr. Middleton's hands, concurs nearly with mine. As to what any one says, since it came out; our people (you must know), are slow of judgment; they wait till some bold body saves them the trouble, and then follow his opinion; or stay till they hear what is said in town, that is at some Bishop's table, or some coffee-house about the Temple. When they are determined I will tell you faithfully their verdict. As for the beauties[2] I am their most humble servant. What shall I say to Mr. Lowth, Mr. Ridley, Mr. Rolle, the Reverend Mr. Brown, Seward, etc.? If I say Messieurs! this is not the thing; write prose, write sermons, write nothing at all; they will disdain me and my advice. What then would the sickly Peer[3] have done, that spends so much time in admiring everything that has four legs, and fretting at his own misfortune in having

[1] Walpole's Epistle to Thomas Asheton, from Florence.

[2] The Epistle to Mr. Eckardt, the painter.

[3] Lord Hervey.

but two; and cursing his own politic head and feeble constitution, that won't let him be such a beast as he would wish? Mr. S. Jenyns[1] now and then can write a good line or two—such as these—

> "Snatch us from all our little sorrows here,
> Calm every grief, and dry each childish tear," etc.

I like Mr. Aston Hervey's Fable; and an Ode (the last of all) by Mr. Mason, a new acquaintance of mine, whose Musæus too seems to carry with it a promise at least of something good to come. I was glad to see you distinguished who poor West was, before his charming Ode,[2] and called it anything rather than a Pindaric. The town is an owl, if it don't like Lady Mary,[3] and I am surprised at it: we here are owls enough to think her eclogues very bad; but that I did not wonder at. Our present taste is Sir T. Fitz-Osborne's Letters.[4]

I send you a bit of a thing for two reasons; first, because it is one of your favourites, Mr. M. Green: and next, because I would do justice. The thought on which my second Ode[5] turns is manifestly stole from hence; not that I knew it at the time, but

[1] Soame Jenyns (1704-1787).

[2] Monody on the death of Queen Caroline.

[3] Lady Mary W. Montagu's Poems.

[4] The book called *Sir Thomas Fitzosborne's Letters on Various Subjects*, which went through many editions during the latter half of the eighteenth century, was originally published anonymously in 1748-49, by its author William Melmoth the younger.—[Ed.]

[5] The *Ode to Spring*.

having seen this many years before, to be sure it imprinted itself on my memory, and, forgetting the Author, I took it for my own. The subject was the Queen's Hermitage.

. . . .

"Tho' yet no palace grace the shore,
To lodge the pair you should adore,
Nor abbeys great in ruins rise,
Royal equivalents for vice;
Behold a grot in Delphic grove,
The Graces' and the Muses' love,
A temple from vain-glory free;
Whose goddess is Philosophy;
Whose sides such licens'd idols crown,
As Superstition would pull down:
The only pilgrimage I know,
That men of sense would choose to go.
Which sweet abode, her wisest choice,
Urania cheers with heavenly voice;
While all the virtues gather round
To see her consecrate the ground.

If thou, the God with winged feet,
In council talk of this retreat;
And jealous Gods resentment show
At altars rais'd to men below.
Tell those proud lords of heaven 'tis fit
Their house our heroes should admit.
While each exists (as poets sing)
A lazy, lewd, immortal thing;
They must, or grow in disrepute,
With earth's first commoners recruit.

Needless it is, in terms unskill'd,
To praise whatever Boyle shall build.
Needless it is the busts to name
Of men, monopolists of fame;

Four chiefs adorn the modest stone,
For virtue, as for learning known:
The thinking sculpture helps to raise
Deep thoughts, the genii of the place:
To the mind's ear, and inward sight,
There silence speaks, and shade gives light:
While insects from the threshold preach,
And minds dispos'd to musing teach;
Proud of strong limbs and painted hues,
They perish by the slightest bruise;
Or maladies begun within
Destroy more slow life's frail machine:
From maggot-youth, thro' change of state,
They feel like us the turns of fate:
Some born to creep have liv'd to fly,
And chang'd earth's cells for dwellings high:
And some that did their six wings keep,
Before they died, been forced to creep.
They politics, like ours, profess;
The greater prey upon the less.
Some strain on foot huge loads to bring,
Some toil incessant on the wing:
Nor from their vigorous schemes desist
Till death; and then they are never mist.
Some frolick, toil, marry, increase,
Are sick and well, have war and peace;
And broke with age in half a day,
Yield to successors, and away."

. . . .

Adieu! I am ever yours,
T. Gray.

LXXXV.—TO HORACE WALPOLE.

November, Tuesday, Cambridge.

It is a misfortune to me to be at a distance from both of you at once. A letter can give one so little idea of such matters, . . . I always believed well of his heart and temper, and would gladly do so still. If they are as they should be, I should have expected everything from such an explanation; for it is a tenet with me (a simple one, you'll perhaps say) that if ever two people, who love one another, come to breaking, it is for want of a timely eclaircissement, a full and precise one, without witnesses or mediators, and without reserving any one disagreeable circumstance for the mind to brood upon in silence.

I am not totally of your mind as to Mr. Lyttleton's elegy, though I love kids and fawns as little as you do. If it were all like the fourth stanza, I should be excessively pleased. Nature and sorrow, and tenderness, are the true genius of such things; and something of these I find in several parts of it (not in the orange-tree): poetical ornaments, are foreign to the purpose; for they only shew a man is not sorry;—and devotion worse; for it teaches him that he ought not to be sorry, which is all the pleasure of the thing. I beg leave to turn your weathercock the contrary way. Your epistle[1] I have not seen a great while, and Dr. M— is not in the way to give me a sight of it: but I remember enough to be sure all the world will be pleased with it, even with all its *faults upon its head*, if you don't care to mend them. I would try to do it myself (however hazardous), rather than it

[1] From Florence to Thomas Asheton. See Walpole's *Works*, vol. i. p. 4.

should remain unpublished. As to my Eton ode, Mr. Dodsley is *padrone.* The second[1] you had, I suppose you do not think worth giving him: otherwise, to me it seems not worse than the former. He might have Selima[2] too, unless she be of too little importance for his patriot-collection; or perhaps the *connections* you had with her may interfere. Che so io? Adieu!—I am yours ever, T. G.

LXXXVI.—TO HORACE WALPOLE.

Cambridge, December, Monday.

THIS comes du fond de ma cellule to salute Mr. H. W. not so much him that visits and votes, and goes to White's and to Court, as the H. W. in his rural capacity, snug in his tub on Windsor-hill, and brooding over folios of his own creation: him that can slip away, like a pregnant beauty (but a little oftener), into the country, be brought to bed perhaps of twins, and whisk to town again the week after, with a face as if nothing had happened. Among the little folks, my godsons and daughters, I cannot choose but enquire more particularly after the health of one; I mean (without a figure) the Memoires. Do they grow? Do they unite, and hold up their heads, and dress themselves? Do they begin to think of making their appearance in the world, that is to say, fifty years hence, to make posterity stare, and all good people

[1] The "Ode on Spring."

[2] The "Ode on Mr. Walpole's Cat," drowned in a tub of gold fishes.

cross themselves? Has Asheton (who will then be Lord Bishop of Killaloe, and is to publish them) thought of an *aviso all' lettore* to prefix to them yet, importing, that if the words church, king, religion, ministry, etc., be found often repeated in this book, they are not to be taken literally, but poetically, and as may be most strictly reconcileable to the faith then established;—that he knew the author well when he was a young man; and can testify upon the honour of his function, that he said his prayers regularly and devoutly, had a profound reverence for the clergy, and firmly believed everything that was the fashion in those days?

When you have done impeaching my Lord Lovat, I hope to hear *de vos nouvelles*, and moreover, whether you have got Colonel Conway yet? Whether Sir C. Williams is to go to Berlin? What sort of a Prince Mitridate may be?—and whatever other tidings you may chuse to refresh an anchoret with. *Frattanto* I send you a scene in a tragedy:[1] if it don't make you cry it will make you laugh; and so it moves some passion, that I take to be enough. Adieu, dear Sir! I am sincerely yours, T. GRAY.

LXXXVII.—TO THOMAS WHARTON.

MY DEAR WHARTON—You are apprised by this time (I don't doubt) that your Mr. Spencer is chose at Pembroke. I received, while I was at Stoke, a letter

[1] The first Scene in *Agrippina*.

from Tuthill, wherein were these words, "Spencer will, I am almost persuaded, be chose at this audit, and perhaps without a quarrel. I shall vote for him with great pleasure, because I believe he may justly claim it, and because I believe Dr. Wharton would, if he knew of our election, desire it; for *he* was maintained by his Mr. Wilkinson." Dr. Long did not make any resistance, when he saw how it would go, so Chapman had little occasion for his *effectual interest.* Oh, by the way I give you joy of that agreeable creature, who has got one of your Prebends of £400 a year, and will visit you soon, with that dry piece of goods, his wife.

Of my house[1] I cannot say much: I wish I could! but for my heart it is no less yours, than it has long been; and the last thing in the world, that will throw it into tumults, is a fine lady. The verses[2] you so kindly try to keep in countenance were wrote to divert that particular family, and succeeded accordingly. But being shewed about in town, are not liked there at all. Mrs. French, a very fashionable personage, told Mr. W[alpole] that she had seen a thing by a friend of his, which she did not know what to make of, for it aimed at everything, and meant nothing. To which he replied, that he had always taken her for a woman of sense, and was very sorry to be undeceived. On the other hand the stanzas,[3] which I now enclose to you, have had the misfortune, by Mr.

[1] The house he was rebuilding in Cornhill.—[*Mason.*]
[2] "The Long Story."—[*Mason.*]
[3] "The Elegy in a Country Church-yard."

W[alpole]'s fault, to be made still more public, for which they certainly were never meant: but is too late to complain. They have been so applauded, it is quite a shame to repeat it. I mean not to be modest; but I mean, it is a shame for those, who have said such superlative things about them, that I can't repeat them. I should have been glad, that you and two or three more people had liked them, which would have satisfied my ambition on this head amply. I have been this month in town, not at Newcastle-house, but diverting myself among my gay acquaintance; and return to my cell with so much the more pleasure. I do not speak of my future excursion to Durham for fear—but at present it is my full intention.

His Prussian Majesty[1] has published the *Suite des Memoirs* pour servir à l'Histoire de la Maison de Brandebourg, which includes a very free account of his Grandfather's Life, who was the first king of that House, reflections on the gradual advance in science, commerce, etc., of his subjects, and on their changes in religion. It is much in Voltaire's manner. The book itself is at present hard to be got, but you may see a good extract of it in the *Mercure Historique*, a work published monthly: whether it is in that for October or September I cannot justly say. There is also an account of the *History of Crusades*, which seems to be Voltaire's, and promises well. I hear talk of a Pamphlet, called *Voix du Sage et du Peuple*, ascribed to Montesquieu; and a book, styled only

[1] Frederick II. of Prussia (1712-1786).

Lettres, by the Procureur General, Fleury, on the power of the clergy in France, but have not seen either of them, being very scarce as yet. Mr. de Buffon has discovered the Speculum of Archimedes, which burns at 200 feet distance; and a chymist in . . .[1]

You mention Stonhewer. I should be glad to know whether he frequents you? whether you find him improved? and what sort of life he leads among your country-folks? Brown, who has been in the midst of tumults and mutinies lately, and Tuthill, desire their best compliments to you. Mine ever wait on Mrs. Wharton.—Adieu! Believe me, most truly yours.

December 18 [Endorsement 1751], Cambridge.

LXXXVIII.—TO THOMAS WHARTON.

My dear Wharton—I should not have made this little journey to town, if I had not imagined the situation of your affairs (after the loss you have lately had) would have prevented your design of coming to Cambridge. The pleasure I have here, is not sufficient, I am sure, to balance a much slighter, than I shall have in seeing you again: my stay therefore, will at farthest not be longer than Wednesday next, when your [2] business will be over, and we shall have time, I hope, to make up in some degree for so many years' separation.

[1] About nine lines of MS. are lost here.—[*Ed.*]

[2] The MS. is torn, but the tail of a stroke can be seen.—[*Ed.*]

My thanks to Mr. Brown for his letter, and I will trouble you to tell him, I see no reason why the person he mentions should refuse the proposal made him. He must necessarily and I think, in prudence sooner or later enter into the profession, that qualifies him for it. And this is perhaps as creditable a way of doing it, as ever will offer, besides that it need not oblige him to anything he dislikes, and may perhaps lead to great advantages . . .[1] if he be returned. I need not tell you that I am ever yours,

T. GRAY.

[April, 1752.]
Endorsement 1753 altered to 1752.

LXXXIX.—TO THOMAS WHARTON.

. . . .[2]

I AM sorry to tell you a sad story of our friend over the way. Young V[ane], who is now chaplain to your new Bishop, and has had the promise of it for some time, applied to his little red Lordship, as a friend to him and to his family, to put him into Orders. He begun by a direct lie, and told him, he knew the bishop was absolutely engaged to two people of Oxford, whom he named. Then he drilled him on with various trifling pretences, and at last went to town without ordaining him, or appointing any time, when he would. In the meantime V[ane] being pressed by letters from home, went to town and

[1] About three words lost here.—[*Ed.*]
[2] Half a page is lost.—[*Ed.*]

was immediately ordained by the Archbishop of York, and soon after appointed chaplain. He was informed from a very sure hand, that all this time his friend of Ch$^{r.}$ had been making interest for R[o]ss against him, and particularly had said, that V[ane] could not have it, for he was a young man, *not in Orders yet:* I assure you, they are very angry (and with reason), at R[aby] Castle;[1] . . . . de Maintenon's Letters; they are undoubtedly genuine. They begin very early in her life, before she married Scarron; and continue after the King's death to within a little while of her own. They bear all the marks of a noble spirit (in her adversity particularly), of virtue, and unaffected devotion, insomuch that I am almost persuaded she indulged Lewis XIV. in no liberties, till he actually married her, and this not out of policy and ambition, but conscience; for she was what we should call a Bigot, yet with great good sense. In short she was too good for a court; misfortunes in the beginning of her life had formed her mind (naturally lively and impatient) to reflexion, and a habit of piety; she was always miserable, while she had the care of Mad. de Montespan's children; timid and very cautious of making use of that unlimited power she rose to afterwards for fear of trespassing on the king's friendship for her; and after his death, not at all afraid of meeting her own. I don't know what to say to you with regard to Racine: it sounds to me as if anybody should fall upon Shakespeare, who indeed lies infi-

[1] Half a page is lost here.—[*Ed.*]

nitely more open to criticism of all kinds, but I should not care to be the person that undertook it. If you don't like Athaliah, or Britannicus, there is no more to be said. I have done.

Ross bears, or dissembles his disappointment better than I expected of him: perhaps indeed it may not turn out to his disadvantage at the end. He is in London about something. Have you seen Bishop Hall's Satyres, called *Virgidemiæ*,[1] republished lately, they are full of spirit and poetry; as much of the first, as Dr. Donne, and far more of the latter. They were wrote at this University, when he was about 23 years old, in Queen Elizabeth's time. Adieu [ ], Brown and Tuthill send their best compliments, with mine, to you and Mrs. Wharton.—I am ever very sincerely yours, T. G.

[Endorsed December 19, 1752.]
[Cambridge Post-mark.]

XC.—TO HORACE WALPOLE.

Stoke, January 1753.

I AM at present at Stoke, to which place I came at half an hour's warning upon the news I received of my mother's illness, and did not expect to have found her alive; but when I arrived she was much better,

[1] Joseph Hall (1574-1656), Bishop of Exeter and then of Norwich, published his *Virgidemiarium Sixe Bookes* in 1597. The edition which Gray mentions was very carelessly produced in 1753, by Dr. W. Thompson of Queen's, at Oxford.—[*Ed.*]

and continues so. I shall therefore be very glad to make you a visit at Strawberry-hill, whenever you give me notice of a convenient time. I am surprised at the print,[1] which far surpasses my idea of London graving:[2] the drawing itself was so finished, that I suppose it did not require all the art I had imagined to copy it tolerably. My aunts seeing me open your letter, took it to be a burying ticket, and asked whether anybody had left me a ring; and so they still conceive it to be, even with all their spectacles on. Heaven forbid they should suspect it to belong to any verses of mine, they would burn me for a poet. On my own part I am satisfied, if this design

[1] A proof print of the Cul de Lampe, which Mr. Bentley designed for the "Elegy in a Country Church-yard," and which represents a village funeral; this occasioned the pleasant mistake of his two aunts. The remainder of the letter relates entirely to the projected publication of Mr. Bentley's designs, which were printed after by Dodsley this same year. The latter part of it, where he so vehemently declares against having his head prefixt to that work, will appear highly characteristical to those readers, who were personally acquainted with Mr. Gray. The print, which was taken from an original picture, painted by Eckardt, in Mr. Walpole's possession, was actually more than half engraved; but afterwards on this account suppressed.—[*Mason.*]

[2] The engravers were John Sebastian Müller (born 1720), who did the exquisite initial letters, and Charles Grignion (1716-1810), to whom the figure-pieces were entrusted. The original drawings by Bentley were for sale in London in 1882, and I can confirm Gray's statement of their high finish. It was difficult, at the first moment, to realise that they were hand-drawings. Among them was a little sketch of Stoke House, drawn by Gray to aid Bentley in realising the scene of "The Long Story."—[*Ed.*]

of yours succeed so well as you intend it; and yet I know it will be accompanied with something not at all agreeable to me.—While I write this, I receive your second letter.—Sure, you are not out of your wits! This I know, if you suffer my head to be printed, you will infallibly put me out of mine. I conjure you immediately to put a stop to any such design. Who is at the expence of engraving it, I know not; but if it be Dodsley, I will make up the loss to him. The thing as it was, I know, will make me ridiculous enough; but to appear in proper person, at the head of my works, consisting of half a dozen ballads in thirty pages, would be worse than the pillory. I do assure you, if I had received such a book, with such a frontispiece, without any warning, I believe it would have given me a palsy: therefore I rejoice to have received this notice, and shall not be easy till you tell me all thoughts of it are laid aside. I am extremely in earnest, and cannot bear even the idea.

I had written to Dodsley if I had not received yours, to tell him how little I liked the title which he meant to prefix; but your letter has put all that out of my head. If you think it necessary to print these explanations for the use of people that have no eyes, I should be glad they were a little altered. I am to my shame in your debt for a long letter, but I cannot think of anything else, till you have set me at ease on this matter.

XCI.—TO ROBERT DODSLEY.

Cambridge, February 12 [1753].

SIR—I am not at all satisfied with the title. To have it conceived that I publish a collection of *Poems*, and half a dozen little matters (four of which too have already been printed again and again) thus pompously adorned would make me appear very justly ridiculous. I desire it may be understood (which is the truth), that the verses are only subordinate and explanatory to the Drawings, and suffered by me to come out thus only for that reason: therefore if you yourself prefixed this title, I desire it may be altered. Or if Mr. W[alpole] ordered it so, that you would tell him why I wish it were changed in the manner I mentioned to you at first, or to that purpose. For the more I consider it, the less I can bear it, as it now stands. I even think there is an uncommon sort of simplicity that looks like affectation, in putting our plain Christian and surnames without a Mr. before them. But this (if it signifies anything) I easily give up, the other I cannot. You need not apprehend that this change in the title will be any prejudice to the sale of the book. A showy title-page may serve to sell a pamphlet of a shilling or two; but this is not of a price for chance customers, whose eye is caught in passing by a window, and could never sell but from the notion the town may entertain of the merit of the drawings, which they will be instructed in by some that understand such things.

I thank you for the offer you make me, but I shall be contented with three copies, two of which you will send me, and keep the third till I acquaint you where to send it. If you will let me know the exact day they will come out a little time beforehand, I will give you a direction. You will remember to send two copies to Dr. Thomas Wharton, M.D. at Durham. Perhaps you may have burnt my letter, so I will again put down the title—"Designs by Mr. R. Bentley for six poems of Mr. T. Gray."—I am, Sir, your humble servant, T. G.

XCII.—TO THOMAS WHARTON.

Stoke, March 15.

MY DEAR WHARTON—I judge by this time you are in town: the reason that I thought would have deprived me of the pleasure of seeing you is now at an end. My poor mother, after a long and painful struggle for life, expired on Sunday morning. When I have seen her buried, I shall come to London, and it will be a particular satisfaction to me to find you there. If you can procure me a tolerable lodging near you, be so good (if you can conveniently) to let me know the night you receive this; if not, I shall go to my old landlord in Jermyn Street. I believe, I shall come on Tuesday, and stay a few days, for I must return hither to pay my aunt her arrears, which she will demand with great exactness.—Adieu, dear Sir, I am ever yours, T. GRAY.

To me at Mrs. Rogers's of Stoke, near Windsor, Bucks.

Endorsed [1752-3.]

XCIII.—TO THOMAS WHARTON.

Cambridge, Thursday, June 28, 1753.

MY DEAR DOCTOR—You may well suppose me no longer here, as I have neglected thus long to answer two very kind letters, and (which is more) to congratulate you on what most of your friends regard as a very happy event: but to me, I own, it has another face, as I have a much greater regard for you than for the young gentleman, whom I never saw; and foresee, that from this time you will never part with your bottle, which is properly the father of this boy. All my rhetorick will be thrown away, the gout may groan at you, and brandish its crutches, the stone rattle, and the palsy shake its head unheeded. We shall be no match for claret, if it can get an heir, as well as carry an election. Now I talk of elections, we have a report here that your friend Mr. V. (I mean Lord Barnard) means to bring in his son-in-law at Durham. Is this true? H. Vane sets out for the North on Saturday, so I suppose the Bishop's entry will be over next week: and next Monday fortnight I hope to set out myself with Stonehewer, who is going down to his father's, in a post-chaise. We shall not come very fast, as I propose to see Burleigh, Bevoir Castle, etc., by the way. But I shall write again before I come, to tell you exactly what day we shall be at York. If the time does not suit you, you will inform me as soon as possible. I did not run away from his Grace, but followed your advice, had a very affectionate squeeze by the hand, and a fine compliment in a corner. Many people here have been curious to know what it was; but I have kept my own secret, for indeed I do not know myself; only I remember it felt warm, and sweated a little. Adieu! You will not fail to present my compliments to Mrs. Wharton. If she drank as much claret, as you have done, we shall have the boy *stand* for the county, as soon as he can walk alone. Mr. Brown (I believe) will be engaged here with Plummer greatest part of the summer; he and Tuthill desire to be remembered to you both.—I am ever, truly yours,

T. Gray.

XCIV.—TO THOMAS WHARTON.

Cambridge, Saturday, July 14, 1752.

My dear Doctor—This is only to tell you, that we set out on Monday morning, and shall travel leisurely, not by the direct road, for we intend to see several houses and places as we go; on Thursday we shall see York, and next morning as early as we can (certainly before ten o'clock) shall hope to meet you at Studley. You will understand all this with Arch-Bishop Potter's proviso, God willing, and provided nothing hinder, for if we are overturned and *tous fracassées*, or if the mob at Leeds cut us off, as friends to turnpikes; or if the waters be out, and drown us; or (as Herodotus says) if we can go no farther for *feathers*,[1] in all these cases, and many more, we may chance to fail you.—My respects to Mrs. Wharton, I am ever yours, T. GRAY.

XCV.—TO THE REV. WILLIAM MASON.

Durham, July 24, Tuesday, 1753.

DEAR SIR—We performed our journey, a very agreeable one, within the time appointed, and left out scarcely anything worth seeing in or near our way. The Doctor and Mrs. Wharton had expected us about two hours, when we arrived at Studley on Friday. We passed that night at Ripon, and the next at Richmond; and on Sunday evening got to Durham. I cannot now enter into the particulars of my travels, because I have not yet gathered up my quotations from the Classics to intersperse, like Mr. Addison;

[1] This passage from the 4th Book of Herodotus is humorously applied, by Swift, to the number of authors existing in England. "A happiness (he says) derived to us, with a great many others, from our Scythian ancestors, among whom the number of pens was so infinite, that the Grecian eloquence had no other way of expressing it than by saying—'That in the regions far to the North it was hardly possible for a man to travel; the very air was so replete with feathers.'"—*Tale of a Tub*, sect. vii.—[*Mit.*]

but I hope to be able soon to entertain you with a dish of very choice erudition. I have another reason, too, which is, that the post is just setting out. Suffice it to tell you, that I have one of the most beautiful vales here in England to walk in, with prospects that change every ten steps, and open something new wherever I turn me, all rude and romantic; in short, the sweetest spot to break your neck or drown yourself in that ever was beheld. I have done neither yet, but I have been twice at the races, once at the assembly, have had a visit from Dr. Chapman, and dined with the Bishop.[1]

I am very shabby, for Stonhewer's box, with my coat in it, which went by sea, is not yet arrived. You are desired therefore to send Lee, the bedmaker at Peterhouse, to the master of the Lynn boats, to enquire what vessel it was sent by, and why it does not come. It was directed to Dr. Stonhewer, of Houghton, to be left with the rector of Sunderland. Another trouble I have to give you, which is to order Barnes to bring any letter Stonhewer[2] or I

[1] Doctor Richard Trevor, translated to Durham from St. David's. He succeeded Dr. Joseph Butler in 1752.

[2] Mr. Stonehewer, son of Dr. Stonehewer, of Houghton, Durham, was Secretary to the Duke of Grafton, in conjunction with Mr. Bradshaw. "He was," says Horace Walpole, "a modest man, of perfect integrity, invariably attached to Lord Grafton from his childhood." He appears to have taken a high degree in 1749-50, by the Cambridge Calendar, as late Fellow of St. Peter's and after of Trinity College. He held for a considerable time the post of Commissioner of Excise, and lived in Curzon Street, in a house nearly opposite to the Chapel. It

may have to you, and direct them hither. The Doctor and Mrs. Wharton desire their particular compliments to you, and are sorry you could not be with us. Adieu. I am ever sincerely yours,

T. G.

P.S.—I have left my watch hanging (I believe) in my bed-room: will you be so good as to ask after it.

XCVI.—TO THE REV. WILLIAM MASON.

Durham, September 21, 1753.

DEAR MASON—It is but a few days since I was informed by Avison,[1] that the alarm you had on your sister's account served but to prepare you for a greater loss, which was soon to follow. I know what it is to lose a person that one's eyes and heart have long been used to, and I never desire to part with the remembrance of that loss, nor would wish you should. It is something that you had a little time to acquaint yourself with the idea beforehand, if I am informed right, and that he probably suffered but little pain, the only thing that makes death terrible.

was through his interest with the Duke of Grafton that Gray obtained the Professorship of Modern History.—[*Mit.*]

[1] Mason, in his *Essays on Church Music*, mentions Mr. *Avison*, the author of the *Essay on Musical Expression, as his friend.* He adopted an opinion of Mason's on ancient and modern music, and published it in his *Works.* "Mason," says Mr. Boaden, in his *Life of Kemble*, i. 184, "was not meanly skilled in choral and scientific composition."—[*Mit.*]

It will now no longer be proper for me to see you at Hull, as I should otherwise have tried to do. I shall go therefore to York, with intention to make use of the stage-coach, either on Friday or Monday. I shall be a week at Cambridge, and then pass through London into Buckinghamshire. If I can be of any use to you in anything it will give me great pleasure. Let me have a line from you soon, for I am very affectionately yours, T. GRAY.

XCVII.—TO THE REV. WILLIAM MASON.

Durham, September 26, 1753.

MY DEAR MASON—I have just received your letter, and am both surprised and angry (if you will suffer me to say so) at the weakness of your father; perhaps I ought not to use such words to a person whose affliction for him is perhaps heightened by that very weakness; for I know it is possible to feel an additional sorrow for the faults of those we have loved, even where that fault has been greatly injurious to ourselves. This is certain, he has been (whether from his illness or some other cause) at least guilty of a great weakness; and it is as sure that there must have been a great fault somewhere, probably in the person who took advantage of his weakness, upon whom your care and kindness is very ill bestowed, though you do not at present shew any resentment, nor perhaps ever will. At least let me desire you not to expose yourself to any further danger in the midst of that scene of sickness and death, but withdraw as soon as possible to some place at a little distance in the country, for I do not at all like the place you are in.

I do not attempt to console you on the situation your fortune is left in; if it were far worse, the good opinion I have of you tells me you will never the sooner do anything mean or unworthy of yourself, and consequently I cannot pity you on this account, but I sincerely do so on the new loss you have had of a good and friendly man,[1] whose memory I honour. May I remind you how like a simpleton I used to talk about him? It is foolish to mention it; but it feels I do not know how like a sort of guilt in me, though I believe you know I could not mean anything by it. I have seen what you describe, and know how dreadful it is; I know, too, I am the better for it. We are all idle and thoughtless things, and have no sense, no use in the world any longer than that sad impression lasts; the deeper it is engraved the better. I am forced to break off by the post.—Adieu, my dear Sir.

I am ever yours, T. G.

P.S.—I shall be at York on Sunday, at the place the stagecoach goes from, having a place taken for Monday. Pray remember James's powder; I have

[1] Dr. Marmaduke Pricket, a young physician of my own age, with whom I was brought up from infancy, who died of the same infectious fever as my father.—[*Mason.*]

great faith in its efficacy; I should take it myself. Here is a malignant fever in the town.

XCVIII.—TO THOMAS WHARTON.

September 29 [1753], Stoke.

My dear Wharton—I shall certainly be in town on Monday next, for Mr. Brown informed me you would arrive there on the 30th, and I ordered my matters here accordingly. You will see me the instant I come, having (I need not tell you) not only nothing I like better to do there, but literally nothing else, than to see you. I have not time to enlarge, as I send this by a person who is just going from our house to Uxbridge, though, to my shame, I stand indebted to you for a very kind letter I received long ago.—Adieu, I am always very truly yours,

T. Gray.

XCIX.—TO THOMAS WHARTON.

October 18 [Endorsed 1753], Stoke.

My dear Doctor—You will wonder not to have heard sooner of me. The reason has been the instability of my own situation. As soon as I arrived at Cambridge, I found a letter informing me my aunt Rogers had had a stroke of the palsy, so that I stayed only a single day, and set out for this place. I found her recovered surprisingly from the greatest danger. Her speech only is not yet quite restored;

but it is easily intelligible to such as are used to her. Is not this something extraordinary at seventy-seven?

I met Mason at York, and passed that evening with him.[1] . . . has absolutely no support at present but his Fellowship; yet he looks more like a hero, than ever I knew him, like one that can stare poverty in the face without being frighted, and instead of growing little and humble before her, has fortified his spirit and elevated his brow to meet her like a man. In short if he can hold it, I shall admire him, for I always maintained, that nobody has occasion for pride but the poor, and that everywhere else it is a sign of folly. My journey was not so bad as usual in a stage-coach. There was a Lady Swinburne, a Roman Catholick, not young, that had been much abroad, seen a great deal, knew a great many people, very chatty and communicative, so that I passed my time very well; and on the third day left them at Stilton, and got to Cambridge that night. As I know, and have heard mighty little to entertain you with, I can only tell you my observations on the face of the country and the season in my way hither, that you may compare them with what you see at Durham. Till I came to York I thought the face of everything rather altered for the worse, certainly not better than that corner of the Bishoprick about Darlington. At Topcliff I saw a large vine full of black grapes, that seemed ripe. At Helperby met a flock of geese in

[1] A line and a half have been cut out of the MS.—[*Ed.*]

full song. If their person had not betrayed them, one might have taken them for nightingales. At York walnuts ripe, twenty for a penny. From thence, especially south of Tadcaster, I thought the country extremely beautiful, broke into fine hills covered with noble woods (particularly towards the east), and everything as verdant almost, as at midsummer. This continued to Doncaster. The hazle and white-thorn were turning yellow in the hedges, the sycamore, lime, and ash (where it was young, or much exposed), were growing rusty, but far greener than in your county. The old ash, the oak, and other timber, shewed no signs of winter. Some few of the lands were in stubble, but for the most part they were ploughed up, or covered with turnips. I find Mr. Evelyn in his book of forest trees, published in Queen Anne's time, takes notice "That Shropshire, and several other counties, and rarely any beyond Stamford to Durham, have the vernacular (or French Elm), or the Mountain Elm (which is what you call the English Elm), growing for many miles together." I cannot say I saw any, but about Scrubey in Nottinghamshire, and they were young ones newly planted near a hedgerow. He also mentions the elm of a more scabrous leaf, harsh and very large, which becomes a huge tree; *mentioned in the* Statue Books *under the name of the*[1] Wych-Hayle. For my part, I could find no sort but the last, at least of any size,

[1] These words in Italics are supplied; one and a half lines of MS. being cut out.—[*Ed.*]

or growing in a wild way, till I came into Northamptonshire. I thought the winter more advanced in Lincolnshire, and so on, till I had passed Huntingdon, than it was in the West Riding of Yorkshire. In Northamptonshire I first observed the appearances of a long drought, which continued quite hither. The turf is everywhere brown and burnt up, as in Italy; even the low meadows want their usual verdure. At Cambridge the finest grapes I ever saw there; the lime trees were only changing colour, but had dropped few of their leaves. In the smoke of London they had almost lost their old leaves, but made fresh shoots, as green as in April. And here before my window are two young sycamores, which have done the same, but still retain all their old leaves too without any change of colour. At Trompington the new rye was green in the fields, and three inches high. It is the same in this county. We are here upon a loam with a bed of gravel below, and rag-stone beneath that. The hay is usually all in by Old Midsummer, this year it was all cut by New Midsummer, but a great deal of it lost for want of rain, which likewise spoiled the tares and peas. In the beginning of August was rain for near three weeks, which saved the corn. Oats were in some places cut before the wheat, which was all got in by the 20th of August. Barley, beans, etc., by the 7th of September. I came hither the 6th of October, and they had then within a mile of the Thames (where the soil is better, than here) begun to sow wheat. For six weeks before my arrival it had been continued fine weather, and the air till sunset was like July. Never almost was such a year known for fruit. The nectarines and best peaches had been all gathered three weeks before. The grapes were then perfectly ripe, and still continue the best I ever eat in England. October 9th, it began to rain, and we have had showers every day since, with brisk winds in the S. and S.W.; to-day it is in the North, clear sunshine, but cold and a little wintry: and so ends my Georgick in prose. Excuse me, if I had nothing better to send you. It is partly from my own eye-sight, and partly from the report of such as have no prejudices in favour of their county, because they hardly know, there is any other.

I write chiefly to draw on a letter from you, for I am impatient to know many things; but remember, this election-time letters are apt to be opened at the offices. Pray, make my sincere acknowledgements to my *kind Hostess:* I trust she was not the worse for her journey. I hope, you know, that I am ever yours, T. G.

At Mrs. Rogers's, of Stoke,
near Windsor, Bucks.

P.S.—Everything resounds with the wood-lark, and robin; and the voice of the sparrow is heard in our land. Remember me to all, that remember there is such a person. Adieu!

C.—TO THE REV. WILLIAM MASON.

Stoke, November 5, 1753.

MY DEAR MASON—I am not in a way of leaving this place yet this fortnight, and consequently shall hardly see you in town. I rejoice in the meantime to think that you are there, and have left, I hope, a part of your disagreeable reflections in the place where they grew.

Stoke[1] has revived in me the memory of many a melancholy hour that I have passed in it, and, though I have no longer the same cause for anxiety, I do not find myself at all the happier for thinking that I have lost it, as my thoughts now signify nothing to any one but myself. I shall wish to change the scene as soon as ever I can.

I am heartily glad to hear Mr. Hutton[2] is so reasonable, but am rather sorry to find that design is known to so many. Dr. Wharton, who, I suppose, heard it from Avison, mentions it in a letter to me. Were I you, I should have taken some pleasure in observing people's faces, and perhaps in putting their kindness a little to the trial; it is a very useful experiment, and very possibly you will never have it

[1] Gray had hastened to Stoke early in October, on being informed that Mrs. Rogers, his aunt, had had a stroke of the palsy. His mother had died March 11, 1753.—[*Ed.*]

[2] Mr. John Hutton, of Marsk, in Yorkshire, who persuaded his cousin Hutton, Archbishop of York, to give the prebend of Holme, in York Cathedral, to Mason, and who on his death in 1758 left Mason an estate.—[*Ed.*]

in your power to put it in practice again. Pray make your bargain with all the circumspection and selfishness of an old hunks; when you are grown as rich as Crœsus, do not grow too good-for-nothing,—a little good-for-nothing to be sure you will grow; everybody does so in proportion to their circumstances, else, indeed, what should we do with one's money? My third sentence is, do not anticipate your revenues, and live upon air till you know what you are worth. You bid me write no more than a scrawl to you, therefore I will trouble you, as you are so busy, with nothing more. Adieu.

I am very sincerely and affectionately yours,

T. G.

I should be obliged to you, if you had time, to ask at Roberts's,[1] or some place in Jermyn Street, whether I could be there about a fortnight hence. I will not give more than half-a-guinea a week, nor put up with a second floor unless it has a tolerable room to the street. Will you acquaint me of this?

CI.—TO THOMAS WHARTON.

Stoke, August 13 [Endorsed 1754].

MY DEAR SIR—Having been some little time absent from hence, I missed of your letter, or I had answered

[1] When Gray came to London he lodged in Jermyn Street, at Roberts's the hosier's, or at Frisby's the oilman's. They are towards the east end, on different sides of the street.—[*Norton Nicholls.*]

it as soon as you desire me. The opportunity of a good house I hope you will not suffer to escape you. Whether the rent be too high, you alone can properly judge. There is great comfort to be sure in a good house. Some appearance of economy I should think would give you credit in that part of the town you are to be well with: they pride themselves in living much within their income. Upon the whole I seem to have a partiality for Mr. Crumpe, but be sure never to repent. If you think you shall; by all means settle yourself in the great house. Beside I do not know, but some great old Doctor may come and squat himself down there at your elbow (for I suppose there may be some convenience in succeeding to a house of the same profession) and then you would be horridly out of humour. In short, you see with your own eyes, you know the quarter, and must necessarily be best qualified to decide. Dr. Fothergill's invitation is very civil. As to the depth of science, which you seem to dread, it always grows shallower, as one comes nearer, though it makes a great noise at a distance. The design of the society at least is a good one. But if they are warm and professed enemies of the College, I should think the same reason, that makes Heberden withdraw himself, should prevent your admission into it. It will be easy to delay it however on various pretences without disobliging any one.

I am glad you agree with me in admiring Mr. Southcote's Paradise, which whenever you see it again, will improve upon you. Do you know, you may have it for £20,000, but I am afraid, the lands are not very improveable. You do not say enough of Esher. It is my other favourite place. It was a Villa of Cardinal Wolsey's, of which nothing but a part of the gateway remained. Mr. Kent[1] supplied the rest, but I think with you, that he had not read the Gothic Classics with taste or attention. He introduced a mixed style, which now goes by the name of the *Battey-Langley manner.*[2] He is an architect, that has published a book of bad designs. If you have seen Mr. Walpole's, pray let me hear your opinion, which I will not anticipate by saying anything about it. To be sure its extreme littleness will be the first thing that strikes you. By all means see Lord Radnor's again. He is a simple old Phobus, but nothing can spoil so glorious a situation, which surpasses everything round it. I take it ill, you should say anything against the Mole. It is a reflection, I see, cast at the Thames. Do you think, that rivers, which have lived in London and its neighbourhood all their days, will run roaring and tumbling about, like your Tramontane torrents in the North. No, they only glide and whisper. In your next expedition you will see Claremont, and

[1] William Kent (1685-1748) the celebrated architect.—[*Ed.*]

[2] Battey Langley (died 1751), a popular architect who endeavoured to reconcile Greek with Gothic architecture, and who introduced five new orders into his art. He was a great corruptor of public taste. The book Gray speaks of was by his brother, Thomas Langley, who survived him.—[*Ed.*]

Lord Portmore's, which joins my Lord Lincoln's, and above all Mr. Hamilton's, at Cobham[1] in Surrey, which all the world talks of, and I have seen seven years ago. The year indeed does not behave itself well, but think, what it must be in the North. I suppose the roads are impassable with the deep snow still.

I could write abundance more, but am afraid of losing this post. Pray let me hear from you as soon as you can, and make my compliments to Mrs. Wharton. Mason is by this time in town again. Tuthill, . . . Brown, I believe, at Cambridge. Adieu! I am ever yours, T. G.

I am obliged to you for sending the tea, which is excellent.

CII.—TO THOMAS WHARTON.

Stoke, September 18, 1754.

DEAR SIR—I rejoice to find you at last settled to your heart's content, and delight to hear you talk of giving your house some *Gothic ornaments* already. If you project anything, I hope it will be entirely within doors; and don't let me (when I come gaping into Coleman Street) be directed to the gentleman's at

[1] Mr. Hamilton formed many of the beautiful scenes in the grounds at Paineshill from the Pictures of Poussin and the Italian Masters: the Waterfall at Bow-wood, the seat of the Marquis of Lansdowne, made by Mr. Hamilton, is from a Picture of G. Poussin.—[*Mit.*]

the ten Pinnacles, or with the church porch at his door. I am glad you enter into the spirit of Strawberry-castle. It has a purity and propriety of Gothicism in it (with very few exceptions) that I have not seen elsewhere. The eating-room and library were not completed, when I was there, and I want to know what effect they have. My Lord Radnor's Vagaries (I see) did not keep you from doing justice to his situation, which far surpasses everything near it, and I do not know a more *laughing* scene, than that about Twickenham and Richmond. Dr. Akenside (I perceive) is no conjurer in Architecture, especially when he talks of the ruins of Persepolis, which are no more Gothic than they are Chinese. The Egyptian style (see Dr. Pococke, not his discourses, but his prints) was apparently the mother of the Greek, and there is such a similitude between the Egyptian, and those Persian ruins, as gave room to Diodorus to affirm, that the old buildings of Persia were certainly performed by Egyptian Artists. As to the other part of his opinion, that the Gothic manner is the Saracen or Moorish, he has a great authority to support him, that of Sir Christopher Wren, and yet (I cannot help thinking) is undoubtedly wrong. The Palaces in Spain, I never saw, but in description, which gives us little or no idea of things; but the Doge's palace at Venice I have seen (which is in the Arabesque manner) and the houses of Barbary you may see in Dr. Shaw's book, not to mention abundance of other eastern buildings in Turkey, Persia, etc., that we have views of, and they seem plainly to be corruptions of the Greek architecture, broke into little parts indeed, and covered with little ornaments, but in a taste very distinguishable from that we call Gothic. There is one thing that runs through the Moorish buildings, that an imitator would certainly have been first struck with, and would have tried to copy, and that is the Cupola's, which cover everything, baths, apartments, and even kitchens—yet who ever saw a Gothic cupola? it is a thing plainly of Greek original. I do not see anything but the slender spires, that serve for steeples, which may perhaps be borrowed from the Saracen minarets on their mosques.

I was in Northamptonshire, when I received your letter, but am now returned hither. I have been at Warwick, which is a place worth seeing. The town is on an eminence surrounded every way with a fine cultivated valley, through which the Avon winds, and at the distance of five or six miles, a circle of hills well wooded, and with various objects crowning them, that close the prospect. Out of the town on one side of it, rises a rock, that might remind one of your rocks at Durham, but that it is not so savage, or so lofty, and that the river, which washes its foot, is perfectly clear, and so gentle, that its current is hardly visible. Upon it stands the castle, the noble old residence of the Beauchamps and Nevilles, and now of Earl Brooke. He has sashed the great apartment that's to be sure (I can't help these things), and being since told, that square sash-windows were not

Gothic, he has put certain whim-wams within side the glass, which appearing through are to look like fret-work. Then he has scooped out a little burrough in the massy walls of the place for his little self and his children, which is hung with paper and printed linen, and carved chimney pieces, in the exact manner of Berkley Square, or Argyle Buildings. What in short can a Lord do now a days, that is lost in a great old solitary Castle, but skulk about, and get into the first hole he finds, as a rat would do in like case. A pretty long old stone-bridge leads you into the town with a mill at the end of it, over which the rock rises with the Castle upon it with all its battlements and queer-ruined towers, and on your left hand the Avon strays through the park, whose ancient elms seem to remember Sir Philip Sidney (who often walked under them), and talk of him to this day. The Beauchamp Earls of Warwick lie under stately monuments in the choir of the great church, and in our lady's chapel adjoining to it. There also lie Ambrose Dudley, Earl of Warwick; and his brother, the famous Lord Leicester, with Lettice, his Countess. This chapel is preserved entire, though the body of the church was burnt down sixty years ago, and rebuilt by Sir C. Wren. I had heard often of Guy Cliff two miles from the town, so I walked to see it; and of all improvers commend me to Mr. Greathead, its present owner. He shewed it me himself, and is literally a fat young man with a head and face much bigger than they are usually worn. It was naturally a very

√agreeable rock, whose cliffs covered with large trees hung beetling over the Avon, which twists twenty ways in sight of it; there was the cell of Guy, Earl of Warwick, cut in the living stone, where he died a hermit (as you may see in a penny history, that hangs upon the rails in Moorfields) there were his fountains bubbling out of the cliff;—there was a chantry founded to his memory in Henry the VIth's time. But behold the trees are cut down to make room for flowering shrubs, the rock is cut up, till it is as smooth and as sleek as satin; the river has a gravel-walk by its side; the cell is a grotto with cockle-shells and looking-glass; the fountains have an iron gate before them, and the chantry is a barn, or a little house. Even the poorest bits of nature, that remain, are daily threatened, for he says (and I am sure, when the Greatheads are once set upon a thing, they will do it) he is determined, it shall be *all new.* These were his words, and they are fate. I have also been at Stow, at Woburn (the Duke of Bedford's), and at Wroxton (Duke of Guilford's) but I defer these chapters till we meet. I shall only tell you for your comfort, that the part of Northamptonshire, where I have been, is in fruits, in flowers, and in corn very near a fortnight behind this part of Buckinghamshire, that they have no nightingales, and that the other birds are almost as silent, as at Durham. It is rich land, but upon a clay, and in a very bleak, high, exposed situation. I hope you have had some warm weather, since you last complained of the south. I have thoughts of seeing you about Michaelmas, though I shall not stay long in town; I should have been at Cambridge before now, if the Duke of Newcastle and his foundation-stone would have let me, but I want them to have done before I go. I am sorry Mr. Brown should be the only one, that has stood upon punctilios with me, and would not write first; pray tell him so. Mason is (I believe) in town, or at Chiswick. No news of Tuthill. I wrote a long letter to him in answer to one he wrote me, but no reply. Adieu, I am ever yours, T. G.

Brown called here this morning before I was up, and breakfasted with me.

CIII.—TO THOMAS WHARTON.

Cambridge, October 10, 1754.

Dear Doctor—I am clear, that you are in the right way and that you ought to make your excuses at the Queen's Arms with all possible civility to Fothergill; and perhaps the civilest excuse is to tell the truth, to him at least, that it would be neither grateful, nor prudent, to hazard disobliging the gentlemen at the Mitre, among whom you have several Friends, and besides it will be always more in your power to recommend moderate measures, while you continue connected with one Party, than if you should lose yourself with both by seeming to divide yourself between them, but how far this is to be said, and to whom, you are best able to determine.[1]

CIV.—TO THOMAS WHARTON.

ODE IN THE GREEK MANNER.

. . . [The "Ode on the Progress of Poesy."] . . .

. . . .

If this be as tedious to you, as it is grown to me, I shall be sorry that I sent it you. I do not pretend to *deballate*[2] any one's pride: I love my own too well to attempt it. As to mortifying their vanity it is too easy and too mean a task for me to delight in. You are very good in shewing so much sensibility on my account. But be assured, my taste for praise is not like that of children for fruit. If there were nothing but medlars and blackberries in the world, I could be very well content to go without any at all. I dare say that M[aso]n (though some years younger than I) was as little elevated with the approbation of Lord D. and Lord M., as I am mortified by their silence. I desire you would by no means suffer this to be copied; nor even shew it, unless to very few, and especially not to mere scholars, that can scan all the measures in Pindar, and say the "Scholia" by heart. The oftener (and in spite of poor Trollope) the *more* you write to me, the happier I shall be. I envy your

[1] Remainder of MS. lost, about sixteen lines.—[*Ed.*]

[2] *Humble* any one's pride.—[*Mason.*]

opera. Your politics I don't understand, but I think matters can never continue long in the situation they now are. *Barbarossa*[1] I have read, but I did not cry; at a modern tragedy it is sufficient not to laugh. I had rather the King's Arms looked askew upon me, than the Mitre; it is enough to be well bred to both of them. You do not mention Lord Strathmore, so that I doubt, if you received my little letter about him. Mason is still here: we are all mighty glad he is in orders, and no better than any of us. Pray inform me, if Dr. Clark is come to town, and where he is fixed, that I may write to him, angry as he is. My compliments to my friend Mrs. Wharton, to your mother, and all the little gentry. I am ever, dear Doctor, most sincerely yours.

Cambridge, December 26, 1754.

CV.—TO THOMAS WHARTON.

Cambridge, March 9, 1755.

MY DEAR DOCTOR—According to my reckoning Mrs. Wharton should have been brought to bed before this time; yet you say not a syllable of it. If you are so loth to publish *your productions*, you cannot wonder at the repugnance I feel to spreading abroad

[1] This play was written by Dr. Brown, the admirer and friend of Warburton; and author of *Athalstan*. Garrick wrote the Epilogue, the following line of which gave the greatest offence to the Author :—

"Let the poor devil eat, allow him that," etc.—[*Mit.*]

mine. But in truth I am not so much against publishing, as against publishing *this*[1] *alone.* I have two or three ideas more in my head. What is to come of them? must they too come out in the shape of little sixpenny flams, dropping one after another, till Mr. Dodsley thinks fit to collect them with Mr. this's song, and Mr. t'other's epigram, into a pretty volume? I am sure Mason must be sensible of this, and therefore can never mean what he says. To be sure, Doctor, it must be owned, that physic, and indeed all professions, have a bad effect upon the mind. This it is my duty, and interest to maintain; but I shall still be very ready to write a satire upon the clergy, and an epode against historiographers, whenever you are hard pressed; and (if you flatter me) may throw in a few lines with somewhat handsome upon Magnesia alba, and Alicant soap. As to humanity you know my aversion to it; which is barbarous and inhuman, but I cannot help it, God forgive me.

I am not quite of your opinion with regard to Strophe[2] and Antistrophe. Setting aside the diffi-

[1] His "Ode on the Progress of Poetry."—[*Mason.*]

[2] He often made the same remark to me in conversation, which led me to form the last Ode of *Caractacus* in shorter stanzas: But we must not imagine that he thought the regular Pindaric method without its use; though, as he justly says, when formed in long stanzas, it does not fully succeed in point of effect on the ear: for there was nothing which he more disliked than that chain of irregular stanzas which Cowley introduced, and falsely called Pindaric; and which from the ex-

culties, methinks it has little or no effect upon the ear, which scarce perceives the regular return of metres at so great a distance from one another. To make it succeed, I am persuaded the stanzas must not consist of above nine lines each at the most. Pindar has several such odes.

Lord S[trathmore] is come, and makes a tall genteel figure in our eyes. His tutors and he appear to like one another mighty well. When we know more of him than his outside, you and the historian shall hear of it. I am going to ask a favour of you, which I have no better pretence for doing, than that I have long been used to give you trouble. It is, that you would go to the London Insurance office in Birchin Lane for me, and pay two insurances, one of my house at Wanstead (Policy, No. 9675), the other of that in Cornhill (No. 23470), from Lady-day next, to Lady-day 1756. The first is twenty shillings; the second, twelve shillings, and be pleased to enclose the two receipts (stamped) in a cover, and send them to me; the sooner the better, for I am always in a little apprehension during this season of conflagrations. I know you will excuse me, and therefore will make

treme facility of execution, produced a number of miserable imitators. Had the regular return of Strophe, Antistrophe, and Epode no other merit than that of extreme difficulty, it ought on this very account, to be valued; because we well know that "Easy writing is no easy reading." It is also to be remarked, that Mr. Congreve, who first introduced the regular Pindaric form into the English language, made use of the short stanzas which Mr. Gray here recommends.—[*Mason.*]

no excuses. I cannot think of coming to town, till some time in April myself.

I know you have wrote a very obliging letter to Tuthill, but as I have not seen it, and he is not in my way at present, I leave him to answer for himself. Adieu, dear Sir, and make my compliments to your family.—I am ever yours, T. G.

CVI.—TO THOMAS WHARTON.

Stoke, August 6, 1755.

DEAR DOCTOR—I was just returned from my Hampshire[1] expedition, and going to enquire after your little family, and how they had got over the measles, when I found a letter from Stonehewer, in which he says nothing on that head; whence I conclude they are out of danger, and you free from anxiety about them. But he tells me, you expect me in town, for which I am at a loss to account, having said nothing to that purpose, at least, I am sure nothing with that meaning. I said I was to go to Twickenham, and am now expecting a letter from Mr. W[alpole], to inform me, when he shall be there. My stay will be at farthest a week with him, and at my return I shall let you know, and if the season be better than it now is, enquire, if you continue inclined to visit Windsor

[1] Mr. Gray went on the 15th of July to Mr. Chute's at the Vine, from thence he went to Portsmouth, and returned to Stoke on the 31st of July, as appears by a journal which he kept.—[*Mit.*]

and its environs. I wished for you often on the Southern coast, where I have been, and made much the same tour, that Stonehewer did before me. Take notice, that the oaks grow quite down to the beach, and that the sea forms a number of bays little and great, that appear glittering in the midst of thick groves of them. Add to this the fleet (for I was at Portsmouth two days before it sailed) and the number of vessels always passing along, or sailing up Southampton river (which is the largest of these bays I mention), and enters about ten miles into the land, and you will have a faint idea of the *South.* From Fareham to Southampton, where you are upon a level with the coast, you have a thousand such peeps and delightful openings, but would you see the whole at once, you must get upon Portsdown, five miles upon this side Portsmouth. It is the top of a ridge, that forms a natural terrass three mile long, literally not three times broader than Windsor Terrass, with a gradual fall on both sides and covered with a turf like Newmarket. To the North, opens Hampshire and Berkshire covered with woods, and interspersed with numerous gentlemen's houses and villages. To the South, Portsmouth, Gosport, etc., just at your foot in appearance, the Fleet, the sea winding, and breaking in bays into the land, the deep shade of tall oaks in the enclosures, which become blue, as they go off to distance, Porchester Castle, Carshot Castle, and all the Isle of Wight, in which you plainly distinguish the fields, hedgerows, and woods, next the shore, and a background of hills behind them. I have not seen a more magnificent or more varied prospect. I have been also at Tichfield, at Nettly Abbey (a most beautiful ruin in as beautiful a situation) at Southampton, at Bevis Mount, at Winchester, etc. My gout is gone, but I am not absolutely well yet. I hear Mason was expected on Monday last, but was not to speak of it, therefore you will say nothing till you see him. I do not understand this; nor what he means by coming. It seems wrong to me. What did you think of the *Morceau*[1] I sent you, pray, speak your mind. My best compliments to Mrs. Wharton. Adieu.—I am ever yours, T. G.

CVII.—TO THOMAS WHARTON.

Stoke, August 21, 1755.

DEAR DOCTOR—Instead of going to Twickenham I was obliged to send my excuses, and the same day Mr. W[alpole] sent a messenger to say he was confined in town with a fever and a rash. He has since wrote me word, that he is well again; but for me I continue much as I was, and have been but once out of the house to walk, since I returned from Hampshire. Being much inclined to bleeding myself, I yet was fearful to venture, lest it should bring on a

[1] A copy of the *first* part of the "Bard," which, I am sorry to say, is not preserved among Dr. Wharton's MSS.

regular fit of the gout, so I sent for advice at last, and expected Dr. Hayes should tell me presently, whether it were Gout or Rheumatism. In his talk he treated it rather as the former, but his prescription appears to me to be meant for the latter. You will judge. He took away 10 or 11 oz. of blood, and ordered these draughts night and morning:—*Sal. Absinth. Succ. Limon finitâ effervescentiâ add. Aqua. Alexit. Simpl., Menth. Piperit. Magnes. alb., Tinct. G. Guiac. Spirituos.* The quantities I can't read; only I think there is a drachm of the Tincture, and half a drachm of Magnesia in each draught. The blood had no sign of Inflammation, but of a bright red; the serum of a dark yellow with little transparency, not viscid to the touch. The draughts (which I took over night only) made me sweat almost immediately, and opened a little in the morning. The consequence is, that I have still many slight complaints, broken and unrefreshing sleeps, as before, less feverish than I was, in a morning. Instead of it a sensation of weariness and soreness in both feet, which goes off in the day, a frequent dizziness and lightness of head, easily fatigued with motion. Sometimes a little pain in my breast, as I had in the winter. These symptoms are all too slight to make an illness; but they do not make perfect health. That is sure.

Though I allow abundance for your kindness and partiality to me, I am yet much pleased with the good opinion you seem to have of the "Bard." You may alter that, "*Robed in* the sable, etc.," almost in your own words, thus,

With fury pale, and pale with woe,
Secure of Fate, the Poet stood, etc.

Though *haggard*, which conveys to you the idea of a *Witch*, is indeed only a metaphor taken from an unreclaimed Hawk, which is called a *haggard*, and looks wild and *farouche*, and jealous of its liberty. I have sent now to Stonehewer a bit more of the *Prophecy*, and desire him to shew it you immediately: it is very rough and unpolished at present. Adieu, dear Sir, I am ever truly yours, T. G.

. . . .

She-wolf of France with unrelenting fangs,
That tear'st the bowels of thy mangled mate;
From thee be born, who o'er thy country hangs
The scourge of Heaven. What terrors round him wait!
Amazement in his van with flight combined,
And Sorrow's faded form and Solitude behind.

ANT. 2.

[*victor*]
Mighty Conqu'ror, mighty Lord,
[*his*]
Low on the funeral couch he lies;
[*No*] [*no*]
What pitying heart, what eye afford
A tear to grace his obsequies?
Is the sable warrior fled?
Thy son is gone, he rests among the dead.
[*in thy noontide beam were born,*]
The swarm, that hover'd in thy noontide ray,
[*morn.*]
Gone to salute the rising day.

Mirrors of Saxon truth and loyalty,
Your helpless old expiring master view,
They hear not. Scarce Religion dares supply
Her mutter'd Requiems, and her holy Dew.
Yet thou, proud Boy, from Pomfret's walls shalt send
A sigh, and envy oft thy happy Grandsire's end.

EPODE 3.

Fill high the sparkling bowl,
The rich repast prepare,
Reft of a crown he yet may share the feast.
Close by the regal chair
Fell Thirst and Famine scowl
A *smile of horror* on their baffled guest.
Heard ye the din of battle bray,
Lance to lance and horse to horse!
Long years of havock urge their destined course,
And thro' the kindred squadrons mow their way.
[*Ye*]
Grim towers of Julius, London's lasting shame,
With many a foul and midnight murther fed,
Revere his Consort's faith, his Father's fame,
And spare the meek Usurper's *hallow'd* head.
Above, below, the Rose of snow,
Twined with her blushing foe we spread:
The bristled boar in infant gore,
Wallows beneath the thorny shade.
Now, Brothers, bending o'er th' accursed loom,
Stamp we our vengeance deep, and ratify his doom.

STROPHE 3.

Edward, lo! to sudden fate,
  (Weave we the woof. The thread is spun),
Half of thy heart we consecrate
  (The web is wove. The work is done).
[*thus*]
Stay, oh stay, nor here forlorn

[*me unbless'd. Unpitied here*]
Leave your despairing Caradoc[1] to mourn !
[*track*]
In yon bright clouds, that fires the western skies,
[*melt*]
They sink, they vanish from my eyes.
But ah ! what *solemn scenes of Heaven* on Snowdon's
height,
[*glitt'ring*]
Descending slow their golden skirts unroll !
Visions of glory, spare my aching sight,
Ye unborn ages, crowd not on my soul.
From Cambria's thousand hills a thousand strains
Triumphant tell aloud, another Arthur reigns.

ANTIST. 3.

[*Girt with many a*]
Youthful Knights, and Barons bold
[*Sublime their starry fronts they rear,*]
With dazzling helm, and horrent spear,
And gorgeous Dames, and Statesmen old,
In bearded majesty appear.
In the midst a Form divine,
Her eye proclaims her of the Briton-Line ;
[*Her*] [*her*]
A Lyon-port, an awe-commanding face,
Attemper'd sweet to virgin-grace.
What strings symphonious tremble in the air !
What strains of vocal transport round her play !
Hear from the grave, great Taliessin, hear,
They breathe a soul to animate thy clay.

---

[1] "The Mountain in Shropshire is called Caer Carădoc ; but Mr. Gray asserts that the middle syllable is long, or he could have used it in his Poem of the Bard."—[*Cradock.*] Joseph Cradock was evidently interested in the name of the mountain because it was so like his own.—[*Ed.*]

Bright Rapture calls, and soaring, as she sings,
Waves in the eye of Heaven her many-coloured wings.

EPODE 3.

The verse adorn again,
Fierce War, and faithful Love,
And Truth severe by Fairy-Fiction drest.
In buskin'd measures move
Pale Grief and pleasing Pain,
With Horrour, tyrant of the throbbing breast.
A voice as of the Cherub-Quire,
Gales from blooming Eden bear;
And distant warblings lessen on my ear,
That lost in long futurity expire.
Fond impious man, think'st thou, yon sanguine cloud,
Rais'd by thy breath has quench'd the orb of day?
To-morrow he repairs the golden flood,
And warms the nations with redoubled ray.
Enough for me, with joy I see
The different doom our fates assign,
Be thine Despair and scepter'd Care.
To triumph and to die are mine.
He spoke, and headlong from the mountain's height
Deep in the roaring tide he sunk to endless night.

CVIII.—TO JOHN CHUTE.

Stoke, August 14, 1755.

DEAR SIR—I write to the Vine, imagining you may be still there, to tell you, that I was to have gone to Strawberry on Monday last; but being ill was obliged to write the day before, and excuse myself. Mr. W. could not receive my letter till Monday afternoon, and had therefore sent a messenger from London, early that morning to say, that he was very ill of a fever, and rash, and unable to go himself to Twickenham. I know this is a dangerous season; and that malignant fevers are now very common, and am therefore something alarmed at his situation. If you have heard anything, you will let me know, and particularly if anything should carry you soon to town. I myself have been ill, ever since I came out of Hampshire. I have had *advice* and been bloodied, and taken draughts of Salt of Wormwood, Lemons, Tincture of Guiacum, Magnesia, and the Devil. You will immediately conclude, they thought me rheumatic and feverish, no such thing! they thought me gouty, and that I had no fever. All I can say, is, that my heats in the morning are abated, that my foot begins to ach again; and that my head achs, and feels light and giddy. So much for me. My compts. to the gentleman with the Moco-smelling-bottle, the Muntz's, the Betties, and the Babies. Adieu, I am ever.

CIX.—TO THOMAS WHARTON.

Endorsed [October 18, 1755].

My dear Doctor—I ought before now to have thanked you for your kind offer, which I mean soon to accept for a reason, which to be sure can be no reason to you or Mrs. Wharton, and therefore I think it my duty to give you notice of it. It is a very possible thing I may be ill again in town, which I would not chuse to be in a dirty inconvenient lodging, where perhaps my Nurse might stifle me with a pillow, and therefore it is no wonder, if I prefer your house. But I tell you of this in time, that if either of you are frighted at the thought of a sick body, you may make a handsome excuse, and save yourselves this trouble. You are not to imagine my illness is in *Esse;* no, it is only in *Posse,* otherwise I should myself be scrupulous of bringing it home to you. I shall be in town in about a fortnight. You will be sorry (as I am) at the destruction of poor Stonehewer's views, which promised so fair: but both he and I have known it this long time, so, I believe, he was prepared, and his old Patron is no bad resource. I am told, it is the fashion to be totally silent with regard to the ministry.[1] Nothing is to be talked of, or even suspected, till the Parliament meets; in the meantime the new *Manager* has taken what appears to me a very odd step. If you do not hear of a thing, which is in it's nature no secret, I cannot well inform you by the Post, to me it is utterly unaccountable.

Pray what is the reason I do not read your name among the Censors of the College? did they not offer it you, or have you refused it? I have not done a word more of *Bard.* Having been in a very listless, unpleasant, and inutile state of mind for this long

[1] This alludes to the dismissal of Pitt, then paymaster of the forces, and the Right Honourable Henry Legge, Chancellor of the Exchequer, on the question of engaging this nation in a continental connection for the defence of Hanover.—[*Mit.*]

while, for which I shall beg you to prescribe me somewhat strengthening and agglutinant, lest it turn to a confirmed Pythisis. To shew you how epidemical self-murther is this year, Lady M. Capel (Lord Essex's sister) a young person, has just cut the veins of both arms across, but (they say) will not die of it, she was well and in her senses, though of a family that are apt to be otherwise. Adieu, dear Doctor, I should be glad of a line from you, before I come.—Believe me ever, most sincerely yours, T. G.

CX.—TO THOMAS WHARTON.

Cambridge, January 9, 1756.

Dear Doctor—I am quite of Mr. Alderman's opinion; provided you have a very fair prospect of success (for I do not love repulses, though I believe in such cases they are not attended with any disgrace) such an employment must necessarily give countenance and name to one in your profession, not to mention the use it must be of in refreshing and keeping alive the ideas of practice you have already got, and improving them by new observation. It cannot but lead to other business too in a more natural way, than perhaps any other; for whatever lucky chance may have introduced into the world here and there a Physician of great vogue, the same chance may hardly befall another in an age; and the indirect and by-ways, that doubtless have succeeded with many, are rather too dirty for you to tread. As to the time it would take up, so much the better. Whenever it interferes with more advantageous practice, it is in your power to quit it. In the meantime it will prepare you for that trouble and constant attendance, which much business requires a much greater degree of. For you are not to dream of being your own master, till old-age, and a satiety of gain shall set you free. I tell you my notions of the matter, as I see it at a distance, which you, who stand nearer, may rectify at your pleasure.

I have continued the Soap every other day from the time I left you, except an interval or two of a week or ten days at a time, which I allow'd in order to satisfy myself, whether the good effects of it were lasting, or only temporary. I think, I may say it has absolutely cured that complaint I used to mention to you, and (what is more) the ill-habit, which perhaps was the cause of that, and of the flying pains I have every now and then felt in my joints. Whenever I use it, it much increases my appetite, and the heart-burn is quite vanished. So I may venture to say, it does good to my stomach. When I shall speak of its bad effects, you are no longer to treat me as a whimsical body, for I am certain now, that it disorders the head, and much disturbs one's sleep. This I now avoid by taking it immediately before dinner; and besides these things are trifles compared with the good it has done me. In short, I am so well, it would be folly to take any other medicine: therefore

I reserve lime water for some more pressing occasion. I should be glad to know the particulars of Lord Northumberland and the Archbishop's illnesses, and how far it has eased them in the gout.

I am glad you admire Machiavel, and are entertained with Buffon, and edified with the divine Ashton. The first (they say) was a good man, as much as he has been abused; and we will hope the best of the two latter. Mr. Bedingfield, who (as Lord Orford sent me word) desired to be acquainted with me, called here (before I came down), and would pay a visit to my rooms. He made Dr. Long conduct him thither, left me a present of a book (not of his own writing) and a note with a very civil compliment. I wrote to him to thank him, and have received an answer, that fifteen years ago might have turned my head. I know [ ] will abuse him to you, but I insist he is a slanderer, and shall write a satire upon him, if he does not do justice to my new admirer. I have not added a line more to old *Caradoc;* when I do, you will be sure to see it. You who give yourself the trouble to think of my health, will not think me very troublesome if I beg you to bespeak me a rope-ladder (for my neighbours every day make a great progress in drunkenness, which gives me reason to look about me) it must be full thirty-six feet long, or a little more, but as light and manageable as may be, easy to unroll, and not likely to entangle. I never saw one, but I suppose it must have strong hooks, or something equivalent, a-top, to throw over an iron bar[1] to be fixed withinside of my window. However, you will chuse the properest form, and instruct me in the use of it. I see an Ephraim Hadden near Hermitage stairs, Wapping, that advertises them, but perhaps you may find a better artisan near you. This with a canister of tea and another of snuff, which I left at your house, and a pound of soap from Mr. Field (for mine is not so good here) will fill a box, which I beg the favour of you to send me when you can conveniently. My best compliments to Mrs. Wharton.—I am ever yours, T. G.

CXI.—TO MR. RICHARD STONEHEWER.[2]

August 21, 1755.

I THANK you for your intelligence about Herculaneum, which was the first news I received of it. I have since turned over Monsignor Baiardi's[3] book,

[1] This iron bar is still to be seen at Peterhouse, in the window of Gray's rooms.—[*Ed.*]

[2] Auditor of Excise. His friendship with Mr. Gray commenced at College, and continued till the death of the latter. —[*Mason.*] Mr. Stonehewer was, while at Cambridge, the Tutor, afterwards the private Secretary, and intimate friend of the late Duke of Grafton.—[*Mit.*]

[3] Ottavo Autonio Baiardi (1690-1765) was a Parmesan antiquary of great pretensions, who was called to Naples by Charles III. to describe the excavations at Herculaneum. He took so long over his task, that the king appointed a Herculaneum Academy, of which Baiardi was to be president, to assist him; but, whether from wounded vanity or conscious incompetence, Baiardi would have none of their help, and left Naples abruptly in stately wrath.—[*Ed.*]

where I have learned how many grains of modern wheat the Roman Congius in the Capitol, holds, and how many thousandth parts of an inch the Greek foot consisted of more or less (for I forget which) than our own. He proves also by many affecting examples, that an Antiquary may be mistaken: that for anything anybody knows, this place under ground might be some other place, and not Herculaneum; but nevertheless, that he can shew for certain that it was this place and no other place; that it is hard to say which of the several Herculeses was the founder; therefore (in the third volume) he promises to give us the memoirs of them all; and after that, if we do not know what to think of the matter, he will tell us. There is a great deal of wit too, and satire, and verses, in the book, which is intended chiefly for the information of the French King, who will be greatly edified without doubt.

I am much obliged to you also for Voltaire's performance; it is very unequal, as he is apt to be in all but his dramas, and looks like the work of a man that will admire his retreat and his Lemon-Lake no longer than till he finds an opportunity to leave it.[1] However, though there be many parts which I do not like, yet it is in several places excellent, and everywhere above mediocrity. As you have the politeness to pretend impatience, and desire I would communi-

[1] I do not recollect the title of this poem, but it was a small one which M. de Voltaire wrote when he first settled at Ferney. —[*Mason.*]

cate, and all that, I annex a piece of the *Prophecy*,[1] which must be true at least, as it was wrote so many hundred years after the events.

CXII.—TO THOMAS WHARTON.

Pembroke Hall, March 25, 1756.

Dear Doctor—Though I had no reasonable excuse for myself before I received your last letter, yet since that time I have had a pretty good one, having been taken up in quarrelling with Peterhouse, and in removing myself from thence to Pembroke.[2] This may be looked upon as a sort of æra in a life so barren of events as mine, yet I shall treat it in Voltaire's manner, and only tell you that I left my lodgings because the rooms were noisy, and the people

[1] The second Antistrophe and Epode, with a few lines of the third Strophe of his Ode entitled the *Bard*, were here inserted.—[*Mason.*]

[2] The reason of Mr. Gray's changing his College, which is here only glanced at, was in few words this: Two or three young men of fortune, who lived in the same staircase, had for some time intentionally disturbed him with their riots, and carried their ill behaviour so far as frequently to awaken him at midnight. After having borne with their insults longer than might reasonably have been expected, even from a man of less warmth of temper, Mr. Gray complained to the governing part of the Society; and not thinking that his remonstrance was sufficiently attended to, quitted the College. The slight manner in which he mentions this affair, when writing to one of his most intimate friends, certainly does honour to the placability of his disposition.—[*Mason.*]

of the house *dirty*:[1] this is all I would chuse to have said about it; but if you in private should be curious enough to enter into a particular detail of facts and minute circumstances, Stonehewer who was witness to them will probably satisfy you. All, I shall say more, is, that I am for the present extremely well lodged here, and as quiet as in the Grande Chartreuse; and that everybody (even the Dr. Longs and Dr. Mays) are as civil, as they could be to Mary de Valence[2] in person. With regard to any advice I can give as to the hospital, I freely own it ought to give way to Dr. Heberden's counsels, who is a much better judge, and (I should think) disinterested. I love refusals no more than you do; but as *to* your effluvia, I maintain, that one sick *rich* has more of pestilence and putrefaction about him, than a whole ward of sick poor.

You should have received Mason's present[3] as last Saturday. I desire you to tell me your critical opinion of the new Ode; and also whether you have found out two lines, which he has inserted in another of them, that are superlative.[4] We do not expect,

[1] Uncivil.—[*Mason.*]

[2] The Lady Mary de Saint Paul, widow of Aymer de Valence, formerly Earl of Pembroke, was foundress of the College, the proper name of which to this day is "the College of Valence-Mary, commonly called Pembroke College." The letters patent granted to Mary de Valence by Edward III. date from 24th Dec. 1347.—[*Ed.*]

[3] The four Odes which I had just published separately. [*Mason.*]

[4] I should leave the Reader to guess (if he thought it worth

that the world, which is just going to be *invaded*, will bestow much attention on them. If you hear anything, you will tell us.

The similitude between the Italian Republicks and ancient Greece has often struck me, as it does you. I do not wonder, that Sully's *Memoirs* have highly entertained you, but cannot agree with you in thinking him or his master two of the *best* men in the world. The king was indeed one of the best natured men, that ever lived. But it is owing only to chance, that his intended marriage with Mad. d'Estrées, or with the Marq$^{se.}$ de Verneuil, did not involve him and the kingdom in the most inextricable confusion; and his design upon the Princess of Condé (in his old age) was worse still. As to the minister, his base application to Concini after the murther of Henry has quite ruined him in my esteem, and destroyed all the merit of that honest surly pride, for which I honoured him before. Yet I own, that as kings and ministers go, they were both extraordinary men. Pray look at the end of Birch's *State Papers of Sir T. Edmondes*, for the character of the French Court at that time, written by Sir George Carew.

his while) what this couplet was which is here commended so much beyond its merit, did not the Ode conclude with a compliment to Mr. Gray, in which part he might probably look for it, as those lines were written with the greater care. To secure, therefore, my friend from any imputation of vanity, whatever becomes of myself, I shall here insert the passage:

"While thro' the west, where sinks the crimson Day,
Meek twilight slowly sails, and waves her banners gray."

[*Mason.*]

Pray don't suspect me of any such *suspicions*, as you mention. I would hardly believe you were tired of me, though you told me so yourself, sensible as I am nevertheless, that you might have reason enough to be so. To prove what I say, I have thoughts of coming to you for three days in April. There is to be a Concerto Spirituale, in which the Mingotti[1] (who has just lain in) and Ricciarelli[2] will sing the *Stabat Mater* of Pergolesi. You and Mason and I are to be at it together, so pray make no excuses, nor put-offs. Saving to you however the liberty of saying whether you have a bed to spare (I mean for me, not for him) in your house. Adieu, dear Sir, I am ever faithfully yours, T. G.

My best compliments to Mrs. Wharton. I give you joy of the divine Ashton; it is indeed a conquest you have made.

[1] Regina Mingotti (1728-1807), one of the most famous singers of the century, was born of German parents at Naples. She came to England about 1754. Burney gives a very interesting account of the powers of her intellect no less than of her organ.—[*Ed.*]

[2] Ricciarelli was a neat and pleasing performer, with a clear, flexible, and silver-toned voice, but so much inferior to Mingotti, both in singing and acting, that he never was in very high favour. It was in the admirable drama of *Demofoonte* that Mingotti augmented her theatrical consequence, and acquired much applause, beyond any period of her performance in England.—[*Burney.*]

CXIII.—TO THE REV. WILLIAM MASON.

Pembroke Hall, Tuesday, 1756.

DEAR SKRODDLES—If all the Greek you transcribe for me were poetry already, I would bestir myself to oblige you and Mr. Rivett;[1] but as it is no more than measured prose, and as unfortunately (in English verse) a tripod with two ears or more has no more dignity than a chamber-pot with one, I do not see why you would have me dress it up with any florid additions, which it must have, if it would appear in rhyme; nor why it will not prove its point as well in a plain prose translation as in the best numbers of Dryden. If you think otherwise, why do not you do it yourself, and consult me if you think fit?

I rejoice to hear the prints succeed so well, and am impatient for the work, but do not approve the fine-lady part of it; what business have such people with Athens? I applaud your scheme for Gaskarth,[2] and wish it could have succeeded. He bears his disappointment like a philosopher, but his health is very bad. I have had the honour myself of some little grumblings of the gout for this fortnight, and yesterday it would not let me put on a shoe to hear the

[1] Nicholas Rivett, the associate of Mr. J. Stuart in the measurement and delineation of the Antiquities of Athens.—[*Mit.*]

[2] Joseph Gaskarth was treasurer of the College of Pembroke; in 1747 he was the fifth senior wrangler.—[*Mit.*]

Frasi in,[1] so you may imagine I am in a sweet amiable humour; nevertheless, I think of being in town (perhaps I may not be able to stir) the middle of next week, with Montagu. You are so cross-grained as to go to Tunbridge just before I come, but I will give you the trouble to enquire about my old quarters at Roberts's, if I can probably have a lodging at that time; if not there, may be I can be in the Oven, which will do well enough for a sinner: be so good to give me notice, and the sooner the better. I shall not stay above a week, and then go to Stoke. I rejoice to know that the genial influences of the spring, which produce nothing but the gout in me, have hatched high and unimaginable fantasies in you. I see, methinks (as I sit on Snowdon), some glimpse of Mona and her haunted shades, and hope we shall be very good neighbours. Any Druidical anecdotes that I can meet with I will be sure to send you. I am of your opinion, that the ghosts will spoil the picture, unless they are thrown at a huge distance, and extremely kept down.

The British Flag,[2] I fear, has behaved itself like a trained-band pair of colours in Bunhill Fields. I think every day of going to Switzerland; will you be of the party, or stay and sing mass at Aston? Adieu! I am stupid, and in some pain; but ever very sincerely yours,

T. G.

[1] An opera-singer not of the first rank. She was pupil to Signor Brivio.—[*Mit.*]

[2] Allusion to the loss of Minorca and Admiral Byng's conduct.

CXIV.—TO THE REV. WILLIAM MASON.

Stoke, July 25, 1756.

DEAR MASON—I feel a contrition for my long silence, and yet perhaps it is the last thing you trouble your head about; nevertheless, I will be as sorry as if you took it ill. I am sorry too to see you so punctilious as to stand upon answers, and never to come near me till I have regularly left my name at your door, like a mercer's wife that imitates people who go a visiting. I would forgive you this, if you could possibly suspect I were doing anything that I liked better, for then your formality might look like being piqued at my negligence, which has somewhat in it like kindness; but you know I am at Stoke, hearing, seeing, doing, absolutely nothing, not such a nothing as you do at Tunbridge, chequered and diversified with a succession of fleeting colours, but heavy, lifeless, without form and void; sometimes almost as black as the moral of Voltaire's "Lisbon,"[1] which angers you so. I have had no more pores and muscular inflations, and am only troubled with this depression of mind; you will not expect therefore I should give you any account of my verve, which is at best, you know, of so delicate a constitution, and has such weak nerves, as not to stir out of its chamber above three days in a year, but I shall enquire after yours, and why it is off again; it

[1] "Poème sur la Desastre de Lisbon, 1755; ou, Examen de cet axiome Tout est bien."

has certainly worse nerves than mine, if your reviewers have frighted it. Sure I (not to mention a score of your uncles and aunts) am something a better judge than all the man midwives and presbyterian parsons that ever were born. Pray give me leave to ask you, do you find yourself tickled with the commendations of such people? for you have your share of these too. I dare say not; your vanity has certainly a better taste; and can, then, the censure of such critics move you? I own it is an impertinence in these gentry to talk of one at all either in good or in bad, but this we must all swallow; I mean not only we that write, but all the we's that ever did anything to be talked of. I cannot pretend to be learned without books, nor to know the Druids from the Pelasgi at this distance from Cambridge. I can only tell you not to go and take the Mona for the Isle of Man; it is Anglesey, a tract of plain country, very fertile, but picturesque only from the view it has of Caernarvonshire, from which it is separated by the Menai, a narrow arm of the sea. Forgive me for supposing in you such a want of erudition.

I congratulate you on our glorious successes in the Mediterranean. Shall we go in time, and hire a house together in Switzerland? it is a fine poetical country to look at, and nobody there will understand a word we say or write. Pray let me know what you are about; what new acquaintances you have made at Tunbridge; how you do in body and in mind; believe me ever sincerely yours, T. G.

Have you read Madame Maintenon's *Letters?* When I saw Lord John[1] in town, he said, if his brother went to Ireland you were to go second chaplain, but it seemed to me not at all certain that the Duke would return thither; you probably know by this time.

CXV.—TO THE REV. WILLIAM MASON.

Stoke, Friday, July 30, 1756.

DEAR MASON—I received your letters both at once yesterday, which was Thursday, such is the irregularity of our post. The affair of Southwell, at this time, is exceedingly unlucky; if it is committed to you by all means defer it. It is even worth while to stop Mrs. Southwell, who will enter into the reason of it. Another thing is, you have very honestly and generously renounced your own interest (I mention it not as a compliment, but *pour la rareté du fait*) to serve Mr. Brown. But what if you might serve him still better by seemingly making interest for yourself? Addison must certainly be a competitor; he will have the old (new) Lord Walpole, of Wolterton, his patron, to back him, the Bishop of Chester,[2] the heads, who know him for a staunch man, and consequently the

[1] Lord John Cavendish, afterwards Chancellor of the Exchequer, and known, from his fair small person, and his classical accomplishment, as "the learned canary-bird."—[*Ed.*]

[2] Dr. Edmund Keene, Master of St. Peter's College, Cambridge; and who, on resigning the Mastership, procured Dr. Law to be elected. He will be mentioned again, more fully.

Duke of Newcastle. If you can divide or carry this interest, and by it gain the dirty part of the college, so as to throw it into Mr. Brown's scale at pleasure, perhaps it may produce an unanimous election. This struck me last night as a practicable thing, but I see some danger in it, for you may disoblige your own friends, and Lord Holdernesse must, I doubt, be acquainted with your true design, who very likely will not come into it. T. and also Mr. B. himself should be acquainted with it immediately; consider therefore well whether this or the plain open way (which, I own, is commonly the best) be most likely to succeed; the former, if it be found impracticable for Mr. B., at least may make it sure for yourself, which is to be wished. In the next place (it is odd to talk thus to a man about himself, but I think I know to whom I am talking), I have puzzled my head about a list of the college, and can make out only these, pray supply it for me: Brown, Gaskarth, May, Cardale, Bedford, Milbourne, Tuthill, Spencer, Forrester, Mapletoft, Delaval, Axton.[1] I do not know if Spencer's Fellowship be vacant or not, or whether a majority only of the whole or two-thirds be required to choose a Master.

I should hope nine of these, and perhaps Maple-

[1] These are the names of the Fellows of Pembroke. Delaval and Cardale appear in the Cambridge Calendar as having taken wranglers' degrees in 1750-1, and Axton, a senior optimé in 1755. Spencer, *late* Fellow of Pembroke, went to Trinity, and took his degree in 1750. Of Bedford and Milbourne I can give no account.—[*Mit.*]

toft too, if Gaskarth pleases, might be got for Mr. Brown, but I can answer only for T[uthill]. Bedford has always professed a friendship for Mr. B. but he is a queer man; his patron is a Mr. Buller of Cornwall, a tory; Delaval, Gaskarth, Milbourne, and Axton, you may soon enquire into yourself; Spencer (if he is one) has promised Dr. Wharton.

I write to Mr. W.[1] (your neighbour over the way) to desire him to speak to Mr. F[raser] or the Duke of Bedford, if it may be of use, and add that if he will let you know he is at home you will come and give him any information necessary. Whether this will signify I cannot say, but I do not see any hurt it can do.

I wish like you I were at Cambridge, but to hurry down on this occasion would be worse than useless, according to my conception. I am glad you think of going, if they approve it. Dr. Long, if he is not dead, will recover,[2]—mind if he don't. I leave my answer to your first letter to another opportunity, and am always yours, T. G.

[1] Horace Walpole, who lived in the same street as Mason, viz. Arlington Street.

[2] He did recover, and lived till December 16, 1770, when he was in his 92d year. In his 88th year he was put in nomination for the office of Vice-Chancellor. He appears in Churchill's "Candidate":

> "Comes Sumner, wise and chaste as chaste can be,
> With *Long* as wise, and not less chaste than he."

[*Mit.*]

CXVI.—TO THOMAS WHARTON.

Stoke, October 15, 1756.

DEAR DOCTOR—I have not been dead, but only gone to [ ][1] seized with a cruel fit of the gout, which held him five weeks, and as he had no other company in the house it was impossible to leave him in that condition. Since my return I have made a visit of four days at Twickenham. I shall probably stay here till the middle of next month and then transplant myself to London, if Mrs. Wharton and you *de bon cœur* have no objection to me. If anything has happened, since I saw you, to make it inconvenient I insist upon being told so. I have heard the story of the *Lyon*, and its consequences, though you say not a word about it. Pray, inform me how Miss Peggy got over her operation. Leicester House is (as I suppose you know) settling upon its own terms. £40,000 a year for the P[rince]; £5000 for P. $E^{d.}$; no removing to St. J[ames]'s; Earl of Bute Groom of the Stole (there is for you), Mr. Stone, Controller of the [ ][1] (a concession by way of thanks). Lords of the Bedchamber I have forgot. Miss Shepherd's Mr. Ingram, and Mr. Onslow, the Speaker's son, Grooms of the Bedchamber. Are you upon the list?

Shew me such another king, as the K. of Prussia. Everybody used to call him coxcomb, and to be sure he is one; but a coxcomb (it is plain) may make a figure far superior to the ordinary run of kings. I

[1] The MS. is imperfect in this place.—[*Ed.*]

delight in his treatment of the K. of Poland. When he first informed him of the necessity he was under to make use of Saxony in his way to Bohemia, he added that if his Majesty chose to retire into his Polish dominions he had ordered relays[1] on the road, and that all the respect in the world should be shewn him. And his last memorial to the Empress-Queen ended with *point de reponse, en stile d'Oracle.*

I recommend two little French books to you, one called *Mémoires de M. de la Porte.* It has all the air of simplicity and truth, and contains some few very extraordinary facts relating to Anne of Austria and Card. Mazarin. The other is two small volumes, *Mémoires de Madame Staël.* The facts are no great matter, but the manner and vivacity of it make it interesting. She was a sort of confidante to the late Dutchess of Maine, and imprisoned a long time in the Bastile on her account during the regency. The first you may buy, and the latter borrow. I desire my compliments to Mrs. Wharton, and am, ever yours, T. G.

CXVII.—TO THOMAS WHARTON.

Cambridge, Thursday.

DEAR DOCTOR—I accept with pleasure your kind invitation, and have agreed to accompany Mr. Balguy and Mr. Hurd to town on Saturday. What I have farther to say, I defer to that time: I need not tell

[1] See Duclos' *Mémoires*, vol. ii. p. 432.—[*Ed.*]

you how much I wish for it, or that I am ever sincerely yours, T. G.

My best compliments to Mrs. Wharton.

Post-mark 4th November.

CXVIII.—TO THOMAS WHARTON.

November 12, 1756.

DEAR DOCTOR—I grow impatient to be in town, and hope for the pleasure of seeing you on Tuesday next. I must confess, the present revolution of affairs, which are settling so slowly, is some spur to my curiosity, though my own interests have no more concern in it, than those of any cottager in the nation. I flatter myself, that necessity will at last throw the management of affairs into more capable, if not more honest hands, than usual. My *Gazette* says, that Mr. P[itt] will be Secretary of State, and has accepted it (though ill of the gout in the country). That the D. of Devonshire has consented (which was one of the conditions of acceptance) to be at the head of the Treasury. Lord Temple, of the Admiralty. G. Grenville, Paymaster. Mr. Legge, Chanc^r. of the Exchequer. Sir G. Lee, Sec. at War. Mr. T.[1] nothing. How far

[1] Mr. T. is (I suppose) Mr. C. Townshend, who wished for the place of Secretary of War in this administration, which was, however, possessed by Lord Barrington. Mr. Townshend unwillingly accepted the place of Treasurer to the Chambers. See *Memoirs of a Celebrated Literary and Political Character*, p. 74. See his character drawn by Walpole in *Memoirs*, p. 296.—[*Mit.*]

all this is fact, you know by this time. I do not forget your letter, when I say this, and to whom it was wrote; but I much doubt, whether you would have received more benefit from his good offices, while he continued in, than now he is in effect out. I am concerned too for another person, who surely can never continue, where he is (if he should, it is a wonderful proof of the force of insignificancy) and if he does not, a good friend of ours must feel it a little in a part very tender to most people, his hopes; but he very wisely has been arming it for some time. I believe, with a reasonable insensibility, and taking, by way of precaution a dose of my sovereign anodyne fastidium.

Don't fancy to yourself, that I have been doing anything here. I am as stupid as a post, and have not added a syllable, but in plain prose am still ever yours, T. G.

CXIX.—TO THE REV. WILLIAM MASON.

December 19, 1756.

DEAR SKRODDLES— . . . The man's name is Joannes Georgius Frickius, *Commentatio de Druidis:* accedunt Opuscula quædam rariora, historiam et antiquitates Druidarum illustrantia itemque Scriptorum de iisdem Catalogus.[1] It was published at Ulm, 1744, 4to.,

[1] Joannis Georgii Frickii, Joan. pl. τοῦ μακαρίτου, A. M. ad æd. S.S. Trinit. Ulm. Pastoris et Gymnas. Visitatoris, itemque Societ. Teutonicæ Leipsicis Sodalis, *Commentatio de Druidis*

and in the *Nova Acta Eruditorum* (printed at Leipsic for 1745), there is some account of it. The rare little works which make the second part of it, are, Peter L'Escalopier's Theologia Vett^{m}. Gallorum; Cæsar. Bulacus, in Historiâ Vett^{m}. Academiarum Galliæ Druidicarum; and two or three more old flams. I do not know what satisfaction you will find in all this, having never seen the book itself. I find a French book commended and cited by Jaques Martin upon the Religion of the Ancient Gauls.

Over leaf you will find a specimen of my Lord Duke of Norfolk's housekeeping. I desire you would enquire of Mr. Noble, or somebody, what the same provisions would cost now-a-days.

I send you a modern curiosity inclosed, a specimen of sturdy begging, which cost me half-a-guinea; if he writes so to strangers, what must he do to particular friends like you. Pray learn a style and manner against you publish your Proposals.

Odikle[1] is not a bit grown, though it is fine mild open weather. Bell Selby has dreamed that you are a Dean or Prebendary; I write you word of it, because

Occidentalium Populorum Philosophis, multo quàm antea auctior et emendatior. Accedunt Opuscula quædam rariora Hist. et Antiq. Druidum illustrantia, itemque Scriptorum de eisdem Catalogus. Recensuit, singula digessit, ac in lucem edidit frater germanus, Albertus Frickius, A. M. V. D. M. Prof. P. P. et Biblioth. Adj. Ulm. itemque M. Prof. P. P. et, etc. Ulmæ, 1744, 4to.—[*Mit.*]

[1] The "Bard."

they say a whore's dreams are lucky, especially with regard to church preferment.

You forget Mr. Senhouse's acoustic warming-pan: we are in a hurry, for I cannot speak to him till it comes. God bless you, come and bring it with you, for we are as merry as the day is short. The squire is gone; he gave us a goose and a turkey, and two puddings of a moderate size. Adieu, dove, I am ever yours.

Gaskyn, and the Viper, etc., desire their civilities.

What prevys, marlings, and oxbirds are I cannot tell, no more than I can tell how to make Stoke fritters; leche is blanc-manger; wardyns are baking-pears; doyse are does. Do not think they lived thus every day. If you would know how they eat on meagre days and in ordinary I will send you word. I shall only add that Lord Surrey loved buttered lyng and targets of mutton for breakfast; and my Lady's Grace used to piddle with a chine of beef upon brewess.

You will wonder what I mean by the half-guinea I talked of above; it was a card from Mr. Frankling, which I meant to inclose, but cannot find it high or low.

Chrystmas Day.

	s.	d.
Empt:—Item, 35 malards, 2½d. a-pece .	7	3
Item, 55 wigyns, 2d. a-pece . . .	10	2
Item, 38 teles, 1d. a-pece	4	9
Item, 2 corlewys	1	0

		S.	D.
Item, 2 prevys,[1] 2d. a-pece	. . .	0	4
Item, 2 plovers, 2d. a-pece	. . .	0	4
Item, 8 woodcocks, 3d. a-pece .	. .	2	0
Item, 42 marlyngs, ½d. a-pece .	. .	1	9
Item, 42 rede-shanks, ½d. a-pece	. .	1	9
Item, 17 doz. and ½ oxbyrdys, 3d. a doz.	.	4	4
Item, 40 grete byrdys, ½d. a-pece	. .	1	8
Item, 40 small byrdys, 4d. a doz.	. .	0	10
Item, 11 pyggs	. . . . . .	3	8
Item, 200 eggs, 8d.	. . . . .	2	8
Item, 31 cople conyse, fett at bery[2]	.	10	4

Presents:—10 cople teles, 3 cople wegyns, 4 cople se-pyse, 8 malards, 3 doz. snytts, 5 doz. oxbyrdys, 6 se-mewys, 2 swanys, 2 pecocks, 14 partridges, 4 woodcoks, 14 doyse, 4 gallons creme, 6 gall. cord, a hundred ½ of wardyns, a bushell apples. Breakfast, to my Ladyse Grace: Braune, and a capon stuyd. To my Lord's Grace, a Crystmas-day dyner: First course (the Duke and Duchess and 24 persons to the same), the borys hede, brawne, pottage, a stuyd capon, a bake-mett with twelve birdys, rostyd vele, a swane, two rostyd capons, a custerde, Stoke-fritter, leeche. (Second course): Gely, three conyse, five teles, a pekoke, twelve rede-shanks, 12 small byrdys, 2 pastyse veneson, a tarte, gynger-brede. (To the Bordys end):

[1] "Prevys" may be the "pivier," or golden plover; "marlyngs," the "morinellus," or dotterel. The "purre," *Tringa cinclus*, is called *provincially* the oxbird, a species of sandpiper.—[*Gray.*]

[2] Thirty-one couple of conies, taken at the *burrow*; Bery, or berrie, means burrow. Thus Dryden:—

"The theatres are *berries* for the fair."

Brawne, a stuyd capon, a bakyd cony, rostyd vele, half a swane, custerde, leche. (Rewarde): Gely, 2 conyse, 4 teles, 12 small byrdys, a pasty venison, a tarte.

There was also a table for the gentlewomen, and 12 persons to the same, and the servants table or tables, at which sate 28 gentlemen, 60 yeomen, 44 gromes, and gentlemen's servants; the meats were much the same with the former. One day this Christmas I see there were 347 people dined at the lower tables. The whole expense of the week (exclusive of wines, spices, salt, and sauce, etc.) amounted to £31 : 9 : 6½.

ODE, p. 32.[1]—"Whom Camber bore." I suppose you say "whom" because the harp is treated as a person; but there is an ambiguity in it; and I should read "that Camber bore." There is a specimen of nice criticism for you!

I much approve the six last lines of this stanza; it is a noble image, and well expressed to the fancy and to the ear.

I. 2.—A rill has no tide of waters to "tumble down amain." I am sorry to observe this just in a place where I see the difficulty of rhyming. I object nothing to the "Symphony of ringdoves and poplars," but that it is an idea borrowed from yourself; and I would not have you seem to repeat your own inventions.

[1] Gray now begins a criticism on the Ode in Mason's *Caractacus*.

I conceive the four last lines to be allegorical, alluding to the brutal ferocity of the natives, which by the power of music was softened into civility. It should not, therefore, be the "wolf-dog," but the "wolf" itself, that bays the trembling moon; it is the wolf that thins the flocks, and not the dog, who is their guardian.

I. 3.—I read "The Fairy Fancy." I like all this extremely, and particularly the ample plumes of Inspiration, that

"Beat on the breathless bosom of the air."

Yet, if I were foolish, I could find fault with this verse, as others will do. But what I do not conceive is, how such wings as those of Inspiration should be mistaken for the wings of Sleep, who (as you yourself tell me presently) "sinks softly down the skies;" besides, is not "her" false English? the nominative case is "she."

II. 3.—This belongs to the second epode. Does the swart-star (that is, Sirius) shine from the north? I believe not. But Dr. Long will tell you.

II. 2.—These are my favourite stanzas. I am satisfied, both mind and ear, and dare not murmur. If Mador would sing as well in the first chorus, I should cease to plague you. Only,—

"Rise at her art's command"

is harsh, and says no more than

"Arise at her command,"

or

"Are born at her command."

II. 3.—I told you of the swart-star before. At the end I read,

"Till Destiny prepare a shrine of purer clay."

Afterwards read, "Resume no more thy strain." You will say I hàve no notion of *tout-ensembles*, if I do not tell you that I like the scheme of this ode at least as well as the execution.

And now I rejoice with you in the recovery of your eyes; pray learn their value, and be sparing of them.[1] I shall leave this place in about a fortnight, and within that time hope to despatch you a packet with my criticalities entire. I send this bit first, because you desire it. Dr. Wharton is in great hopes that Mr. Hurd will not treat Dr. Akenside so hardly as he intended, and desires you would tell him so, as his request is founded on mere humanity (for he pretends no friendship, and has but a slight acquaintance with the doctor). I present it to you, and wish you would acquaint Mr. Hurd with it, the sooner the better.

I am well and stupid, but ever unalterably yours,

T. G.

[1] Mason's eyes were weak, a complaint that lasted more or less through his life. The place in his library was pointed out to me by Mr. Alderson, where he usually sat and wrote, and which was the most distant from the light. His poetical chair —*sedes beata*—was kindly bequeathed to me; and I have left it by will to the Poet Laureate of the day, that it may rest among the sacred brotherhood:—

———"lætumque choro *Pæana* canentes,
Inter odoratum *Lauri* nemus."—[*Mit.*]

I do not understand if Fraser is recovered; I wish he was. Do you know anything of Stonhewer?

P. 2.—I liked the opening as it was originally better than I do now, though I never thoroughly understood "how blank he frowns." And as to "black stream," it gives me the idea of a river of mud.[1] I should read "dark stream," imagining it takes its hue only from the rocks and trees that overhang it. "These cliffs, these yawning," etc., comes in very well where it stood at first, and you have only removed it to another place, where, by being somewhat more diffused, it appears weaker. You have introduced no new image in your new beginning but one, "utters deep wailings," which is very well: but as to a "trickling runlet," I never heard of such a thing, unless it were a runlet of brandy.

Yet I have no objection at all to the reflection Didius makes on the power objects of the sight have over the soul; it is in its place, and might even be longer, but then it should be more choicely and more feelingly expressed. He must not talk of dells and streams only, but of something more striking, and more corresponding to the scene before him. Intellect is a word of science, and therefore is inferior to any more common word.

P. 3.—For the same reason I reject "philosophy,"

[1] Mason has, in accordance with Gray's criticism, given "How *stern* he frowns," and the "*dark* stream." The "trickling runlet" has entirely disappeared.—[*Mit.*]

and read "studious they measure, save when contemplation," etc., and here you omit two lines, relating to astronomy, for no cause that I discern.

P. 4.—What is your quarrel to "shallops?" I like "Go bid thine eagles soar," perhaps from obstinacy, for I know you have met with some wise gentleman who says it is a false thought, and informs you that these were not real eagles, but made of metal or wood painted. The word "seers," comes over too often: here, besides, it sounds ill. Elidurus need not be so fierce. "Dost thou insult us, Roman?" was better before. Sure "plan'd" is a nasty stiff word.

P. 6.—It must be Cæsar[1] and Fate; the name of Claudius carries contempt with it.

P. 7.—

> "Brother, I spurn it, better than I scorn it.
> Misjudging Boy!"

is weakly. He calls him coward because such a reproach was most likely to sting him. "I'll do the deed myself," is bolder, more resolute, more hearty, than the alteration. "Lead forth the saintly," etc., better, shorter, and more lively at first. "What have I to do with purple robes and arraignments?"—like a trial at York assizes.

P. 8.—"Try, if 'twill bring her deluging," etc., better so, only I do not like "strait justice:" "modest mounds" is far worse.

[1] So it is printed,

> "Cæsar and Fate demand him at your hand."

P. 9.—"Do this and prosper, but pray thee," etc. Oh! how much superior to the cold lines for which you would omit them. It is not you but somebody else that has been busy here and elsewhere. "Come from their caves." I read, "Are issuing from their caves. Hearest thou yon signal?" and put "awful" where it was before. "I'll wait the closing," etc. Leave it as it was. "Do thou as likes thee best, betray, or aid me:" it is shorter and more sulky. Elidurus too must not go off in silence; and what can he say better?

P. 10.—I do not dislike the idea of this ceremony, but the execution of it is careless and hasty. The reply of the Semi-chorus is stolen from Dryden's *Œdipus*, which, perhaps, you never saw, nor I since I was a boy, at which time it left an impression on my fancy. Pray look at it. This "dread ground" breaks my teeth. "Be it worm, or aske, or toad:" these are things for fairies to make war upon but not Druids, at least they must not name them. An *aske*[1] is something I never heard of. "Full five fathom under ground." Consider, five fathom is but thirty feet; many a cellar lies deeper. I read, "Gender'd by the autumnal moon;" by its light I mean. "Conjoined" is a bad word. "Supernal art profound" is negligent. Indeed I do not understand the image, how the snakes in copulation should heave their egg to the sky; you will say it is an old British fancy.

[1] "Asker," in old language, was a *water-newt*, which Mason probably meant.—[*Mit.*]

I know it of old; but then it must be made picturesque, and look almost as if it were true.

P. 13.—"Befit such station." The verse wants a syllable. "Even in the breast of Mona," read "the heart of Mona." "Catches fresh grace;" the simile is good, but not this expression. The Tower is more majestic, more venerable, not more graceful. I read,

> "He looks as doth the Tower
> After the conflict of Heaven's angry bolts;
> Its nodding walls, its shatter'd battlements,
> Frown with a dignity unmark'd before,
> Ev'n in its prime of strength."[1]

P. 13.—I do not desire he should return the Druid's salute so politely. Let him enter with that reflection, "This holy place," etc., and not stand upon ceremony. It required no alteration, only I hate the word "vegetate," and would read,

> "Tell me, Druid,
> Is it not better to be such as these
> Than be the thing I am?"

I read, too, "Nor show a Prætor's edict," etc., and "pestilent glare," as they were before. Add, too, "See to the altar's base the victims led," etc. And then, whether they were bulls or men, it is all one. I must repeat again, that the word "Seers" is repeated for ever.

[1] The text of Mason stands thus:

> "He looks, as doth the Tower, whose nodding walls,
> After the conflict of Heaven's angry bolts,
> Frown with a dignity unmark'd before,
> Ev'n in its power of strength."——

P. 15.—"I know it, rev'rend Fathers," etc. This speech is sacred with me, and an example of dramatic poetry. Touch not a hair of its head, as you love your honour.

P. 16.—I had rather some of these personages, "Resignation, Peace, Revenge, Slaughter, Ambition," were stript of their allegorical garb.[1] A little simplicity here in the expression would better prepare the high and fantastic strain, and all the unimaginable harpings that follow. I admire all from "Eager to snatch thee," etc., down to the first epode of the chorus. You give these Miltonic stanzas up so easily that I begin to waver about Mador's song. If you have written it, and it turn out the finest thing in the world, I rejoice, and say no more. Let it come though it were in the middle of a sermon; but if not, I do confess, at last, that the chorus may break off, and do very well without a word more. Do not be angry at the trouble I have given you; and now I have found the reason why I could not be pleased with Mador's philosophic song. The true lyric style, with all its flights of fancy, ornaments, and heightening of expression, and harmony of sound, is in its nature superior to every other style; which is just the cause why it could not be borne in a work of great length, no more than the eye could bear to see all this scene that we

[1] *Chorus.* ——"that Resignation meek,
That dove-ey'd Peace, handmaid of Sanctity,
Approached the altar with thee; 'stead of these
See I not gaunt Revenge, ensanguined Slaughter,
And mad Ambition," etc.——

constantly gaze upon,—the verdure of the fields and woods, the azure of the sea and skies, turned into one dazzling expanse of gems. The epic, therefore, assumed a style of graver colours, and only stuck on a diamond (borrowed from her sister) here and there, where it best became her. When we pass from the diction that suits this kind of writing to that which belongs to the former, it appears natural, and delights us; but to pass on a sudden from the lyric glare to the epic solemnity (if I may be allowed to talk nonsense) has a very different effect. We seem to drop from verse into mere prose, from light into darkness. Another thing is, the pauses proper to one and the other are not at all the same; the ear therefore loses by the change. Do you think if Mingotti stopped in the middle of her best air, and only repeated the remaining verses (though the best Metastasio ever wrote), that they would not appear very cold to you, and very heavy?

P. 24.—"Boldly dare" is tautology.

P. 27.—"Brigantum:" there was no such place.

P. 28.—"The sacred hares." You might as well say "the sacred hogs."

P. 29.—There is an affectation in so often using the old phrase of "or ere" for "before."

P. 30.—"Rack" is the course of the clouds, "wreck" is ruin and destruction. Which do you mean? I am not yet entirely satisfied with the conclusion of this fine allegory. "That blest prize redeem'd" is flatly expressed; and her sticking the pages over the arch of her bower is an idea a little burlesque; besides, are we sure the whole is not rather too long for the place it is in, where all the interests of the scene stand still for it? and this is still drawn out further by the lines you have here put into the mouth of Caractacus. Do not mistake me; I admire part of it, and approve almost all; but consider the time and place.

P. 31.—"Pensive Pilgrim." Why not? there is an impropriety in "wakeful wanderer." I have told you my thoughts of this chorus already; the whole scheme is excellent, the 2d strophe and antistrophe divine. Money (I know) is your motive, and of that I wash my hands. Fame is your second consideration; of that I am not the dispenser, but if your own approbation (for every one is a little conscious of his own talents) and mine have any weight with you, you will write an ode or two every year, till you are turned of fifty, not for the world, but for us two only; we will now and then give a little glimpse of them, but no copies.

P. 37.—I do not like "maidenhood."

P. 38.—Why not "smoke in vain" as before? the word "meek" is too often repeated.

P. 42.—The only reason why you have altered my favourite speech is, that "surging and plunging," "main and domain," come too near each other; but could not you correct these without spoiling all? I read

"Cast his broad eye upon the wild of ocean,
And calm'd it with a glance; then, plunging deep
His mighty arm, pluck'd from its dark domain," etc.

Pray have done with your "piled stores and coral floors."

P. 43.—"The dies of Fate," that is, "the dice of Fate." Find out another word.

P. 44.—I cannot say I think this scene improved: I had no objection before, "but to harm a poor wretch like me;" and what you have inserted is to me inferior to what it was meant to replace, except p. 47, "And why this silence," which is very well; the end of the scene is one of my favourite passages.

P. 49.—Why scratch out, "Thou, gallant boy"? I do not know to what other scene you have transferred these rites of lustration, but methinks they did very well here. Arviragus's account of himself I always was highly pleased with.

P. 51.—"Fervid" is a bad word.

CXX.—TO THOMAS WHARTON.

DEAR DOCTOR—I cannot help thanking you for your kind letter, though I have nothing essential to inform you of in return. Lord S[trathmore] and his brother are come back, and in some measure rid me of my apprehensions for the College. S[tonehewe]r is gone to town, but (as he assures me) not to stay above a week. You advise me to be happy, and would to God it depended upon your wishes. A part of what

I imagined,[1] has already happened here, though not in the way I expected. In a way indeed, that confutes itself, and therefore (as I am told) makes no impression on the hearers. But I will not answer for the truth of this: at least such, as are strangers to me, may be influenced by it. However, though I know the quarter, whence it comes, I cannot interpose at present, lest I make the matter worse. Judge you of my happiness, may yours never meet with any cloud or interruption. Adieu! I beg you to write to me.

February 17, 1757.

CXXI.—TO THOMAS WHARTON.

Sunday, April 17, 1757.

Dear Doctor—If I did not immediately answer your kind enquiry, you will attribute it to the visit, which I was obliged to do the honours of for two or three days, and which is now over. I find nothing new to add to my uneasiness here; on the contrary it is considerably abated, and quiet, and hope, is gradually returning. I am extremely glad to hear your country residence promises so well, and has been so serviceable to Mrs. Wharton already.

You desire to know how I like my visit. Lord N[uneham] is a sensible well-bred young man, a little too fine even for me, who love a little finery: he

[1] This seems to refer to the ejection of Henry Tuthill from his fellowship.—[*Ed.*]

never will bo popular, and it is well, if he be not very much hated. His party were Lord Villiers, and Mr. Spencer, but I did not see a great deal of them. Lord John has been with me all this morning. The Duke of Bedford is now here to settle his son at Trinity, and Mr. Rigby is come to assist him with his advice. Adieu, I am interrupted, but will write again soon. Believe me ever yours, T. G.

CXXII.—TO THE REV. WILLIAM MASON.

April 23, 1757.

DEAR MASON—I too am set down here with something greater hopes of quiet than I could entertain when I saw you last; at least nothing new has happened to give me any disturbance, and the assurances you gave me in your letter from hence are pretty well confirmed by experience. I shall be very ready to take as much of Mr. Delap's[1] dulness as he chooses to part with at any price he pleases, even with his want of sleep and weak bowels into the bargain; and I will be your curate, and he shall live here with all

[1] Mr. or Dr. Delap was curate in his earlier life to Mason at Aston in 1756. The first entry of his name appears in a marriage 14th November 1756, his last signature in May 1758. In 1759 he was succeeded by Mr. John Wood. His portrait I have seen in the dining-room at Aston rectory, and it is now in Mrs. Alderson's possession. He was the author of a tragedy, *Hecuba*, acted with very indifferent success at Drury Lane Theatre in 1762, and *The Captives*, which was endured for three nights and then was gathered to its fathers.—[*Mit.*]

my wit and power of learning. Dr. Brown's book[1] (I hear) is much admired in town, which I do not understand. I expected it would be admired here; but they affect not to like it, though I know they ought. What would you have me do? There is one thing in it I applaud, which is the dissertation against trade, for I have always said it was the ruin of the nation. I have read the little wicked book about Evil,[2] that settled Mr. Dodsley's conscience in that point, and find nothing in it but absurdity: we call it Soame Jenyns's, but I have a notion you mentioned some other name to me, though I have forgotten it. Stonhewer has done me the honour to send me your friend Lord Nuneham hither, with a fine recommendatory letter written by his own desire, in Newmarket-week. Do not think he was going to Newmarket; no, he came in a solitaire, great sleeves, jessamine-powder, and a large bouquet of jonquils, within twelve miles of that place, on purpose not to go thither. We had three days' intercourse, talked about the beaux arts, and Rome, and Hanover, and Mason,—whose praises we celebrate *à qui mieux mieux*,—vowed eternal friendship, embraced, and parted. I promised

[1] This is the well-known *Estimate of the Manners and Principles of the Times*, by Dr. John Brown, a book which occupied for a time a very large share of public attention and applause; several editions were called for in the course of a year, and a second volume followed the first.—[*Mit.*]

[2] *The Origin of Evil*, by Soame Jenyns. Dr. Johnson exposed the absurdity of this book by his famous review in the *Literary Magazine.*—[*Ed.*]

to write you a thousand compliments in his name. I saw also Lord Villiers and Mr. Spencer, who carried him back with them; *en passant*, they did not like me at all. Here has been too the best of all Johns[1] (I hardly except the Evangelist and the Divine), who is not, to be sure, a bit like my Lord Nuneham, but full as well, in my mind. The Duke of Bedford has brought his son,[2] aye, and Mr. Rigby too; they were at church on Sunday morning, and Mr. Sturgeon[3] preached to them and the heads, for nobody else was present. Mr. F——n is not his tutor.[4] These are the most remarkable events at Cambridge.

Mr. Bonfoy has been here; he had not done what you recommended to him before he came out of town, and he is returned thither only the beginning of this week, when he assured me he certainly would do it. Alas! what may this delay occasion; it is best not to think. Oh happy Mr. Delap! Adieu, my best Mason; I am pleased to think how much I am obliged to you, and that, while I live, I must be ever yours.

CXXIII.—TO THE REV. WILLIAM MASON.

Cambridge, Tuesday, May . ., 1757.

DEAR MASON—You are so forgetful of me, that I should not forgive it, but that I suppose Caractacus

[1] Lord John Cavendish.

[2] Francis Marquess of Tavistock, of Trinity College, M.A. 1759; he died before his father in 1767.

[3] Roger Sturgeon, M.A., Fellow of Caius.

[4] Perhaps Thomas Francklyn, of Trinity, who was Greek Professor from 1750 to 1759.—[*Ed.*]

may be the better for it; yet I hear nothing from him neither, in spite of his promises. There is no faith in man, no, not in a Welch-man, and yet Mr. Parry[1] has been here and scratched out such ravishing blind harmony, such tunes of a thousand years old, with names enough to choke you, as have set all this learned body a-dancing, and inspired them with due reverence for Odikle, whenever it shall appear. Mr. Parry (you must know) it was that has put Odikle in motion again, and with much exercise it has got a tender tail grown, like Scroddles, and here it is; if you do not like it, you may kiss it.

You remember the "Visions of Glory," that descended on the heights of Snowdon, and unrolled their glittering skirts so slowly.[2]

ANTIST. 3.

Haughty knights and barons bold,
With dazzling helm and horrent spear,
And gorgeous dames and statesmen old,
Of bearded majesty, appear;
In the midst a form divine:
Her eye proclaims her born of Arthur's line
Her lion-port, her awe-commanding face,
Attemper'd sweet to virgin grace.
What strings symphonious tremble in the air,

---

[1] A Welsh harper of considerable eminence, who had been blind from his infancy. He died in 1782. He was the father of John Parry, A.R.A.—[*Ed.*]

[2] This copy of the unfinished text of the "Bard" varies in several places from that sent two years before to Dr. Wharton. —[*Ed.*]

What strains of vocal transport round her play!
Hear, from the grave, great Taliesin, hear!
They breathe a soul to animate thy clay.
Bright Rapture wakes, and, soaring as she sings,
Waves in the eye of Heaven her many-coloured wings.

EPODE 3.

The verse adorn again
Fierce War and faithful Love,
And Truth severe, by fairy Fiction drest.
In mystic measures move
Pale Grief and pleasing Pain,
With Horror wild that chills the throbbing breast.
A voice, as of the Cherub choir,
Gales from blooming Eden bear,
And distant warblings lessen on my ear,
That lost in long futurity expire.
Fond, impious man! think'st thou yon sanguine cloud,
Rais'd by thy breath, has quench'd the orb of day?
To-morrow he repairs the golden flood,
And warms the nations with redoubled ray.
Enough for me, with joy I see
The diff'rent doom our Fates assign:
Be thine Despair, and sceptred Care;
To triumph and to die are mine!
He spoke, and headlong from the mountain's height,
Deep in the roaring tide he sunk to endless night.[1]

I am well aware of many weakly things here, but I hope the end will do. Pray give me your full and true opinion, and that not upon deliberation, but

[1] The Moses of Parmegiano, and Raphael's figure of God in the vision of Ezekiel, are said by Mr. Mason to have furnished Gray with the head and action of his "Bard;" if that was the case, he would have done well to acquaint us with the Poet's method of making *Placidis coire immitia.*—[*Fuseli.*]

forthwith. Mr. Hurd[1] himself allows that "lion-port" is not too bold for Queen Elizabeth. All here are well, and desire their respects to you. I read yesterday of a canonry of Worcester vacant in the newspaper. Adieu, dear Mason, and believe me most truly yours.

It will not be long before I shall go to London.

CXXIV.—TO THE REV. WILLIAM MASON.

Cambridge, Saturday, June.

Dear Mason—I send you inclosed the breast and merry-thought and guts and garbage of the chicken, which I have been chewing so long that I would give the world for neck-beef or cow-heel. I thought, in spite of *ennui*, that the ten last lines would have escaped untouched; for all the rest that I send you I know is weakly, and you think so too. But you want them to be printed and done with; not only Mr. Hurd, but Mr. Bonfoy too and Neville[2] have seen them. Both these like the first Ode (that has no *tout-ensemble*), the best of the two, and both somehow dislike the conclusion of the "Bard," and mutter something about antithesis and conceit in "to triumph,

[1] "I asked Mr. Gray, what *sort of a man Dr. Hurd* was; he answered, 'The last person who left off *stiff-topped gloves.*'"—[*Norton Nicholls.*]

[2] Thomas Neville, of Jesus' College, published Imitations of Horace, 1758, and of Juvenal and Persius in 1769, in which he attacked the heads of houses. He died September 9, 1781.—[*Ed.*]

to die," which I do not comprehend, and am sure it is altered for the better. It was before—

> "Lo! to be free to die, are mine."

If you like it better so, so let it be. It is more abrupt, and perhaps may mark the action better; or it may be—

> "Lo! liberty and death are mine."

whichever you please. But as to breaking the measure, it is not to be thought of; it is an inviolable law of the Medes and Persians. Pray think a little about this conclusion, for all depends upon it; the rest is of little consequence. "In bearded majesty," was altered to "of" only because the next line begins with "In the midst," etc. I understand what you mean about "The verse adorn again." You may read—

> "Fierce War and faithful Love
> Resume their," etc.

But I do not think it signifies much, for there is no mistaking the sense, when one attends to it. "That chills the throbbing," etc. I dislike as much as you can do. "Horror wild," I am forced to strike out, because of "wild dismay" in the first stanza. What if we read

> "With Horror, tyrant of the throbbing breast."

Why you would alter "lost in long futurity" I do not see, unless because you think "lost" and "expire" are tautologies, or because it looks as if the end of the prophecy were disappointed by it, and that people may think that poetry in Britain was some time or other really to expire, whereas the meaning is only that it was lost to his ear from the immense distance. I cannot give up "lost," for it begins with an *l*.

I wish you were here, for I am tired of writing such stuff; and besides, I have got the old Scotch ballad[1] on which Douglas was founded; it is divine, and as long as from hence to Aston. Have you never seen it? Aristotle's best rules are observed in it in a manner that shews the author never had heard of Aristotle. It begins in the fifth act of the play. You may read it two-thirds through without guessing what it is about; and yet, when you come to the end, it is impossible not to understand the whole story. I send you the two first verses—

Gil Maurice was an Earle's son,
His fame it wexed wide.
It was nae for his grete riches,
Nae for his mickle pride;
But it was for a ladie gay
That lived on Carron's side.
"Where shall I get a bonny boy
That will win hose and shoon,
That will gae to Lord Barnard's ha',
And bid his ladie come?
Ye maun rin this errand, Willie,
And ye maun rin with pride;
When other boys gae on their feet,
On horseback ye sal ride,"
"Ah na, ah na, my master dear," etc. etc.

You will observe in the beginning of this thing I send you some alterations of a few words, partly

[1] "Gil Morrice" or "Child Maurice."

for improvement, and partly to avoid repetitions of like words and rhymes; I have not got rid of them all. The six last lines of the fifth stanza are new; tell me if they will do.

I have seen your friend the Dean of S[alisbur]y[1] here to-day in the theatre, and thought I should have spewed. I am very glad you are to be a court chaplain nevertheless; for I do not think you need be such a one,—I defy you ever to be.

I have now seen your first Chorus, new-modelled, and am charmed with it. Now I am coming with my hoe. Of all things I like your idea of "the sober sisters, as they meet and whisper with their ebon and golden rods on the top of Snowdon;" the more because it seems like a new mythology peculiar to the Druid superstition, and not borrowed of the Greeks, who have another quite different moon. But yet I cannot allow of the word "nod," though it pictures the action more lively than another word would do. Yet, at the first blush, "See the sober sisters nod," taken alone without regard to the sense, presents a ridiculous image, and you must leave no room for such ideas; besides, a word that is not quite familiar to us in the sense it is used should never form a rhyme; it may stand in any other part of a line. The rest is much to my palate, except a verse (I have it not now before me) towards the end. I think it is "Float your saffron vestments here,"

[1] Thomas Green, D.D., succeeded Dr. John Clerke in 1757, and died 1780.

because one does not at once conceive that "float" is "let them float;" and besides, it is a repetition of the idea, as you speak of the "rustling of their silken draperies" before, and I would have every image varied as the rest are. I do not absolutely like "Hist ye all," only because it is the last line. These are all the faults I have to find; the rest is perfect. I have written a long letter of poetry, which is tiresome, but I could not help it. My service to Mr. Delap. Adieu! Do write soon; love and compliments. R. For:r's[1] sister Dolly is dead, and he has got £1400, a man, and two horses. I go to town next week. If you could write directly, it would be clever; but, however, direct hither, it will be sent me, if you cannot write so soon.

CXXV.—TO HORACE WALPOLE.

Stoke, July 11, 1757.

I WILL not give you the trouble of sending your chaise for me. I intend to be with you on Wednesday in the evening. If the press stands still all this time for me, to be sure it is dead in child-bed. I do not love notes, though you see I had resolved to put two or three.[2] They are signs of weakness and obscurity. If a thing cannot be understood without them, it had

[1] Richard Forester, a Fellow of Pembroke College, afterwards Rector of Passenham, Northamptonshire. He died in April 1769.—[*Mit.*]

[2] To the "Bard."

better be not understood at all. If you will be vulgar, and pronounce it *Lunnun*, instead of London,[1] I can't help it. Caradoc[2] I have private reasons against; and besides it is in reality Carādoc, and will not stand in the verse.

I rejoice you can fill all your *vuides;* the Maintenon could not, and that was her great misfortune. Seriously though, I congratulate you on your happiness, and seem to understand it. The receipt is obvious; it is only, Have something to do; but how few can apply it. Adieu! I am ever yours,

T. GRAY.

CXXVI.—TO THE REV. JAMES BROWN.

Stoke, July 25, 1757.

DEAR SIR—I thank you for the second little letter, for your Cambridge Anecdotes, and, suffer me to say too, for the trouble you have had on my account. I am going to add to it, by sending you my poetical cargo to distribute; though, whatever the advertisement says, it will not be this fortnight yet, for you must know (what you will like no more than I do, yet it was not in my power anyhow to avoid it), Mr. Walpole, who has set up a printing-press in his own house at Twickenham, earnestly desired that he might

[1] Ye towers of Julius, *London's* lasting shame.
"Bard," v. 87.

[2] Gray alludes to the line "Leave your despairing *Caradoc* to mourn," which he afterwards altered to "Leave me unblessed, unpitied here to mourn."—[*Ed.*]

print it for Dodsley, and, as there is but one hand employed, you must think it will take up some time to despatch 2000 copies. As soon as may be you will have a parcel sent you, which you will dispose of as follows: Mrs. Bonfoy, Mr. Bonfoy, Dr. Long, Gaskarth, and all the Fellows resident; Mr. Montagu and Southwell, if they happen to be there; Master of St. John's[1] (I know he is at Rochester, but it suffices to send it to his lodge); Master of Bennet,[2] Mr. Hurd, Mr. Balguy,[3] Mr. Talbot, Mr. Nourse,[4] Mr. Neville of Jesus, Mr. Bickham,[5] Mr. Hadley,[6] Mr. Newcome. If you think I forget anybody, pray send it them in my name; what remain upon your hands you will hide in a corner. I am sorry to say I know no more of Mason than you do. It is my own fault, I am afraid, for I have not yet answered that letter.

His Prussian Majesty wrote a letter to the King owning himself in a bad situation, from which, he said, nothing but a *coup-de-maître* would extricate him. We have a secret expedition going forward; all I know is, that Lord Ancram, Sir John Mordaunt, and

[1] John Newcome, Master of St. John's, 1734 to 1765. He was known by the nickname of Belshazzar.—[*Ed.*]

[2] John Green, Master of Ben'et, 1750 to 1764.—[*Mit.*]

[3] Thomas Balguy, of St. John's.—[*Ed.*]

[4] Peter Nourse, of St. John's.—[*Ed.*]

[5] James Bickham, junior tutor of Emmanuel. He had been a bruiser in his youth, and now was a brawling Tory.—[*Ed.*]

[6] Probably Dr. J. Hadley, of Queen's, the Chemistry Professor.—[*Ed.*]

General Conway are to bear a part in it. The Duke[1] has been very ill, with his leg; Ranby was sent for, but countermanded, the Marshall d'Etrées having sent him his own surgeons. I would wish to be like Mr. Bonfoy, and think that everything turns out the best in the world, but it won't do, I am stupid and low-spirited, but ever yours, T. G.

CXXVII.—TO THE REV. WILLIAM MASON.

Stoke, Monday, August 1.

DEAR MASON—If I did not send you a political Letter forthwith, it was because Lord Holdernesse came in again so soon that it was the same thing as if he had never gone out, excepting one little circumstance, indeed, the anger of old Priam;[2] which, I am told, is the reason, that he has not the blue riband, though promised him before. I have been here this month or more, low-spirited and full of disagreeablenesses, and, to add to them, am at this present very ill, not with the gout, nor stone (thank God), nor with blotches, nor blains, nor with frogs nor with lice, but with a painful infirmity, that has to me the charms of novelty, but would not amuse you much in the description.

I hope you divert yourself much better than I do. You may be sure Dodsley had orders to send you some Odes[3] the instant they were off the spit; indeed

[1] Duke of Cumberland. [2] George the Second.

[3] *Odes by Mr. Gray*, published August 8, 1757.—[*Ed.*]

I forgot Mr. Fraser, so I fear they will come to Sheffield in the shape of a small parcel by some coach or waggon; but if there is time I will prevent it. They had been out three weeks ago, but Mr. Walpole having taken it into his head to set up a press of his own at Twickenham, was so earnest to handsel it with this new pamphlet that it was impossible to find a pretence for refusing such a trifle. You will dislike this as much as I do, but there is no help; you understand, it is he that prints them, not for me, but for Dodsley. I charge you send me some *Caractacus* before I die; it is impossible this weather should not bring him to maturity.

If you knew how bad I was you would not wonder I could write no more. Adieu, dear Mason; I am ever most truly yours, T. G.

CXXVIII.—TO THE REV. JAMES BROWN.

August 14, 1757.

DEAR SIR—Excuse me if I begin to wonder a little that I have heard no news of you in so long a time. I conclude you received Dodsley's packet at least a week ago, and made my presents. You will not wonder therefore at my curiosity, if I enquire of you what you hear said; for, though in the rest of the world I do not expect to hear that anybody says much, or thinks about the matter, yet among *mes confrères*, the learned, I know there is always leisure, at least to find fault, if not to commend.

I have been lately much out of order, and confined at home, but now I go abroad again. Mr. Garrick and his wife have passed some days at my Lady Cobham's,[1] and are shortly to return again; they, and a few other people that I see there, have been my only entertainment till this week, but now I have purchased some volumes of the great *French Encyclopedie*, and am trying to amuse myself within doors. Pray tell me a great deal, and believe me ever most faithfully yours, T. G.

CXXIX.—TO THOMAS WHARTON.

Stoke, August 17, 1757.

DEAR DOCTOR—It feels to me as if it were a long while, since I heard from you. Not a word to flatter or to abash the vanity of an author! suffer me then to tell you, that I hear, we are not at all popular. The great objection is obscurity, nobody knows what we would be at. One man (a Peer) I have been told of, that thinks the last stanza of the 2d Ode relates to Charles the first, and Oliver Cromwell, in short the Συνετὸι[2] appear to be still fewer, than even I expected.

You will imagine all this does not go very deep; but I have been almost ever since I was here exceedingly dispirited, besides being really ill in body. No

[1] At Stoke.

[2] This is a reference to the motto on the half-title of the *Odes*, Φωνάντα συνετοῖσι.—[*Ed.*]

gout, but something feverish, that seems to come almost every morning, and disperses soon after I am up. The Cobhams are here, and as civil as usual. Garrick and his wife have been down with them some days, and are soon to come again. Except the little amusement they give me, and two volumes of the *Encyclopedia* now almost exhausted, I have nothing but my own thoughts to feed upon, and you know they are of the gloomy cast. Write to me then for *sweet St. Charity*, and remember, that while I am my own, I am most faithfully yours, T. G.

My best services to Mrs. Wharton.

CXXX.—TO RICHARD HURD.

Stoke, August 25, 1757.

DEAR SIR—I do not know why you should thank me for what you had a right and title to; but attribute it to the excess of your politeness, and the more so because almost no one else has made me the same compliment. As your acquaintance in the University (you say) do me the honour to admire, it would be ungenerous in me not to give them notice that they are doing a very unfashionable thing, for all people of condition are agreed not to admire, nor even to understand: one very great man, writing to an acquaintance of his and mine, says that he had read them seven or eight times, and that now, when he next sees him, he shall not have above thirty questions to ask. Another, a peer, believes that the last stanza of the Second Ode relates to King Charles the First and Oliver Cromwell. Even my friends tell me they do not succeed, and write me moving topics of consolation on that head; in short, I have heard of nobody but a player and a doctor of divinity[1] that profess their esteem for them. Oh yes! a lady of quality, a friend of Mason's, who is a great reader. She knew there was a compliment to Dryden, but never suspected there was anything said about Shakspeare or Milton, till it was explained to her; and wishes that there had been titles prefixed to tell what they were about.

From this mention of Mason's name you may think, perhaps, we are great correspondents; no such thing; I have not heard from him these two months. I will be sure to scold in my own name as well as in yours. I rejoice to hear you are so ripe for the press, and so voluminous,[2]—not for my own sake only, whom you flatter with the hopes of seeing your labours both public and private,—but for yours too, for to be employed is to be happy. This principle of mine, and I am convinced of its truth, has, as usual, no influence on my practice. I am alone and *ennuyé* to the last degree, yet do nothing; indeed I have one excuse; my health, which you so kindly enquire after, is not extraordinary, ever since I came hither. It is no

[1] Garrick and Dr. Warburton. Garrick wrote some verses in their praise.

[2] Alluding probably to the "Moral and Political Dialogues" then composing, and published in 1759.—[*Mit.*]

great malady, but several little ones, that seem brewing no good to me.

It will be a particular pleasure to me to hear whether Content dwells in Leicestershire,[1] and how she entertains herself there; only do not be too happy, nor forget entirely the quiet ugliness of Cambridge. I am, dear sir,

Your friend and obliged humble servant.

T. GRAY.

If Mr. Brown falls in your way, be so good to shew him the beginning of this letter, and it will save me the labour of writing the same thing twice. His first letter, I believe, was in the mail that was robbed, for it was delayed many days; his second I have just received.

CXXXI.—TO THE REV. WILLIAM MASON.

DEAR MASON—You are welcome to the land of the living, to the sunshine of a court, to the dirt of a chaplain's table,[2] to the society of Dr. Squire[3] and Dr.

[1] Mr. Hurd was settled in Leicestershire February 16, 1757, on the College living of Thurcaston.—[*Mit.*]

[2] Mason was appointed, by the Duke of Devonshire, Chaplain in ordinary to George II. 1757.—[*Mit.*]

[3] "And leave Church and State to Charles Townshend and *Squire*,"

is a line which concludes Gray's sketch of his own character. Dr. Samuel Squire, of St. John's, made an abortive attempt to encourage the study of Anglo-Saxon at Cambridge. He was Chaplain to the Duke, and was successively made Rector of St.

Chapman. Have you set out, as Dr. Cobden ended, with a sermon against adultery? or do you, with deep mortification and a Christian sense of your own nothingness, read prayers to Princess Emily while she is putting on her dress? Pray acquaint me with the whole ceremonial, and how your first preachment succeeded; whether you have heard of anybody that renounced their election, or made restitution to the Exchequer; whether you saw any woman trample her pompons under foot, or spit upon her hankerchief to wipe off the rouge.

I would not have put another note to save the souls of all the owls in London. It is extremely well as it is—nobody understands me, and I am perfectly satisfied. Even the *Critical Review*[1] (Mr. Franklin, I am told), that is rapt and surprised and shudders at me, yet mistakes the Æolian lyre for the harp of Æolus, which, indeed, as he observes, is a very bad instrument to dance to. If you hear anything (though it is not very likely, for I know my day is over), you will tell me. Lord Lyttleton and Mr. Shenstone[2]

Anne's, Soho, afterwards Dean of Bristol, and then Bishop of St. David's in 1761; he died 7th May 1766. Warburton told Tucker, Dean of Gloucester, that never Bishopric was so *bedeaned*, for that one (Squire) made *religion his trade*, and that he (Tucker) made *trade his religion*. Squire was so swarthy that he was nicknamed "The Man of Angola."—[*Ed.*]

[1] See *Critical Review*, vol. iv. p. 167. "Such an instrument as the *Æolian harp*, which is altogether uncertain and irregular, must be very ill adapted to the dance, which is one continued, regular movement," etc.—[*Mit.*]

[2] "Mr. Gray, of manners very delicate, yet possessed of a

admire me, but wish I had been a little clearer. Mr. (Palmyra) Wood[1] owns himself disappointed in his expectations. Your enemy, Dr. Brown,[2] says I am the best thing in the language. Mr. Fox, supposing the Bard sung his song but once over, does not wonder if Edward the First did not understand him. This last criticism is rather unhappy, for though it had been sung a hundred times under his window, it was absolutely impossible King Edward should understand him; but that is no reason for Mr. Fox, who lives almost 500 years after him. It is very well; the next thing I print shall be in Welch,—that's all.

I delight in your Epigram, but dare not show it anybody, for your sake; but I more delight to hear from Mr. Hurd that *Caractacus* advances. Am I not to see Mador's song? Could not we meet some day, —at Hounslow, for example, after your waiting is over? Do tell me time and place. I am most truly yours, T. G.

P.S.—If you write to Lord Jersey, commend me to him. I was so civil to send a book to Lord Nuneham, but hear nothing of him. Where is Stonhewer? I am grown a stranger to him. You will oblige me by sending to Dodsley's, to say I wonder

poetical vein fraught with the *noblest and sublimest images,* and a mind fraught with the more masculine parts of learning."—[*Shenstone.*]

[1] Mr. Palmyra Wood accompanied the Duke of Bridgewater in his travels through Italy.—[*Mit.*]

[2] The author of *The Estimate.*

the third and fourth volumes of the *Encyclopedie* are not come. If you chance to call yourself, you might enquire if many of my 2000 remain upon his hands. He told me a fortnight ago about 12 or 1300 were gone.

You talk of writing a comment. I do not desire you should be employed in any such office; but what if Delap (inspired by a little of your intelligence) should do such a matter; it will get him a shilling; but it must bear no name, nor must he know I mentioned it.

CXXXII.—TO HORACE WALPOLE.

I HAVE been very ill this week with a great cold and a fever, and though now in a way to be well, am like to be confined some days longer: whatever you will send me that is new, or old, and long, will be received as a charity. Rousseau's people do not interest me; there is but one character and one style in them all, I do not know their faces asunder. I have no esteem for their persons or conduct, am not touched with their passions; and as to their story, I do not believe a word of it—not because it is improbable, but because it is absurd. If I had any little propensity, it was to Julie; but now she has gone and (so hand over head) married that Monsieur de Wolmar, I take her for a *vraie Suissesse*, and do not doubt but she had taken a cup too much like her lover. All this does not imply that I will not read it out, when you can spare the rest of it.

CXXXIII.—TO THOMAS WHARTON.

Stoke, September 7, 1757.

DEAR DOCTOR—I am greatly obliged to your care and kindness for considering with more attention, than it deserves, the article of my health. At present I am far better, and take long walks again, have better spirits, and am more capable of amusement. The offer you make me of your lodgings for a time I should gladly embrace, both for the sake of seeing you, and for variety, and because it will answer another end by furnishing me with a reason for not going into the country to *a place, where I am invited.* (I think, you understand me.) But the truth, is I cannot afford to hurry about from place to place; so I shall continue, where I am, and trust to *illness*, or some other cause for an excuse, since to *that place* I am positive, I will not go. It hurts me beyond measure, that I am forced to make these excuses, but go I cannot, and something must be said. These are cruel things!

The family you mention near me are full as civil as ever; Miss Sp[eed] seems to understand; and to all such, as do not, she says—*φωνάντα συνετοῖσι*—in so many words. And this is both my motto and comment. I am afraid, you mistake Mr. Roper's complaisance for approbation. Dr. Brown (I hear) says, they are the best odes[1] in our language. Mr. Garrick,

[1] From a note communicated to me by my friend Mr. James Boswell, I find that on the 29th June 1757, Gray received forty guineas for his two Odes.—[*Mit.*]

the best in ours, or *any other*. I should not write this immodest panegyric, did not you guess at the motive of their applause. Lord Lyttleton and Mr. Shenstone admire, but wish they were a little clearer. Lord Barrington's explanation, I think, I told you before, so will not repeat it. Mr. Fox thinks if the Bard sung his song but once over, King Edward could not possibly understand him. Indeed I am of his opinion, and am certain, if he had sung it fifty times, it was impossible the king should know a jot the more about Edward the III., and Queen Elizabeth, and Spencer, and Milton, etc. . . . Mr. Wood (Mr. Pitt's Wood) is disappointed in his expectations. Dr. Akenside criticises opening a *source*[1] with a *key*. The *Critical Review* you have seen, or may see. He is in raptures (they say, it is Professor Franklin) but mistakes the Æolian Lyre for the *Harp of Æolus*, and on this mistake founds a compliment and a criticism. This is, I think, all I have heard, that signifies.

The *Encyclopedia*, I own, may cloy one, if one sits down to it. But you will own, that out of one great good dinner, a number of little good dinners may be made, that would not cloy one at all. There is a long article *sur le Beau* that for my life I cannot understand. Several of the geographical articles are carelessly done, and some of the Antiquities, or Ancient History.

[1] Yet Akenside himself had twice used the analogous expression "to *unlock* the *springs*" of Wisdom or of the Muse. —[*Ed.*]

My best compliments to Mrs. Wharton. I hope the operation going forward on your children will succeed to your wishes. Adieu, dear Sir, and believe me ever yours, T. G.

This letter is to *yourself* only. Our best Mason, I suppose you know is in town, and in *waiting*. Do you know any thing of St[onehewe]r? Pray desire Mason to repeat an Epigram to you.

CXXXIV.—TO THE REV. WILLIAM MASON.

Stoke, September 28, 1757.

DEAR MASON—I have, as I desired Stonhewer to tell you, read over *Caractacus* twice, not with pleasure only, but with emotion.[1] You may say what you will, but the contrivance, the manners, the interests, the passions, and the expression, go beyond the dramatic part of your *Elfrida* many, many leagues. I even say (though you will think me a bad judge of this) that the world will like it better. I am struck with the Chorus, who are not there merely to sing and dance, but bear throughout a principal part in the action, and have (beside the costume, which is excellent) as much a character of their own as any

[1] Mr. Mason has published another drama called *Caractacus*. There are some incantations poetical enough, and odes so Greek as to have very little meaning. But the whole is laboured, uninteresting, and no more resembling the manners of Britons than of the Japanese.—[*Walpole.*]

other person. I am charmed with their priestly pride and obstinacy, when, after all is lost, they resolve to confront the Roman General, and spit in his face. But now I am going to tell you what touches me most. From the beginning the first opening is greatly improved. The curiosity of Didius is now a very natural reason for dwelling on each particular of the scene before him, nor is the description at all too long. I am glad to find the two young men are Cartismandua's sons; they interest me far more. I love people of condition. They were men before that nobody knew; one could not make them a bow if one had met them at a public place.

I always admired that interruption of the Druids to Evelina, "Peace, Virgin, peace," etc.; and chiefly the abstract idea personified (to use the words of a critic), at the end of it. That of "Caractacus would save my Queen," etc., and still more, that, "I know it, reverend Fathers, 'tis heaven's high will," etc., to "I've done, begin the rites!" This latter is exemplary for the expression (always the great point with me); I do not mean by expression the mere choice of words, but the whole dress, fashion, and arrangement of a thought. Here, in particular, it is the brokenness, the ungrammatical position, the total subversion of the period, that charms me. All that ushers in the incantation, from "Try we yet what holiness can do," I am delighted with in quite another way, for this is pure poetry, as it ought to be, forming the proper transition, and leading on the mind to that still purer poetry that follows it. You have somehow mistaken my meaning about the sober Sisters: the verb "nod," before "only," seemed to be a verb neuter; now you have made it absolutely such, which was just my objection to it; but it is easily altered, for if the accusative case come first, there is no danger of ambiguity. I read

See! their gold and ebon rod
Where the sober Sisters nod,
And greet in whispers sage and slow.
Snowdon, mark! 'tis Magic's hour;
Now the mutter'd spell hath power,
Power to rift thy ribs of rock,
To burst thy base with thunder's shock,
But, etc., etc.
                    Than those that dwell
In musick's, etc.

You will laugh at my "these's" and "those's," but they strike my ear better. What Mador sings must be the finest thing that ever was wrote; and the next chorus, where they all go to sleep, must be finer still.

In the beginning of the succeeding act I admire the chorus again, "Is it not now the hour, the holy hour," etc.: and their evasion of a lie, "Say'st thou, proud boy," etc.: and "Sleep with the unsunn'd silver," which is an example of a dramatic simile. The sudden appearance of Caractacus, the pretended respect and admiration of Vellinus, and the probability of his story, the distrust of the Druids, and their reasoning with Caractacus, and particularly that, "'Tis meet thou should'st; thou art a king," etc. etc.; "Mark me, Prince, the time will come when destiny," etc., are well and happily imagined. Apropos of the last striking passage I have mentioned, I am going to make a digression.

When we treat a subject where the manners are almost lost in antiquity our stock of ideas must needs be small, and nothing betrays our poverty more than the returning to and harping frequently on one image; it was therefore I thought you should omit some lines before, though good in themselves, about the scythed car, that the passage now before us might appear with greater lustre when it came; and in this, I see, you have complied with me. But there are other ideas here and there still that occur too often, particularly about the oaks, some of which I would discard to make way for the rest.

But the subjects I speak of, to compensate (and more than compensate) that unavoidable poverty, have one great advantage when they fall into good hands: they leave an unbounded liberty to pure imagination and fiction (our favourite provinces), where no critic can molest or antiquary gainsay us. And yet (to please me) these fictions must have some affinity, some seeming connection with that little we really know of the character and customs of the people. For example, I never heard in my days that midnight and the moon were sisters, that they carried rods of ebony and gold, or met to whisper on the top of a mountain; but now, I could lay my life it is all true, and do not doubt it will be found so in some Pantheon of the Druids that is to be discovered in the library at Herculaneum. The Car of Destiny and Death is a very noble invention of the same class, and, as far as that goes, is so fine, that it makes me more delicate than, perhaps, I should be. About the close of it, Andraste, sailing on the wings of Fame, that snatches the wreaths from oblivion to hang them on her loftiest amaranth, though a clean and beautiful peace of unknown mythology, has too Greek an air to give me perfect satisfaction.

Now I proceed. The preparation to the Chorus, though so much akin to that in the former act, is excellent. The remarks of Evelina, and her suspicions of the brothers, mixed with a secret inclination to the younger of them (though, I think, her part throughout wants re-touching), yet please me much; and the contrivance of the following scene much more. "Masters of wisdom, no," etc., I always admired, as I do the rocking-stone and the distress of Elidurus. Evelina's examination of him is a well-invented scene, and will be, with a little pains, a very touching one; but the introduction of Arviragus is superlative. I am not sure whether those few lines of his short narrative, "My strength repaired, it boots not that I tell," etc., do not please me as much as anything in the whole drama. The sullen bravery of Elidurus; the menaces of the Chorus, that "Think not, Religion," etc.; the trumpet of the Druids; that "I'll follow him, though in my chains," etc.; "Hast thou a brother, no," etc.; the placability of the Chorus when they see the motives of Elidurus' obstinacy, give me great contentment. So do the reflections of the Druid on the necessity of lustration, and the reasons for Vellinus' easy escape; but I would not have him seize on a spear, nor issue hastily through the cavern's mouth. Why should he not steal away unmarked and unmissed till the hurry of passions in those that should have guarded him was a little abated? But I chiefly admire the two speeches of Elidurus:—"Ah! Vellinus, is this thee," etc., and "Ye do gaze on me, Fathers," etc. The manner in which the Chorus reply to him is very fine, but the image at the end wants a little mending. The next scene is highly moving; it is so very good that I must have it made yet better.

Now for the last Act. I do not know what you would have, but to me the design and contrivance of it is at least equal to any part of the whole. The short-lived triumph of the Britons—the address of Caractacus to the Roman victims—Evelina's discovery of the ambush—the mistake of the Roman fires for the rising sun—the death of Arviragus—the interview between Didius and Caractacus—his mourning over his dead son—his parting speech (in which you have made all the use of Tacitus that your plan would admit)—everything, in short, but that little dispute between Didius and him, "'Tis well, and therefore to increase that reverence," etc., down to "Give me a moment" (which must be omitted, or put in the mouth of the Druid), I approve in the highest degree. If I should find any fault with the last Act it could only be with trifles and little expressions. If you make any alterations I fear it will never improve it, I mean as to the plan. I send you back the two last sheets, because you bid me. I reserve my nibblings and minutiæ for another day. Adieu, I am most truly yours, T. G.

I have had a printed Ode sent me, called "Melpomene." Pray who wrote it? I suspect Mr. Bedingfield,[1] Montagu,[2] young Pitt,[3] or Delap. Do say I like it.

CXXXV.—TO THE REV. WILLIAM MASON.

Friday, October 13, 1757.

DEAR MASON—I thank you for your history of Melpomene, which is curious and ought to be remembered; the judgment of knowing ones ought always to be upon record, that they may not be suffered to

[1] In Dodsley's *Collection of Poems*, vol. iii. p. 119, is a poem, "The Death of Achilles," by Mr. Bedingfield. See on him a letter of Dr. J. Warton to his brother, 1753, "Give my compliments to Bedingfield. I am glad he is emerging into life from Hertford College," in Dr. Wooll's *Life of Dr. Warton*, p. 217; and one from Dodsley, "Mr. Bedingfield has actually refined his taste to a degree that makes him dissatisfied with almost every composition," p. 225; and another from him of the year 1757 to Dr. Warton, p. 244, on Milton.—[*Mit.*]

[2] Frederick Montagu, son of Charles Montagu, of Paplewick, in Northamptonshire.

[3] Mr. Thomas Pitt, of Boconnock, nephew of Lord Chatham, afterwards Lord Camelford, died at Florence in 1793.

retract and mitigate their applause. If I were Dodsley I would sue them, and they should buckle my shoe in Westminster Hall. What is the reason I hear nothing of your waiting, and your performances in public? Another thing,—why has Mr. Hurd's Letter[1] to you never been advertised? and why do not I hear what anybody says about it?

I go from hence for three days on Wednesday next, and hope your installation will not be so over that you should come to Windsor before I return; if I had notice in due time, I would meet you at the Christopher in Eton, or, if you choose it,—you know the worst, having been already here,—shall rejoice to see you at Stoke. In town I shall hardly be till next month. Our expedition is extremely *à l'Anglaise*, but I have given up all thoughts of England, and care for nobody but the King of Prussia. Pray do not suffer your megrims to prevail over you; it is good for you that you should come to school for a few months now and then. I must say no one has profited more in so few lessons. Common sense nowhere thrives better than in the neighbourhood of nonsense. Take care of your health, and believe me ever yours, T. G.

Send me Elegy,[1]—my hoe is sharp.

[1] In 1757 Hurd published a letter to Mason, "on the marks of Imitation," which he afterwards incorporated as a dissertation into his *Horace*.

[1] Mason's "Elegy in the Garden of a Friend."

CXXXVI.—TO THOMAS WHARTON.

October 7, 1757.

DEAR DOCTOR—I heartily rejoice with you, that your little family are out of danger, and all apprehensions of that kind over with them for life. Yet I have heard, you were ill yourself, and kept your bed: as this was (I imagine) only by way of regimen, and not from necessity; I hope soon to be told, you have no farther occasion for it. Yet take care of yourself, for there is a bad fever now very frequent, it is among the boys at Eton, and (I am told), is much spread about London too. My notion is, that your violent quick pulse, and soapy diet, would not suit well with feverish disorders. Though our party at Slough turned out so ill, I could not help being sorry, that you were not with us.

Have you read Mr. Hurd's (printed) letter to Mason, on the "Marks of Imitation?" You do not tell me your opinion of it. You bid me send you criticisms on myself, and even *compliments.* Did I tell you, what the Speaker says? the second Ode, he says, is a good pretty tale, but nothing to the *Churchyard.* Mr. Bedingfield in a golden shower of panegyric writes me word that at York Races he overheard three people, whom by their dress and manner he takes for lords, say, that I was impenetrable and inexplicable, and they wished, I had told them in prose, what I meant in verse, and then they bought me (which was what most displeased him) and put me in their pocket. Dr. Warburton is come to town, and likes them extremely. He says the world never passed so just an opinion upon anything as upon them: for that in other things they have affected to like or dislike, whereas here they own, they do not understand, which he looks upon to be very true; but yet thinks, they understand them as well as they do Milton or Shakespeare, whom they are obliged by fashion to admire. Mr. G[arric]k's compliment you have seen; I am told it was printed in the *Chronicle* of last Saturday. The Review I have read, and admire it, particularly that observation, that the "Bard" is taken from *Pastor, cum traheret*, and the advice to be more an *original*, and in order to be so, the way is (he says) to cultivate the native flowers of the soil, and not introduce the exotics of another climate.

I am greatly pleased with M[aso]n's *Caractacus* in its present state. The contrivance and arrangement of events, the manners of the country, the characters and passions, strike me wonderfully. The difficult part is now got over, nothing remains, but to polish, and retouch a little: yet only the beginning of the first chorus is done of the lyric part. Have you seen it? Adieu! dear Sir, and believe me ever yours,

T. G.

I shall be in town probably sooner than you come to stay there.

CXXXVII.—TO THOMAS WHARTON.

DEAR DOCTOR—I should be extremely sorry to think that you or Mrs. Wharton came a day the sooner to town on my account this fine season. If you are already come, I shall come to you: if not, you will let me know some day this week (for I shall hardly stay here much longer) that I may write for a lodging. I rejoice to hear you are all well.

If there be really any enquiry into the expedition (which I believe will scarcely be, unless it be very hard press'd) many things will appear, as well with regard to the design as the execution, that do not yet seem to be generally known.[1] The design, for which the soldiers were put into the boats, was to attack a fort, called *Fourasse*, at the mouth of the Charante (for Rochefort itself lies five miles up the river), it was necessary, they should be masters of this place not only to clear their way to the town, but to have some place of security for their first embarkation of about 1200 men, who must remain for four hours exposed to the enemy, before any reinforcement could join them (as the admirals declared), and (I have heard) this design was laid aside in great measure upon Captain Howe's saying it would be, if practicable at all,

[1] This passage refers to the unsuccessful result of the expedition, under the command of Sir Edward Hawke, and Sir John Mordaunt, against Rochefort, in the month of September, 1757. For which Sir John Mordaunt was afterwards tried by a court martial, and acquitted.—[*Mit.*]

a very bloody, and difficult attempt. If therefore he asserts what you have been told, it is very strange. When I see you, I shall tell you more; and even this, if you do not hear it publicly said, I should wish you would not mention.

I want to know what is said of our captain-general's resignation[1] and the causes of it, for this seems a more extraordinary thing than the other. Adieu, dear Sir, I am ever faithfully yours.

October 31, 1757.

CXXXVIII.—TO THOMAS WHARTON.

December 8, 1757.

Dear Doctor—I have received the draught you were so good to send me, and the money is paid. You apprehend too much from my resolutions about writing: they are only made to be broken, and after all it will be just as the maggot bites. You have a very mean opinion of the epic, if you think it consists only in laying out a plan. In four and twenty years at a moderate computation I may have finished twelve books, and nine years after I hope to publish. I shall then be 74 years old, and I shall get £500 for the copy to make me easy for the remainder of my days. Somebody has directed a letter to the *Revd.* Mr. G. at Strawberry Hill, which was sent me yesterday

[1] I suppose that this relates to the resignation of the command of the army by the D. of Cumberland, after the capitulation of Closter-Seven.—[*Mit.*]

hither. It is anonymous, consists of above nine pages, all about the "Bard," and if I would hear as much more about his companion, I am to direct to the Post House at Andover.[1] I do not know but I may have that curiosity, for his observations (whoever it is) are not nonsense. He takes the liberty of a person unknown, and treats me with abundance of freedom. I guess it to be some *reading* clergyman. Mr. Brown and I join in our best compliments to Mrs. Wharton, and I am, dear Sir, most sincerely yours, T. G.

CXXXIX.—TO THE REV. WILLIAM MASON.

December 19, 1757.

DEAR MASON—Though I very well know the bland emollient saponaceous qualities both of sack and silver, yet if any great man would say to me, "I make you

[1] Gray's, then unknown, critic and correspondent was, I believe, "Mr. J. Butler, of Andover." In a MS. letter from Gray to Dodsley (which Mr. Bindley purchased at the sale of Mr. Isaac Reed's books, subsequently bought by Mr. Rogers at Bindley's sale for eighteen guineas), after he has mentioned how he wishes his poems to be printed, and added some notes, etc., he says, "When you have done, I shall desire you to present, in my name, a copy to Mr. Walpole, in Arlington Street; another to Mr. Daines Barrington (he is one of the Welsh judges) in the Inner Temple; and a third, to *Mr. J. Butler, at Andover.* Whether this latter gentleman is living or not, or in that neighbourhood, I am ignorant; but you will oblige me in making the enquiry. If you have no better means of knowing, a line directed to the post mistress, at Andover, will bring you information; after this you may, if you please, bestow another copy or two on me. I am, etc."—[*Mit.*]

rat-catcher to his Majesty, with a salary of £300 a year and two butts of the best Malaga; and though it has been usual to catch a mouse or two, for form's sake, in public once a year, yet to you, sir, we shall not stand upon these things," I cannot say I should jump at it; nay, if they would drop the very name of the office, and call me Sinecure to the King's Majesty, I should still feel a little awkward, and think everybody I saw smelt a rat about me; but I do not pretend to blame any one else that has not the same sensations; for my part I would rather be serjeant trumpeter or pinmaker to the palace. Nevertheless I interest myself a little in the history of it, and rather wish somebody may accept it that will retrieve the credit of the thing, if it be retrievable, or ever had any credit. Rowe was, I think, the last man of character that had it. As to Settle,[1] whom you mention, he belonged to my lord mayor not to the king. Eusden[2] was a person of great hopes in his youth, though at last he turned out a drunken parson. Dryden was as disgraceful to the office, from his character, as the poorest scribbler could have been from his verses. The office itself has always humbled the professor hitherto (even in an age when kings were somebody), if he were a

[1] Elkanah Settle, born 1646, died 1724; the *last* of the city poets.

[2] Appointed poet-laureate by Lord Halifax, in 1716. He was rector of Coningsby in Lincolnshire (which afterwards received another poet, Dyer, the author of the *Fleece*), where he died in 1730.

poor writer by making him more conspicuous, and if he were a good one by setting him at war with the little fry of his own profession, for there are poets little enough to envy even a poet-laureat.

I am obliged to you for your news; pray send me some more, and better of the sort. I can tell you nothing in return; so your generosity will be the greater;—only Dick[1] is going to give up his rooms, and live at Ashwell. Mr. Treasurer[2] sets Sir M. Lamb[3] at nought, and says he has sent him reasons half a sheet at a time; and Mr. Brown attests his veracity as an eye-witness. I have had nine pages of criticism on the "Bard" sent me in an anonymous letter, directed to the Reverend Mr. G. at Strawberry Hill; and if I have a mind to hear as much more on the other Ode, I am told where I may direct. He seems a good sensible man, and I dare say a clergyman. He is very frank, and indeed much ruder than he means to be. Adieu, dear Mason, and believe me that I am too.

[1] Dick is the Rev. Richard Forester, mentioned before, in Letter CXXIV., son of Poulter Forester, Esq. of Broadfield, Herts. He vacated his fellowship at the end of the year 1757, and went to Ashwell in his own county.—[*Mit.*]

[2] Mr. Joseph Gaskarth was the college treasurer, but the subject of his disagreement with Sir M. Lamb does not appear to be known.—[*Mit.*]

[3] Probably Sir Matthew Lamb, of Brocket Hall, Herts, created a Baronet in 1755; father of the first Lord Melbourne. He died 6th November 1768.—[*Mit.*]

CXL.—TO THE REV. WILLIAM MASON.

January 3, 1758.

Dear Mason—A life spent out of the world has its hours of despondence, its inconveniences, its sufferings, as numerous and as real (though not quite of the same sort) as a life spent in the midst of it. The power we have, when we will exert it, over our own minds, joined to a little strength and consolation, nay, a little pride we catch from those that seem to love us, is our only support in either of these conditions. I am sensible I cannot return to you so much of this assistance as I have received from you. I can only tell you that one who has far more reason than you (I hope) will ever have to look on life with something worse than indifference, is yet no enemy to it, and can look backward on many bitter moments partly with satisfaction, and partly with patience, and forward too, on a scene not very promising, with some hope and some expectations of a better day. The conversation you mention seems to me to have been in some measure the cause of your reflection. As you do not describe the manner (which is very essential, and yet cannot easily be described), to be sure I can judge but very imperfectly of it. But if (as you say) it ended very amicably, why not take it as amicably? In most cases I am a great friend to *éclaircissements*; it is no pleasant task to enter upon them, therefore it is always some merit in the person who does so. I am in the dark too as to what you have said of ——. To whom, where, before whom, how did it come round? for you certainly would not do it indiscriminately, nor without a little reserve. I do not mean on your own account (for he is an object of contempt, that would naturally tempt any one to laugh, or —— *himself*), but for the person's sake with whom you so often are, who (merely from his situation) must neither laugh nor —— *himself*, as you and I might do. Who knows? any little imprudence (which it is so pleasant to indulge) might really be disagreeable in its consequences to him; for it would be said infallibly, though very unjustly, that you would not dare to take these liberties without private encouragement, at least, that he had no aversion to hear in secret what you ventured to say in public. You do not imagine that the world (which always concludes wrong about the motives of such minds as it has not been used to) will think you have any sentiments of your own; and though you (if you thought it worth while) might wish to convince them of their mistake, yet you would not do it at the expense of another, especially of this other; in short, I think (as far as I know) you have no reason from this to take any such resolution as you meditate. Make use of it in its season, as a relief from what is tiresome to you, but not as if it was in consequence of something you take ill; on the contrary, if such a conference had happened about the time of your transmigration, I would defer it, to avoid that appearance merely: for the frankness of this proceeding has to me an appearance of friendliness that one would by no means wish to suppress.

I am ashamed not to have returned Mr. Hurd my thanks for his book;[1] pray do it for me in the civilest manner, and tell him I shall be here till April, when I must go for a short time to town, but shall return again hither. I rejoice to hear he is again coming out, and had no notion of his being so ready for the press.

I wrote to the man (as you bid me), and had a second criticism; his name (for I desired to know it) is Butler. He is (he says) of the number of those who live less contented than they ought, in an independent indolence, can just afford himself a horse for airings about Harewood Forest (the scene of Elfrida), half a score new books in a season, and good part of half an acre of garden-ground for honeysuckles and roses. Did you know that Harewood was near Andover? I think that you had some friend in that neighbourhood,—is it not Mr. Bourne? however, do not enquire, for our correspondence is to be a profound secret. Adieu! I am ever truly yours, T. G.

[1] It appears by the dates of his life that Hurd printed in 1757 his *Remarks on Hume's Natural History of Religion*; or the book which he gave to Gray might be the new edition of his *Commentary of Horace*.—[*Mit.*]

CXLI.—TO THOMAS WHARTON.

Dear Doctor—You will wonder why I trouble you so soon with another letter; it is about the great box which I committed to the care of your John, and which does not yet make its appearance at Cambridge. In it are all my shoes, clogs, *Encyclopedia*, and other rich moveables, and I begin to fear it has miscarried. I shall be much obliged to you, if you will let him make enquiry after it.

What are we to believe about Silesia?[1] am I to make bonfires, or keep a general fast? pray, rid me of this suspense, for it is very uneasy to me. I am ever yours, T. G.

Cambridge, December 12, 1757.

CXLII.—TO THE REV. WILLIAM MASON.

January 13, 1758.

Dear Mason—Why you make no more of writing an Ode, and throwing it into the fire, than of buckling and unbuckling your shoe. I have never read Key-

[1] This alludes to the various turns of fortune in the contest then taking place between the King of Prussia and the Austrians. The latter, it will be recollected, took Schweidnitz, and afterwards defeated the Prince, of Bevern, at Breslaw by which they got possession of that town. They were, however, defeated by the K. of Prussia himself, at Lissa; who then retook Schweidnitz and Breslaw, and thus became master of Silesia.—[*Mit.*]

sler's book,[1] nor you neither, I believe; if you had taken that pains, I am persuaded you would have seen that his Celtic and his septentrional antiquities are two things entirely distinct. There are, indeed, some learned persons who have taken pains to confound what Cæsar and Tacitus have taken pains to separate, the old Druidical or Celtic belief, and that of the old Germans, but nobody has been so learned as to mix the Celtic religion with that of the Goths. Woden himself is supposed not to have been older than Julius Cæsar; but let him have lived when he pleases, it is certain that neither he nor his Valhalla were heard of till many ages after. This is the doctrine of the Scalds, not of the Bards; these are the songs of Hengist and Horsa, a modern new-fangled belief in comparison of that which you ought to possess. After all, I shall be sorry to have so many good verses and good chimæras thrown away. Might we not be permitted (in that scarcity of Celtic ideas we labour under) to adopt some of these foreign whimsies, dropping however all mention of Woden and his Valkhyrian virgins, etc.? To settle this scruple of conscience, I must refer you to Dr. Warburton: if this should be his opinion (which I doubt), then I go on to tell you (first premising that a dirge is always a funeral service sung over persons already

[1] This was probably the second English edition, of 1757, of Johann Georg Keysler's *Travels through Germany, Hungary, Bohemia, Switzerland, Italy, and Lorrain*, originally published in German in 1740.—[*Ed.*]

dead), that I would have something striking and uncommon in the measures, the rhythm, and the expression of this Chorus; the two former are not remarkable here, and the third is so little antiquated, that "murky"[1] and "dank" look like two old maids of honour got into a circle of fleering girls and boys. Now for particulars. I like the first stanza; the image of Death in arms is very fine and gallant, but I banish "free-born train," and "glory and luxury" here (not the ideas, but the words), and "liberty and freedom's cause," and several small epithets throughout. I do no see how one person can *lift* the voice of another person. The imagery of the second stanza too is excellent. A dragon *pecks!* why a cock-sparrow might do as much: in short, I am pleased with the Gothic Elysium. Do you think I am ignorant about either that, or the *hell* before, or the *twilight*. I have been there, and have seen it all in Mallet's *Introduction to the History of Denmark* (it is in French), and many other places. "Now they charge," etc., looks as if the coursers rode upon the men. A ghost does not fall. These are all my little objections, but I have a greater. Extreme conciseness of expression, yet pure, perspicuous, and musical, is one of the grand beauties of lyric poetry. This I have always aimed at, and never could attain; the necessity of rhyming is one great obstacle to it: another and perhaps a stronger is, that way you have

[1] "Haste with light spells the *murky* foe to chase."
Chorus in *Caractacus*.

chosen of casting down your first ideas carelessly and at large, and then clipping them here and there, and forming them at leisure; this method, after all possible pains, will leave behind it in some places a laxity, a diffuseness; the frame of a thought (otherwise well invented, well turned, and well placed) is often weakened by it. Do I talk nonsense, or do you understand me? I am persuaded what I say is true in my head, whatever it may be in prose,—for I do not pretend to write prose.

I am extremely pleased with your fashionable Ode, and have nothing to find fault there, only you must say "portray'st" in the first stanza; and "it looks at best but skin," in the fourth, is not right. I have observed your orders, but I want to shew it everybody. Pray tell me when I may have the credit of doing so. I have never seen a prettier modernism: let it be seen while it is warm. You are in the road to fame; but do not tell your name at first, whatever you may venture to do afterwards.

Fobus is a treat; desire Lord Holdernesse to kiss him on both ears for me. I forgive Lord B. for taking the Tudors for the Restoration. Adieu, dear Mason, and remember me; and remember too that I have neither company, nor pleasure, nor spirits here, and that a letter from you stands in all the place of all these. Adieu!

So you have christened Mr. Dayrolles'[1] child, and

[1] Mr. Dayrolles was the intimate friend and correspondent of Lord Chesterfield and the Resident at the Hague. His

my Lady Y.[1] they say. Oh, brave Dupp.[2] how comes he to be the Chancellor of the Exchequer? What is going to be now?

CXLIII.—TO THE REV. WILLIAM MASON.

Sunday, January . .,[3] 1758.

DEAR MASON—I am almost blind with a great cold, and should not have written to you to-day if you did not hurry me to send back this Elegy. My advices are always at your service to take or to refuse, therefore you should not call them severe. You know I do not love, much less pique myself, on criticism, and think even a bad verse as good a thing or better than the best observation that ever was made upon it. I like greatly what you have now sent me, particularly the spirit and sentiment of it; the disposition of the whole too is natural and elegiac. As to the expres-

daughter eloped with Leonidas Glover's youngest son. He was protected by the Richmond and Grafton families. From a MS. memorandum of Horace Walpole's, relating to Mr. Dayrolles, I find that some scandal existed with regard to Mr. Stanhope, to whom he was gentleman at the Hague, and to which Gray silently pointed in his mention of Mr. Dayrolles' child.—[*Mit.*]

[1] I suppose that Lady Yarmouth is meant. She had a son called Master Louis, but not owned, 1758.—[*Mit.*]

[2] Thomas Henry, Viscount Dupplin, afterwards Earl of Kinnoul.

[3] Mason has not given the date of the day of the month in this letter; but as it was on a Sunday subsequent to the 16th, it must have been either on the 22d or the 29th,—most probably the former.—[*Mit.*]

sion, I would venture to say (did you not forbid me) that it is sometimes too easy. The last line I protest against. This, you will say, is worse than blotting out rhymes. The descriptive part is excellent, yet I am sorry for the name of Cutthorpe. I had rather Vertumnus and Flora did not appear in person. The word "lopt" sounds like a farmer, or a man of taste. "A mountain hoar," "The savage," etc., is a very good line: yet I always doubt if this ungrammatical construction be allowable; in common speech it is usual, but not in writing even prose; and I think Milton (though hard pressed by his short metre in the Penseroso) yet finds a way to bring in his *that's*, his *who's*, and his *which's*.[1] "Fair unfold the wide-spread," etc.; "fair," is weakly, "wide-spread" is contained in "unfold." By "amber mead," I understand the yellow gleam of a meadow covered with marsh-marigolds and butterflowers,—is it not so? the two first lines (the second especially) I do not admire. I read, "Did Fancy wake not—refuse one votive strain;" you will ask me why? I do not know. As to votive, it is like delegated, one of the words you love. I also read, "How well does Memory," etc.—for the same no reason. "It all was his," etc. I like the sense, but it is not sufficiently clear. As to the versification, do not you perceive that you make

[1] Mason seems to have profited by Gray's judicious criticisms. The name "*Cutthorpe*" does not appear in the printed copy. "*Pierced*" is substituted for "lopped."—"That yon wild peak," for "*savage peak*," etc.

the pause on the fourth syllable in almost every other line?

Now I desire you would neither think me severe, nor at all regard what I say any further than it coincides with your own judgment; for the child deserves your partiality; it is a healthy well-made boy, with an ingenuous countenance, and promises to live long. I would only wash its face, dress it a little, make it walk upright and strong, and keep it from learning paw words.

I never saw more than two volumes of Pelloutier, and repent that I ever read them. He is an idle man of some learning, who would make all the world Celts whether they will or no. *Locus est et pluribus umbris,* is a very good motto; you need look no further. I cannot find the other passage, nor look for it with these eyes. Adieu! dear Mason, I am most sincerely yours.

You won't find me a place like Mr. Wood's.

ELEGY I.[1]

"Favour'd steps," useless epithet! Write "choir." Read "rank'd and met." "Cull living garlands," etc., too verbose. You love "garlands which pride nor gains:" odd construction. "Genuine wreath—Friendship twine;" a little forced. "Shrink" is usually a verb neuter; why not "blight" or "blast"? "Fervid;" read "fervent." "When sad reflection;"

[1] "To a young nobleman (Lord John Cavendish) leaving the University, 1753."

read "till sad," etc. "Blest bower," "call on;" read "call we." "In vain to thee;" read "in vain to him," and "his" for "thy." Oh, I did not see: what will become of "thine?" "Timid" read "fearful." "Discreter part;" "honest part" just before "explore." "Vivid," read "warmest."

There is too much of the Muse here. "The Muse's genuine wreath," "the Muse's laurel," "the Muse full oft," "the Muse shall come," "the Muse forbids,"—five times.

Elegy II.[1]

"Laurel-circled;" "laurel-woven" sounds better. "Neglect the strings" is somehow naked: perhaps

"That rules my lyre, neglect her wonted strings."

Read "re-echo to my strain." "His earliest blooms" should be "blossoms." "Then to thy sight," "to the sight." Read "he pierced." "Modestly retire," I do not like. "Tufts" sounds ill.

"To moral excellence:" a remnant of bad books you read at St. John's; so is the "dignity of man."

"Of genuine man glowing,"

a bad line. "Dupe" I do not approve. "Taste" too often repeated.

"From that great Guide of Truth,"

hard and prosaic.

[1] This stands as Elegy III., "Written in the Garden of a Friend." Mason accepted all these corrections.—[*Ed.*]

Elegy III.[1]

"Attend the strain," "quick surprise," better than "sweet." "Luxuriant Fancy, pause," "exulting leap." —Read

> "The wint'ry blast that sweeps ye to the tomb."

"Tho' soon,"—query? "His patient stand," better before. Read "that mercy." "Trace then by Reason's,"—blot it out. "Dear as the sons," perhaps, "yet neither sons," etc.

> "They form the phalanx," etc.
> "Is it for present fame?"

From hence to "peasant's life," the thought seems not just, because the questions are fully as applicable to a prince who does believe the immortality of the soul as to one who does not; and it looks as if an orthodox king had a right to sacrifice his myriads for his own ambition, because they stand a chance of going to heaven, and he of going to hell.

Indeed these four stanzas may be spared, without hurting the sense at all. After "brave the torrent's roar," it goes on very well. "Go, wiser ye," etc.; and the whole was before rather spun out and weakly.

[1] This is placed as Elegy V. (p. 107), "On the death of a Lady," *i.e.* the beautiful Lady Coventry.—[*Mit.*]

CXLIV.—TO THOMAS WHARTON.

February, 21, 1758.

Dear Doctor—I feel very ungrateful (which is the most uneasy of all feelings) in that I have never once enquired, how you and your family enjoy the region of air and sunshine, into which you are removed, and with what contempt you look back on the perpetual fogs, that hang over Mrs. Payne and Mrs. Paterson. Yet you certainly have not been the less in my mind. That at least has packed up with you, has helped Mrs. Wharton to arrange the mantle-piece, and drank tea next summer in the grotto. But I am much puzzled about the bishop and his fixtures, and do not stomach the loss of that money.

Would you know, what I am doing? I doubt, you have been told already, and hold my employment cheap enough: but every one must judge of his own *capabilities*, and cut his amusements according to his disposition. The drift of my present studies, is to know, wherever I am, what lies within reach, that may be worth seeing, whether it be building, ruin, park, garden, prospect, picture, or monument; to whom it does, or has belonged, and what has been the characteristic, and taste of different ages. You will say, this is the object of all antiquaries. But pray, what antiquary ever saw these objects in the same light, or desired to know them for a like reason? In short say what you please, I am persuaded, whenever my List[1] is finished, you will approve it, and think it of no small use. My spirits are very near the *freezing point*, and for some hours of the day this exercise by its warmth and gentle motion serves to raise them a few degrees higher. I hope the misfortune, that has befallen Mrs. Cibber's canary-bird will not be the ruin of *Agis.*[2] It is probable you will have curiosity enough to see it, as it comes from the writer of *Douglas:* I expect your opinion. I am told, that Swift's *History of the Tory Administration* is in the press, and that Stuart's *Attica*[3] will be out this spring. Adieu, dear Sir, I am ever yours, T. G.

Mr. Brown joins his compliments with mine to you and Mrs Wharton.

CXLV.—TO THOMAS WHARTON.

Sunday, April 9, 1758.

My dear Sir—I am equally sensible of your affliction,[4] and of your kindness, that made you think of

[1] A Catalogue of the Antiquities, Houses, etc., in England and Wales; which Gray drew up in the blank pages of Kitchen's English Atlas: after his death Mr. Mason printed a few copies, and distributed them among the friends of Gray; and in 1787 a new edition was printed for sale.—[*Mit.*]

[2] A tragedy by John Home, performed at the Theatre Royal, Drury Lane, in 1758. It would have been a failure but for the antitheologian zeal of the author's admirers, who resented the action of the Scotch elders in the matter of *Douglas.*—[*Ed.*]

[3] Gray was a subscriber to this book, as appears by a note in one of his pocket journals.—[*Ed.*]

[4] Occasioned by the death of his eldest (and at the time his

me at such a moment. Would to God, I could lessen the one, or requite the other with that consolation, which I have often received from you, when I most wanted it! but your grief is too just, and the cause of it too fresh, to admit of any such endeavour. What indeed is all human consolation, can it efface every little amiable word or action of an object we loved, from our memory? Can it convince us that all the hopes we had entertained, the plans of future satisfaction we had formed, were ill-grounded and vain, only because we have lost them? The only comfort (I am afraid) that belongs to our condition is to reflect (when time has given us leisure for reflection) that others have suffered worse, or that we ourselves might have suffered the same misfortune at times and in circumstances, that would probably have aggravated our sorrow. You might have seen this poor child arrive at an age to fulfil all your hopes, to attach you more strongly to him by long habit, by esteem, as well as natural affection, and that towards the decline of your life, when we most stand in need of support, and when he might chance to have been your *only* support; and then by some unforeseen and deplorable accident, or some painful lingering distemper you might have lost him. Such has been the fate of many an unhappy father! I know, there is a sort of tenderness, which infancy and innocence alone

only) son.—[*Mason.*] Gray wrote an epitaph on the child, in verse, which is for the first time printed in vol. i. of the present edition.—[*Ed.*]

produce, but I think, you must own the other to be a stronger and more overwhelming sorrow.

I am glad Mrs. Wharton has fortitude enough not to suffer this misfortune to prevail over her, and add to the natural weakness of her present condition. Mr. Brown sincerely sympathises with you, and begs to be kindly remembered to you both. I have been . . .[1] in town by this time, had I not heard Mason was coming hither soon, and I was unwilling to miss him. Adieu, my dear Wharton, and believe me ever most sincerely yours, T. G.

CXLVI.—TO THE REV. WILLIAM MASON.

Good Friday, 1758.

DEAR MASON—I have full as much *ennui* as yourself though much less dissipation, but I cannot make this my excuse for being silent, for I write to you *pour me desennuyer*, though I have little enough to say. I know not whether I am to condole with you on this Canterbury business, for it is not clear to me that you or the Church are any great losers by it; if you are be so good as to inform me, and I will be sorry; however, there is one good thing in it, it proves the family are mortal.

You do not seem to discover that Mons. Mallet is but a very small scholar, except in the erudition of the Goths. There are, *à propos*, two Dissertations on the "Religion and Opinions of the Gauls," published in the *Mémoires de l'Acad. des Belles Lettres et des Inscriptions*, vol. xxiv. 4to. one by the Abbé Fénel, in which he

[1] About two lines of MS. are lost here.—[*Ed.*]

would shew that, about Tiberius' and Claudius' times the Druids, persecuted and dispersed by the Romans, probably retired into Germany, and propagated their doctrines there. This is to account for some similitude to the Gaulish notions which the religion of Germany seems to bear, as Tacitus has described it, whereas Julius Cæsar makes them extremely different, who lived before this supposed dispersion of the Druids; the other by Monsieur Freret, is as to shew the reverse of all this,—that there was no such dispersion, no such similitude, and that, if Cæsar and Tacitus disagree, it is because the first knew nothing but of those nations that bordered on the Rhine, and the other was acquainted with all Germany. I do not know whether these will furnish you with any new matter, but they are well enough written and easily read. I told you before, that, in a time of dearth, I would venture to borrow from the Edda without entering too minutely on particulars; but, if I did so, I would make each image so clear, that it might be fully understood by itself, for in this obscure mythology we must not hint at things, as we do with the Greek fables, that everybody is supposed to know at school. However, on second thoughts, I think it would be still better to graft any wild picturesque fable, absolutely of one's own invention, upon the Druid stock; I mean upon those half-dozen of old fancies that are known to have made their system: this will give you more freedom and latitude, and will leave no hold for the critics to fasten on.

Pray, when did I pretend to finish, or even insert passages into other people's works? as if it were equally easy to pick holes and to mend them. All I can say is, that your Elegy must not end with the worst line in it; it is flat, it is prose; whereas that above all ought to sparkle, or at least to shine. If the sentiment must stand, twirl it a little into an apophthegm, stick a flower in it, gild it with a costly expression; let it strike the fancy, the ear, or the heart, and I am satisfied.

Hodges is a sad fellow; so is Dr. Akenside,[1] and Mr. Shenstone, our friends and companions. Your story of Garrick is a good one; pray is it true, and what came of it? did the tragic poet call a guard?[2] It was I that hindered Mr. Brown from sending the pamphlet. It is nonsense, and that nonsense all stolen from Dr. Stukeley's book about Abury and Stonehenge; yet if you will have it, you may. Adieu, and let me hear soon from you.—I am ever yours,

T. G.

CXLVII.—TO THOMAS WHARTON.

Dear Doctor—I am much concerned to hear the account you give of yourself, and particularly for

[1] Gray alludes to the two additional volumes to Dodsley's *Collection of Poems*, which came out in the year 1758, and contained his two Odes, and some poems by Mason, Shenstone, Akenside, etc. Gray disliked Akenside, and in general all poetry in blank verse, except Milton.—[*Mit.*]

[2] This may allude to the disputes with Arthur Murphy regarding "The Orphan of China."—[*Mit.*]

that dejection of spirits, which inclines you to see everything in the worst light possible, and throw a sort of voluntary gloom not only over your present, but future days, as if even your situation now were not preferable to that of thousands round you, and as if your prospect hereafter might not open as much of happiness to you, as to any person you know. The condition of our life perpetually instructs us to be rather slow to hope, as well as to despair, and (I know, you will forgive me, if I tell you) you are often a little too hasty in both, perhaps from constitution. It is sure, we have great power over our own minds, when we choose to exert it; and though it be difficult to resist the mechanic impulse and bias of our own temper, it is yet possible; and still more so, to delay those resolutions it inclines us to take, which we almost always have cause to repent.

You tell me nothing of Mrs. Wharton's, or your own state of health. I will not talk to you more on this subject, till I hear you are both well, for that is the grand point, and without it we may as well not think at all. You flatter me in thinking, that anything, I can do,[1] could at all alleviate the just concern your late loss has given you: but I cannot flatter myself so far, and know how little qualified I am at present to give any satisfaction to myself on this head, and in this way, much less to you. I by no means pretend to inspiration, but yet I affirm, that

[1] Dr. Wharton had requested him to write an epitaph on the child.—[*Mason.*]

the faculty in question is by no means voluntary. It is the result (I suppose) of a certain disposition of mind, which does not depend on oneself, and which I have not felt this long time. You that are a witness, how seldom this spirit has moved me in my life, may easily give credit to what I say.

I am in hopes of seeing you very soon again in my way to Stoke. Mrs. Rogers has been very ill this Spring, and my other aunt writes me word, that she herself has had something (which she takes for a paralytic stroke) which came as she walked in the garden, and is afraid, she shall lose the use of one leg: so that it looks to me, as if I should have perhaps some years to pass in a house with two poor bed-ridden women, a melancholy object, and one that in common humanity I cannot avoid. I shall be glad to know, whether I can be in Gloucester Street for a week, ten or twelve days hence.

I had wrote to you sooner, but that I have been on a little expedition lately to see Ely, Peterborough, Crowland Abbey, Thorney, Fotheringay, and many other old places, which has amused me a little.

Poor Mason is all alone at Aston (for his Curate is gone to be Tutor to somebody) with an inflammation in his eyes, and could scarce see to write me a few lines. Adieu, dear Sir, I am ever yours, T. G.

June 18, 1758.

CXLVIII.—TO THE REV. WILLIAM MASON.

June 20, 1758.

DEAR MASON—I sympathise with your eyes, having been confined at Florence with the same complaint for three weeks, but (I hope) in a much worse degree, for, besides not seeing, I could not sleep in the night for pain; have a care of old women (who are all great oculists), and do not let them trifle with so tender a part.

I have been exercising my eyes at Peterborough, Crowland, Thorney, Ely, etc.; am grown a great Fen antiquary; this was the reason I did not answer you directly, as your letter came in my absence. I own I have been all this while expecting *Caractacus* or at least three choruses, and now you do not so much as tell me it is finished: sure your spiritual functions, and even your attentions to the Duchess of Norfolk and Sir Conyers,[1] might have allowed you some little intervals for poetry; if not (now Queen

[1] The Right Honourable Sir Conyers d'Arcy, K.B., younger son of John Lord d'Arcy, by the Hon. Bridget Sutton, only surviving daughter of Robert Lord Lexington. He was appointed Master of the King's Household 1719-20; K.B. 1725; Comptroller of the Household and a Privy Counsellor 1730; Lord Lieutenant of the North Riding during the minority of his nephew, Robert Earl of Holdernesse; M.P. for Richmond from 1728 to 1747, and for Yorkshire from 1747 to his death, in 1758. "Lady M. W. Montagu.—Her father fell in love with Lady Anne Bentinck, who forsook for him Sir Conyers Darcy, who had long been HER lover, and on whose despair Rowe wrote the ballad of 'Colin's Complaint.'"—MS. note by Horace Walpole.—[*Mit.*]

Hecuba is gone), I utterly despair, for (say what you will) it was not retirement, it was not leisure, or the summer, or the country, that used to make you so voluminous; it was emulation, it was rivalry, it was the collision of tragedy against tragedy, that kindled your fires, and set old Mona in a blaze. You do not say who succeeds her Trojan Majesty;[1] it ought to be well considered. Let me have none of your prosaic curates. I shall have you write sermons and private forms, and "heaven's open to all men."

That old *fizzling* Duke[2] is coming here again (but I hope to be gone first) to hear speeches in his new library, with the Bishop of Bristol, to air his close-stool; they have fitted it up—not the close-stool, nor the Bishop, but the library, with classes, that will hold anything but books, yet books they must hold, and all the bulky old Commentators, the Synopses and *Tractatus Tractatuums*,[3] are washed with white-of-eggs, gilt and lettered, and drawn up in review before his Grace. Your uncle Balguy takes his doctor's degree, and preaches the commencement sermon at Dr. Green's request.

[1] Dr. Delap, the author of *Hecuba*, who had left Mason's curacy.

[2] Duke of Newcastle. "The old *Hubble-bubble* Duke" is Dr. Warner's expression for the same peculiarity of manner which Gray describes by *fizzling*.—[*Mit.*]

[3] A collection of legal dissertations, *Tractatus universi juris*, published by Zilettus, the bookseller at Venice, in 1564, in 18 folio volumes, usually bound in 25, to which there are additional volumes of Index, making in all 28 folios.—[*Mit.*]

Mr. Brown sends his love, and bids me tell you that Dr. Warburton has sent you his *New Legation*, with its dedication to Lord Mansfield; would you have it sent you? Lord Strathmore goes to-morrow into the North to come of age.[1] I keep an owl in the garden as like me as it can stare; only I do not eat raw meat, nor bite people by the fingers. This is all the news of the place. Adieu, dear Mason! and write to me directly if it will not hurt you, or I shall think you worse than you are.—I am ever yours,

T. G.

CXLIX.—TO THOMAS WHARTON.

Stoke, August 9, 1758.

DEAR DOCTOR—I have been, since I saw you in town, pretty much on the wing, at Hampton, Twickenham, and elsewhere. I staid at the first of these places with the Cobhams two days and should (I own) gladly have done so longer, but for the reason we talked about. The place spite of the weather is delightful: every little gleam of sunshine, every accident of light, opens some new beauty in the view, and I never saw in so small a spot so much variety, and so many natural advantages, nor ever hardly wished more for your company to partake of them. We were also at Hampton Court, Sion, and several places in the neigh-

[1] John, ninth Earl of Strathmore and Kinghorne, succeeded to the title 1755, and died in April 1776; in 1767 he married the great heiress, daughter of G. Bowes, Esq., of Streatlam Castle, in the western part of the county of Durham.—[*Mit.*]

bourhood again, particularly at Lord Lincoln's, who (I think) is hurting his view by two plantations in front of his terrace, that regularly answer one another, and are of an oval form with rustic buildings in the middle of them, a farm, dairies, etc. They stand on the opposite side of the water, and (as they prosper) will join their shade to that of the hills in the horizon, exclude all the intermediate scene of enclosures, meadows, and cattle feeding, and reduce that great distance to nothing. This seems to be the advice of some new gardener, or director of my Lord's taste; his successor perhaps may cut all down again.

I shall beg the favour of you (as you were so kind to offer it) to buy us a Lottery Ticket, if you find the market will not be much lower than at present; and (if you think it has no great hazard in it) enclose it to me here: I will take care to repay you as soon as I come to town, or (if you choose it) directly. My best respects to Mrs. Wharton. Pray let me hear soon, how you both are.—Believe me, ever yours,

T. G.

CL.—TO THE REV. WILLIAM MASON.

Stoke, August 11, 1758.

DEAR MASON—I was just leaving Cambridge at the time when I received your last letter, and have been unfixed and flitting about almost ever since, or you had heard of me sooner. You do not think I could stay to receive Fobus; no more did Mr. Hurd, he was gone into Leicestershire long before. As to uncle Balguy,[1] pray do him justice; he stayed, indeed, to preach the commencement sermon, but he assured me (in secret) it was an old one, and had not one word in it to the purpose. The very next morning he set out for Winchester, and I do really think him much improved since he had his residence there; freer and more open, and his heart less set upon the mammon of unrighteousness. *A propos,*—would you think it?—Fobus has wit. He told Young,[2] who was invited to supper at Doctor L.'s, and made all the company wait for him,—"Why, Young, you make but an awkward figure now you are a bishop; this time last year you would have been the first man here." I cannot brag of my spirits, my situation, my employments, or my fertility; the days and the nights pass, and I am never the nearer to anything but that one to which we are all tending. Yet I love people that leave some traces of their journey behind them, and have strength enough to advise you to do so while you can. I expect to see *Caractacus* completed, not so much from the opinion I entertain of your industry as from the consideration that another winter approaches, which is the season of harvest to an author; but I will conceal the secret of your motives, and join in the common applause. The books you enquire after are not

[1] Doctor Thomas Balguy, prebendary of Winchester, and archdeacon; the friend of Warburton and Hurd.

[2] Philip Yonge, Residentiary of St. Paul's, consecrated Bishop of Bristol 1758; translated to Norwich 1761; died 1783. He resigned the Public Oratorship in 1752.—[*Mit.*]

worth your knowledge. Parnell[1] is the dunghill of Irish Grub Street. I did hear who Lancelot Temple[2] was, but have really forgot. I know I thought it was Mr. Greville. Avon is nothing but a type.[3] The Duchess of Queensberry's advertisement[4] has moved my impatience; yet, after all, perhaps she may curl her gray hair with her grandfather's golden periods. Another object of my wishes is, the King of Prussia's account of the Campaign, which Niphausen talked of

[1] The posthumous and dubious collection of Parnell's *Remains*, published in Dublin in 1758.—[*Ed.*]

[2] A name assumed by Dr. Armstrong, the poet and physician.

[3] "Avon," a poem in three parts, 4to. Birmingham, printed in the *new types* of Mr. Baskerville.

[4] The *Public Advertiser*, July 10, 1758.—"Whereas a spurious, incorrect edition of a work represented to contain the history of the reign of his Majesty King Charles the Second, from the Restoration to the end of the year 1667, by the late Lord Chancellor Clarendon, has been attempted to be imposed on the public; to prevent which, their Graces the Duke and Dutchess of Queensberry have preferred a bill in the High Court of Chancery, and obtained an injunction to restrain the printing and publishing the same; and, in order to prevent the abuse which will arise to the public from such a publication, they think it incumbent on them to signify that a correct edition from the original manuscript in the hand of Lord Chancellor Clarendon, of his Lordship's life, from his birth to his banishment (and which includes the history of the Last Seven Years attempted to be imposed on the public), is now preparing for the press, and will soon be published, the profits of which have been appropriated by the family for a public benefaction to the University of Oxford." The Duchess was the wife of Douglas, third Duke of Queensberry. She was the friend of Pope, and patroness and protector of Gay, for whom she quarrelled with the Court. She retained in age the dress of her youth, which was one of her many eccentricities. She died in 1772.—[*Mit.*]

six weeks ago as just coming over, but it is not come; perhaps he waits for a better catastrophe. The Tickenham Press is in labour of two or three works (not of the printer's own). One of them is an *Account of Russia* by a Lord Whitworth,[1] who, I think, was minister there from King William.

I seem to have told you all I know, which you will think very little, but *a nihilo nil fit.* If I were to coin my whole mind into phrases they would profit you nothing, nor fill a moderate page. Compassionate my poverty, shew yourself noble in giving me better than I bring, and ever believe me most sincerely yours, T. G.

I find you missed of Stonhewer by going to Sir Conyers Darcy's. Can you tell me if he is still at Harrowgate, for I do not know how to direct to him there?

CLI.—TO RICHARD STONEHEWER.

Cambridge, August 18, 1758.

I AM as sorry as you seem to be, that our acquaintance harped so much on the subject of materialism, when I saw him with you in town, because it was plain to

[1] This little work was printed at Strawberry Hill in 1758. The MS. was given by Richard Owen Cambridge, Esq., who had purchased *Mr. Zolman's* Library, which related solely to *Russian* History. In the Preface, written by Walpole, some account may be found of Lord Whitworth. The title is, "Account of Russia as it was in 1710."—[*Mit.*]

which side of the long-debated question he inclined. That we are indeed mechanical and dependent beings, I need no other proof than my own feelings; and from the same feelings I learn, with equal conviction, that we are not *merely* such: that there is a power within that struggles against the force and bias of that mechanism, commands its motion, and, by frequent practice, reduces it to that ready obedience which we call *Habit;* and all this in conformity to a preconceived opinion (no matter whether right or wrong) to that least material of all agents, a Thought. I have known many in his case who, while they thought they were conquering an old prejudice, did not perceive they were under the influence of one far more dangerous; one that furnishes us with a ready apology for all our worst actions, and opens to us a full license for doing whatever we please; and yet these very people were not at all the more indulgent to other men (as they naturally should have been); their indignation to such as offended them, their desire of revenge on anybody that hurt them was nothing mitigated: in short, the truth is, they wished to be persuaded of that opinion for the sake of its convenience, but were not so in their heart; and they would have been glad (as they ought in common prudence) that nobody else should think the same, for fear of the mischief that might ensue to themselves. His French Author I never saw, but have read fifty in the same strain, and shall read no more. I can be wretched enough without them. They put me in mind of the Greek Sophist that got immortal honour by discoursing so feelingly on the miseries of our condition, that fifty of his audience went home and hanged themselves; yet he lived himself (I suppose) many years after in very good plight.

You say you cannot conceive how Lord Shaftesbury came to be a Philosopher in vogue; I will tell you: First, he was a Lord; 2dly, he was as vain as any of his readers; 3dly, men are very prone to believe what they do not understand; 4thly, they will believe anything at all, provided they are under no obligation to believe it; 5thly, they love to take a new road, even when that road leads nowhere; 6thly, he was reckoned a fine writer, and seemed always to mean more than he said. Would you have any more reasons? An interval of above forty years has pretty well destroyed the charm. A dead Lord ranks but with Commoners: Vanity is no longer interested in the matter, for the new road has become an old one. The mode of free-thinking is like that of Ruffs and Farthingales, and has given place to the mode of not thinking at all; once it was reckoned graceful, half to discover and half conceal the mind, but now we have been long accustomed to see it quite naked: primness and affectation of style, like the good breeding of Queen Anne's Court, has turned to hoydening and rude familiarity.

CLIL—TO THOMAS WHARTON.

DEAR DOCTOR—I ought to have informed you sooner, that I had received the Ticket you were so good to buy for me, but I have been obliged to go every day to Stoke House, where the Garricks have been all the last week. They are now gone, and I am not sorry for it, for I grow so old, that, I own, people in high spirits and gaiety overpower me, and entirely take away mine. I can yet be diverted with their sallies, but if they appear to take notice of my dullness, it sinks me to nothing. I do not know whether you will blame me, but I found so good an opportunity given me of entering into the quarrel between Mason and him, that I could not help seizing it, and trying to shew him the folly of hearkening to half-witted friends and tale-bearers; and the greater folly of attempting to hurt, or merely to pique, so worthy and so estimable a man. If I did nothing else, I at least convinced him that I spoke entirely from myself; and that I had the most entire good opinion and most unalterable respect as well as kindness for M[aso]n.

I congratulate you on our successes, and condole with you on our misfortunes: but do you think we draw the nearer to any happy conclusion of the war, or that we can bear so great a burden much longer. The King of Prussia's situation embarrasses me, surrounded as he is, and reduced to the defence of his own little marquisate.

Your *Encyclopedia* is the object of my envy. I am reduced to French Plays and Novels, Willis's *Mitred Abbies*, and the *History of Norfolk* in 3 volumes folio. These *latter* Authors have, I think, the most wit, though the others know rather more of the world.

I wish the air of Hampstead were not so necessary to you all, but am glad you always know where to find health, and that she lives so near you. I continue better than has been usual for me in the summer, though I neither walk, nor take anything: 'tis in mind only, that I am weary and disagreeable. Mrs. R[ogers] is declining every day, her stomach gone, very weak, sometimes giddy, and subject to disorders in her bowels: yet I do not apprehend any immediate danger, but believe she will be reduced to keep her bed entirely.

My best compliments to Mrs. Wharton. Pray let me hear from you as often as you are in a humour for writing, though from hence I can requite your kindness with so little to amuse you.—I am ever truly yours,

T. G.

Stoke, August 31, 1758.

CLIII.—TO THE REV. JAMES BROWN.

September 7, 1758.

DEAR SIR—It is always time to write (whether Louisbourg be taken or not), and I am always alike glad to hear from you. I am glad however to repay you with "the King of Prussia:" there is a man for you at a dead lift, that has beat and baffled his three most powerful enemies, who had swallowed him up in idea: not that I look upon this last exploit, however seasonable, as his most heroic exploit: I suppose it was only butchering[1] a great flock of slaves and savages, a conquest that, but for the necessity of it, he would have disdained. What use our little supply is like to be of in Germany I cannot say. I only know that my Lord Granby, with his horse, had a bridge which broke under them, and that he (the Marquess) was sore bruised and laid up; but I think the Electorate may be saved for all this.

Old Pa.[2] wrote to me from Scarborough three weeks ago; he had seen more in his journey than ever he saw before in his life, and was to see twice as much more in his way to Glamis. He is become acquainted with rocks and precipices, and despises the tameness and insipidity of all we call fine in the South. Mr. Pitt and he did not propose being at Glamis till the end of August.

If I had been at the great gambling dinner, I should have desired somebody would help me to a collop of the other great turtle, though I believe it is vile meat. You tell me nothing about the good family at Ripton, that were to come together from all quarters[3] and be so happy this summer; has any

[1] This alludes to the King of Prussia's victory over the Russian army at Zorndorf, August 25; "as the Prussians gave no quarter, the slaughter was terrible."—[*Mit.*]

[2] The Rev. William Palgrave.

[3] Nicholas Bonfoy, Esq., married Elizabeth, a daughter of William Hall, Esq., of King's Walden. She was one of a

ill chance hindered their meeting, or have you not paid them a visit this vacation? It is an infinite while since I heard from Mason; I know no more of him than you do; but I hope *Caractacus* will profit of our losses; if pleasure or application take up his thoughts I am half content.

My health I cannot complain of, but as to my spirits they are always many degrees below changeable, and I seem to myself to inspire everything around me with *ennui* and dejection; but some time or other all these things must come to a conclusion, till which day I shall remain very sincerely yours,

T. G.

Commend me to any that enquire after me, particularly Mr. Talbot.

CLIV.—TO WILLIAM PALGRAVE.[1]

[Stoke,] September 6, 1758.

I do not know how to make you amends, having neither rock, ruin, or precipice near me to send you; they do not grow in the South: but only say the word, if you would have a compact neat box of red brick with sash windows, or a grotto made of flints

family of ten sons and four daughters; he resided at Abbot's Ripton, in the county of Huntingdon. Gray said that Mrs. Bonfoy taught him to pray.—[*Ed.*]

[1] Known as "Old Pa" (1735-1799). He was a fellow of Pembroke College, and Rector of Palgrave and Thrandeston in Suffolk. Mason says that he was making a tour in Scotland when this letter was written to him.—[*Ed.*]

and shell-work, or a walnut-tree with three mole-hills under it, stuck with honey-suckles round a basin of gold-fishes, and you shall be satisfied; they shall come by the Edinburgh coach.

In the meantime I congratulate you on your new acquaintance with the *savage*, the *rude*, and the *tremendous.* Pray, tell me, is it anything like what you had read in your book, or seen in two-shilling prints? Do not you think a man may be the wiser (I had almost said the better) for going a hundred or two of miles; and that the mind has more room in it than most people seem to think, if you will but furnish the apartments? I almost envy your last month, being in a very insipid situation myself; and desire you would not fail to send me some furniture for my Gothic apartment, which is very cold at present. It will be the easier task, as you have nothing to do but transcribe your little red books, if they are not rubbed out; for I conclude you have not trusted everything to memory, which is ten times worse than a lead pencil: half a word fixed upon or near the spot, is worth a cartload of recollection. When we trust to the picture that objects draw of themselves on our mind, we deceive ourselves; without accurate and particular observation, it is but ill-drawn at first, the outlines are soon blurred, the colours every day grow fainter; and at last, when we would produce it to anybody, we are forced to supply its defects with a few strokes of our own imagination. God forgive me, I suppose I have done so myself before now, and misled many a good body that put their trust in me. Pray, tell me (but with permission, and without any breach of hospitality), is it so much warmer on the other side of the Swale (as some people of honour say) than it is here? Has the singing of birds, the bleating of sheep, the lowing of herds, deafened you at Rainton! Did the vast old oaks and thick groves of Northumberland keep off the sun too much from you? I am too civil to extend my enquiries beyond Berwick. Everything, doubtless, must improve upon you as you advanced northward. You must tell me, though, about Melross, Rosslin Chapel, and Arbroath. In short, your Port-feuille must be so full, that I only desire a loose chapter or two, and will wait for the rest till it comes out.

CLV.—TO THOMAS WHARTON.

[Stoke,] September 16, 1758.

DEAR DOCTOR—Having been for a considerable time without any news of you, I have taken it into my head, that you are ill, or that Mrs. Wharton is so. You will not wonder, if I grow a little superstitious, when you know, that I have not been a step out of the house for this fortnight or more past, for Mrs. Rogers has been at the point of death with a disorder in her stomach accompanied with continual and laborious retchings, and a total loss of appetite, that has reduced her to the weakness of an infant, I mean, her body, though her senses are still perfect, and (what I think remarkable) she has recovered the use of her speech (which for several years had been hardly intelligible), and pronounces almost as plain, as ever she did. She is now, for three days past, such is the strength of her constitution, in a way of recovery: medicine has had nothing to do in it, for she will take nothing prescribed her. When I say recovery, I do not mean, that she will ever recover her strength again, but, I think, she may live a good while in this helpless state; however it is very precarious, and Dr. Hayes believes her quite worn out. I certainly do not put on (to you) more tenderness, than I really feel on this occasion, but the approaches of death are always a melancholy object, and common humanity must suffer something from such a spectacle.

It is an age since I heard anything from Mason. If I do not mistake, this should be his month of waiting, unless he has exchanged his turn with somebody. If he be in town, you must probably have heard of him, and can give me some intelligence. My old new acquaintance Lady Denbigh is here at Stoke-house; but I do not believe, I shall be able to get out, or have any opportunity of seeing her, while she stays.

If my fancies (which I hope in God are mere fancies) should prove true, I hope you will let somebody tell me, how you do. If not, I shall beg you to tell me yourself, as soon as possible, and set my understanding to rights. Adieu, dear Sir, I am ever most sincerely yours, T. G.

CLVI.—TO THE REV. JAMES BROWN.

October 28, 1758.

Dear Sir—You will not imagine me the less grateful for the long letter you were so good to write me some time since, because I have omitted to answer it, especially if you know what has since happened. Mrs. Rogers died in the end of September; and what with going to town to prove her will and other necessary things, what with returning back hither to pay debts, make inventories, and other such delightful amusements, I have really been almost wholly taken up. I might perhaps make a merit even of writing now, if you could form a just idea of my situation, being joint executor with another aunt, who is of a mixed breed between —— and the Dragon of Wantley. So much for her. I next proceed to tell you that I saw Mason in town, who stayed there a day on my account, and then set out (not in a huff) with a laudable resolution to pass his winter at Aston, and save a curate.[1] My Lord[2] has said something to him, which I am glad of, that looked like an excuse for his own dilatoriness in preferring him; but this is a secret. He told me he had seen you, and that you were well. Dr. Wharton continues dispirited, but a little better than he was.

[1] I presume that he did so; for there appears a vacancy in the curacy between Mr. Delap's leaving Aston and Mr. Wood coming in 1759, by the Aston Register.—[*Mit.*]

[2] Lord Holdernesse.

The first act of *Caractacus* is just arrived here, but I have not read it over.

I am very disagreeable; but who can help that? Adieu, my best Mr. Brown; I am ever yours,

T. G.

I shall hardly be at Cambridge before Christmas. I recollect that it is very possible you may have paid my bills; if so, pray inform me what they amount to, that I may send the money when I get to London, or sooner, if you please.

CLVII.—TO THOMAS WHARTON.

Stoke, November 1758.

DEAR DOCTOR—My judgement is, that if your picture possess but any one of the beauties you see and describe in it, it must certainly be worth eight or ten times as much as you gave for it. I only wonder, you should forget to say by what lucky chance you came by it. Old *Frank*[1] was a Dutch master of some note: the history of that school I am very little acquainted with, but if I am not mistaken, there was lately published a French account of their lives in two or more volumes, 4to., which I have seen at Nourse's, in which you may meet with better information.

I am agreeably employed here in dividing *nothing*

[1] Jerome Franck or Francken, called old Franck, died about 1620. He was a Flemish painter of minor merit, a pupil of Floris.—[*Ed.*]

with an *old Harridan*,[1] who is the Spawn of Cerberus and the Dragon of Wantley. When I shall get to town, I cannot divine, but doubtless it will be between this and Christmas. You were so good to offer me house-room for some of my lumber: I am therefore packing up certain boxes and baskets, which I believe you will be troubled with. But I beg Mrs. Wharton to consider well first, whether it will be inconvenient to her. If she assures me, it will not, I shall inform you shortly of their shapes and numbers. At present it seems to me, that there will be three or four large boxes; and five baskets of china: the rest Madame Forster shall accommodate.

Ah, poor King of Prussia![2] what will become of him? I am told here, that matters are much worse, than is yet avowed. I also hear that seven Generals have refused the command, which Hopson[3] is now gone with, who has been before censured for ill-conduct, and is besides so infirm, that he will not live the voyage. Adieu, dear Sir, I am ever yours, T. G.

1 Gray's aunt, Mrs. Oliffe, who was his joint executor.—[*Ed.*]

2 Gray's lamentation was excited, I conclude, by the defeat of the King of Prussia at Hochkirchen, by the Austrians under Marshal Daun, the 14th of October 1758. In this battle he lost 7000 men, his tents, and baggage; and the day was rendered memorable by the death of Marshal Keith, who was shot through the heart.—[*Mit.*]

3 Major-General Hopson was appointed to the command of an expedition against Martinique, which sailed on the 12th of November 1758. The attack on this Island failed, and the armament directed its course to Guadaloupe, where General Hopson died.—[*Mit.*]

CLVIII.—TO THE REV. WILLIAM MASON.

Stoke, November 9, 1758.

DEAR MASON—I should have told you that *Caradoc* came safe to hand, but my critical faculties have been so taken up in dividing nothing with "The Dragon of Wantley's Dam," that they are not yet composed enough for a better and more tranquil employment; shortly, however, I will make them obey me. But am I to send this copy to Mr. Hurd, or return it to you? Methinks I do not love this travelling to and again of manuscripts by the post. While I am writing, your second packet is just arrived. I can only tell you in gross that there seem to me certain passages altered, which might as well have been let alone; and that I shall not be easily reconciled to Mador's own song. I must not have my fancy raised to that agreeable pitch of heathenism and wild magical enthusiasm, and then have you let me drop into moral philosophy and cold good sense. I remember you insulted me when I saw you last, and affected to call that which delighted my imagination nonsense. Now I insist that sense is nothing in poetry but according to the dress she wears, and the scene she appears in. If you should lead me into a superb Gothic building with a thousand clustered pillars, each of them half a mile high, the walls all covered with fretwork, and the windows full of red and blue saints, that had neither head nor tail, and I should find the Venus of

Medici in person perked up in a long niche over the high altar, as naked as ever she was born, do you think it would raise or damp my devotions. I say that Mador must be entirely a Briton, and that his pre-eminence among his companions must be shewn by superior wildness, more barbaric fancy, and a more striking and deeper harmony, both of words and numbers. If British antiquity be too narrow, this is the place for invention; and if it be pure invention, so much the clearer must the expression be, and so much the stronger and richer the imagery—there's for you now.[1]

I am sorry to hear you complain of your eyes. Have a care of candle-light, and rather play at hot-cockles with the children than either read or write. Adieu! I am truly and ever yours, T. G.

CLIX.—TO THOMAS WHARTON.

DEAR DOCTOR—You are so hospitable in your offers, that my Cargo is preparing to set out on Monday next, and will (I imagine) present itself at your door on Tuesday or Wednesday next: it comes by water, and the Man undertakes the whole together, so that I need not trouble any one to send to the wharf about them. I have divided this incumbrance between yourself and Mrs. Forster, yet am afraid you will find your share of it more than enough. It consists of

[1] The fourth Ode was afterwards new written.—[*Mason.*]

1. A Chest cover'd with leather and bound with iron. No. 1, full of Bed and Table Linen.
2. A large wainscot Box with iron handles, No. 2, full of the same and other furniture.
3. A long deal Box, No. 3, of the same.
4, 5, 6, 7, 8. Five large Baskets, of China, No. 5, 6, 7, 8, 9.
9. A wainscot Chest of Drawers, matted up, No. 10, with table-linen, covers for chairs, curtains, and some little Plate.
10. A middling deal-box, of sheets, quilts, etc, No. 13.
11. A square India-Cabinet, of odd nameless things, No. 16.

The numbers you see at the end (which are also inscribed on the parcels) relate to the whole and not to your part of them, therefore you need not take any notice of them. As to the danger of fire, nothing can be more combustile than the China-Baskets, being of wicker and pack'd full of Tow, Paper, Shavings, and Hay; wherever they are disposed, I should hope nobody would come with a candle. If the matted things fright you on the same account, the coverings may be taken off, and laid by in some dry place. I like mightily your proposal of insuring; but I thought, they would not do it for China, Glasses, or Linen. The value (including Mrs. Forster's parcels) I should set at about £250. I could not perhaps sell the contents for so much, but it is certain, that I could never buy them for that money. If it could be done immediately, I should be glad (supposing it be not any great trouble) tho' in about ten days I shall be in town myself. Will you let your Servant enquire, if my old lodgings will be vacant at that time?

It may be necessary to add a list of the remaining

parcels, supposing you should think it right to insure all together. At Mrs. Forster's:

1. An old leather Trunk nail'd, No. 4, with Beds, Quilts, and table-linen, etc.
2. A Hand-Basket, with a Kettle, Pewter, and kitchen utensils, No. 11.
3. An old Portmanteau, with servant's linen, etc., No. 12.
4. A Walnut-tree Escritoire, upper half, with quilting, a bed, toilettes, and some china, matted, No. 14.
5. Lower Part of ye same, with Cushions, Curtains, Blankets, and a few Books, No. 15.
6. Large Deal Case with Looking-Glasses, Pictures, etc., No. 19.

7, 8, 9, 10. Six Chairs, and a Settee, matted, No. XX., 1, 2, 3, and 4.

11\. A deal Chest of Books, No. 21.

There are some other trifles, but this is all worth mention.

I am glad you are master of a "*Pieta.*" I could have said *Pieta* myself, if I had not left off being a coxcomb or a connoisseur. Palma (that is the *old* one) was a good colorist, like most of the Venetians, but remarkable for bad drawing, particularly of hands and arms. What you say of Dr. Ak[enside] I fully agree with you in, and have mentioned it to Mason. As soon as I can write to Mr. H[urd], I shall repeat to him a *part* of your own words, which I think will prevail, besides I know he thinks himself obliged to you in Dr. Hn.'s affair. I have seen no Rousseau, nor anybody else: all I can tell you is, that I am to dine with my lady Carlisle to-morrow, who is a melancholy Dowager reduced from Castle Howard and ten thousand pounds a year to £1500, her jewels, plate, and a fine house in town excellently well furnished. She has just discovered too (I am told in confidence) that she has been long the object of calumny, and scandal. What am I to say to comfort her?

I do not dislike the Laureate at all, to me it is his best Ode,[1] but I don't expect any one should find it out, for Otbert and Ateste are surely less known than Edward the Ist, and Mount Snowdon. It is no imitation of me; but a good one of

Pastor, cum traheret, etc.

which was falsely laid to my charge. Adieu, dear Sir, I am ever yours.

December 2, 1758.

P.S.—If the China arrives safe and without rattling, the Men will deserve something to drink, which I shall be careful to repay: they promise to bring it on biers not in a cart. In No. 6 is the best of it.

Pray, do you know anything of Stonhewer? is he in London?

CLX.—TO THE REV. WILLIAM MASON.

London, January 18, 1759.

DEAR MASON—You will think me either dead, or in that happy state which is that of most people alive,

[1] "Ode for his Majesty's Birthday," November 10, 1758.

of forgetting everything they ought to remember; yet I am neither one nor the other. I am now in town, having taken leave of Stoke, and hoping to take leave of my other incumbrances in a few months hence. I send you in short my opinion of *Caractacus*, so far, I mean, as I have seen of it; I shall only tell you further, that I am charmed with the idea you give me of your fourth Ode; it is excellently introduced, and the specimen you send me even sublime. I am wrapped in it; but the last line of the stanza falls off, and must be changed, "Courage was in his van," etc., for it is ordinary when compared with the rest; to be sure, the immortality of the soul and the happiness of dying in battle are Druid doctrines; you may dress them at pleasure, so they do but look wild and British.

I have little to say from hence but that *Cleone*[1] has succeeded very well at Covent Garden, and that people who despised it in manuscript went to see it, and confess—they cried so. For fear of crying too I did not go. Poor Smart is not dead, as was said, and *Merope*[2] is acted for his benefit this week, with a new farce, *The Guardian.*[3] Here is a very agreeable opera of Cocchi's, the *Cyrus*,[4] which gave me some

[1] Written by Dodsley, and acted in 1758 at Covent Garden.

[2] Written by Aaron Hill, and acted in 1749.

[3] A farce written by Garrick, acted 1759, in two acts, and taken in great measure from the *Pupille* of Fagan.

[4] *Il Ciro Riconosciuto* is the title of an opera composed by Cocchi, produced at the King's Theatre in 1759, and said by Dr. Burney to be the best of Cocchi's productions during his

pleasure; do you know I like both Whitehead's Odes in great measure, but nobody else does.

I hear matters will be made up with the Dutch, and there will be no war. The King of Portugal has slily introduced troops into Lisbon, under pretence of clearing away the rubbish, and seized the unsuspecting conspirators in their own houses; they are men of principal note, in particular the family of Tavora, who have some pretensions to the crown; and it is thought the Jesuits have made use of their ambition to execute their own revenge. The story of the king's gallantries, and the jealousy of some man of quality, who contrived the assassination, is said to be all false.

Adieu! I rejoice to hear you use your eyes again. Write to me at Dr. Wharton's, for perhaps I may go to Cambridge for some weeks, and he will take care I shall have your letter.

CLXI.—TO THE REV. WILLIAM MASON.

Cambridge, March 1, 1759.

DEAR MASON—Did I tell you I had been confined in town with the gout for a fortnight? well, and since I came hither, it is come again. Yesterday I came

residence in England. In the British Museum is a copy of the opera in Italian and English, as used in the theatre at the time; and it is curious to observe how materially it varies from the text of the *Ciro Riconosciuto* in the modern editions of Metastasio's *Works*. The wording of whole scenes is different.—[*Mit.*]

abroad again, for the first time, in a great shoe, and very much out of humour; and so I must return again in three days to town about business, which is not like to add much to the sweetness of my temper, especially while stocks are so low.

I did not remember ever to have seen the joint criticism[1] from Prior Park that you speak of, so little impression did it make; nor should I believe now that I had ever seen it, did I not recollect what a prejudice the parsons expressed to human sacrifice, which is quite agreeable to my way of thinking; since Caractacus convinced me of the propriety of the thing, it is certain that their fancies did in no sort influence me in the use of my tomahawk. Now you must know I do not much admire the chorus of the rocking-stone, nor yet much disapprove it; it is grave and solemn, and may pass. I insist, however, that "deigns" (though it be a rhyme) should be "deign'st," and "fills" "fill'st," and "bids" "bid'st." Do not blame me, but the English tongue. The beginning of the antistrophe is good. I do not like "meandring way,"

"Where Vice and Folly stray,"

nor the word "sprite." The beginning too of the epode is well; but you have used the epithet "pale" before in a sense somewhat similar, and I do not love repetitions. The line

"Or magic numbers"

interrupts the run of the stanza, and lets the measure drop too short. There is no beauty in repeating

[1] Of Hurd and Warburton.

"ponderous sphere." The two last lines are the best.[1]

The sense of your simile about the "distant thunder" is not clear, nor well expressed; besides, it implies too strong a confession of guilt.

The stanza you sent me for the second Ode is very rude; and neither the idea nor verses touch me much. It is not the gout that makes me thus difficult. Finish but your Death-song as well as you imagined and begun it, and mind if I won't be more pleased than anybody. Adieu! dear Mason, I am ever truly yours,

T. G.

Did I tell you how well I liked Whitehead's two Odes? they are far better than anything he ever wrote.[2]

Mr. Brown and Jemmy Bickham[3] lament your indolence, as to the degree, in chorus; as to me, I should have done just so for all the world.

CLXII.—TO THE REV. WILLIAM MASON.

April 10, 1759.

Dear Mason—This is the third return of the gout in the space of three months, and worse than either of the former. It is now in a manner over, and I am so much the nearer being a cripple, but not at all the

[1] By reference to the poem it will be seen that Mason adopted some of Gray's proposed alterations and rejected others.—[*Mit.*]

[2] "Ode for his Majesty's Birth-day," and "Ode for the New Year, 1759."

[3] James Bickham, Fellow of Emanuel College.

richer. This is my excuse for long silence; and, if you had felt the pain, you would think it an excuse for a greater fault. I have been all the time of the fit here in town, and doubtless ought to have paid my court to you and to Caractacus. But a critic with the gout is a devil incarnate, and you have had a happy escape. I cannot repent (if I have really been any hindrance) that you did not publish this spring. I would have it mellow a little longer, and do not think it will lose anything of its flavour; to comfort you for your loss, know that I have lost above £200 by selling stock.

I half envy your situation and your improvements (though I do not know Mr. Wood),[1] yet am of your opinion as to prudence; the more so because Mr. Bonfoy tells me he saw a letter from you to Lady H.,[2] and that she expressed a sort of kindness; to which my Lord added, that he should write a rattling epistle to you that was to fetch you out of the country. Whether he has or not don't much signify: I would come and see them.

I shall be here this month at least against my will, unless you come. Stonhewer is here with all his sisters, the youngest of which has got a husband. Two matches more (but in a superior class) are going to be soon:—Lord Weymouth[3] to the Duchess of

[1] The author of the "Essay on Homer."

[2] Lady Holdernesse.

[3] Thomas, third Viscount Weymouth on May 22, 1759, married the Lady Elizabeth Cavendish Bentinck, eldest daughter of William, second Duke of Portland.—[*Mit.*]

Portland's homely daughter, Lady Betty, with £35,000; and Lord Waldegrave to Miss Maria Walpole, with £10,000. It is impossible for two handsomer people ever to meet.[1]

All the cruelties of Portugal are certainly owing to an amour of the King's (of long standing) with the younger Marquess of Tavora's wife. The Jesuits made their advantage of the resentments of that family. The disturbances at Lisbon are all false.

This is my whole little stock of news.

Here is a very pretty opera, the *Cyrus*;[2] and here is the Museum, which is indeed a treasure. The trustees lay out £1400 a-year, and have but £900 to spend. If you would see it you must send a fortnight beforehand, it is so crowded. Then here are Murdin's *Papers*,[3] and Hume's *History of the Tudors*, and Robertson's *History of Mary Stuart and her Son*, and what not. Adieu, dear Mason, I am most faithfully yours, T. G.

[1] In 1759 he (Lord Waldegrave) married the natural daughter of Sir Edward Walpole, a lady of great beauty and merit.—[*Mit.*]

[2] *Il Ciro Riconosciuto* of Cocchi.

[3] "*A Collection of State Papers in the reign of Queen Elizabeth*, from 1571 to 1596, from the library at Hatfield House; by William Murdin, etc.," folio, 1759. The collection is a continuation of that published by Dr. Haynes in 1740.—[*Mit.*]

CLXIII.—TO THOMAS WHARTON.

Saturday, July 21, 1759.

DEAR DOCTOR—I have at last found rest for the sole of my gouty foot in your own old dining-room,[1] and hope in spite of the damnation denounced by the bishop's two chaplains, that you may find at least an equal satisfaction and repose at Old Park. If your bog prove as comfortable as my oven, I shall see no occasion to pity you; and only wish that you may *brew* no worse than I *bake*. You totally mistake my talents, when you impute to me any magical skill in planting roses.[2] I know, I am no conjuror in these things; when they are done, I can find fault, and that is all. Now this is the very reverse of genius, and I feel my own littleness. Reasonable people know themselves better, than is commonly imagined; and therefore (though I never saw any instance of it) I believe Mason, when he tells me he understands planting better, than anything whatever. The *prophetic eye of taste* (as Mr. Pitt call'd it) sees all the beauties, that

[1] The house in Southampton Row, where Mr. Gray lodged, had been tenanted by Dr. Wharton; who, on account of his ill health, left London the year before; and was removed to his paternal estate at Old Park, near Durham.—[*Mason.*]

[2] I once called on Mr. Hurd, at Thurcaston, and he said to me: I wish you had come sooner, for *Mason* has just left me, he is going to Aston. I think you must have passed him in the gateway. He got up very early this morning to plant those roses opposite, and otherwise decorate my grounds; he boasts that he knows exactly where every rose ought to be planted.—[*Cradock.*]

a place is susceptible of, long before they are born; and when it plants a seedling, already sits under the shadow of it, and enjoys the effect it will have from every point of view, that lies in prospect. You must, therefore invoke Caractacus, and he will send his spirits from the top of Snowdon to Cross Fell or Warden Law.

The thermometer is in the passage window (where the sun never comes) near the head of the back stairs. Since you went, I have never observed it lower than 68, most part of the day at 74, and yesterday at 5 in the afternoon it was at 79, the highest I have ever seen it. It now is prepared to correspond regularly with you at the hours you mention. The weather for this fortnight has been broiling without interruption, one thunder-shower excepted, which did not cool the air at all. Rye (I am told) is begun to be cut near London. In Cambridgeshire a fortnight ago the promise of harvest was the finest I ever saw, but the farmers complain (I hear) that the ears do not fill for want of wet. The wheat was then turning yellow. Duke-cherries are over in London; three days ago they sold for half-a-crown a pound. Caroons[1] and Blackhearts very large and fine drive about the streets in wheel-barrows a penny a pound. Raspberries a few are yet remaining, but in a manner over. Melons are ripe, and apricots and Orleans-plums are to be seen in the fruit-shops. Roses are (I think) over a week ago. The jessamine (at Mrs. Dod's, on a S. W. wall) was in full bloom (if you remember) long before

[1] A sort of cherries.—[*Ed.*]

you went from hence, and so it continues. That below in the garden on a N. E. wall has been all this week covered with flowers. My nosegays from Covent Garden consist of nothing but scarlet-martagons, everlasting-peas, double-stocks, pinks, and flowering-marjoram. As I have kept no exact account hitherto this year, I can say no more of July, that now is. Therefore, I shall annex one for the year 1754, which I observed day by day at Stoke. Observe, it had been then a cold rainy summer.

The heat was very moderate this month, and a great deal of rain fell. The sown hay was all got in by the first day, but the meadow-hay was not before the 23d. It was very good and in plenty, but sold at 40 shillings a load in the field on account of the scarcity the year preceding. Barley was in ear on the first day; grey and white peas in bloom. The bean flowers were going off. Duke-cherries in plenty on the 5th; hearts were also ripe. Green melons on the 6th, but watry and not sweet. Currants begun to ripen on the 8th, and red gooseberries had changed colour; tares were then in flower, and meadow-hay cutting. Lime-trees in full bloom on the 9th. Mushrooms in perfection on the 17th. Wheat and oats had changed colour, and buck-wheat was in bloom on the 19th. The vine had then opened its blossoms, and the end of the month grapes were near the size of small peas. Turnips appeared above ground on the 22d; and potatoes were in flower. Barley had changed its hue, and rye was almost ripe on the 23d.

The pine-apple-strawberry was then in perfection. Black caroons were ripe, and some duke-cherries still remained on walls the 26th, but the hearts were then all spoiled by the rain. Gooseberries red and white were then ripe, and currants in abundance.

On the 1st.

Haws, turned red.
Honey-suckles, in full bloom.
Broomflower went off.

On the 2d.

Phlomis, or yellow-tree-sage.

On the 3d.

Virginia flowering Raspberry, blew.
Shrub Cinque-foil.
Spiræa-frutex.
Syringa went off.

On the 7th.

Balm of Gilead blowing.

On the 8th.

Common Jasmine blew.
Moss-Provence Rose.
Yellow and Austrian, Rose go off.

On the 9th.

Yellow Jasmine blows.
White, and Gum Cistus.
Tamarisk in Flower.
Coccygria.
Virginia-Sumach.
Tutsan, or Park-leaves.
Spanish-Broom.
Scarlet, and painted Geraniums.

On the 11th.

Pyracantha, in berry.
Mountain-Ash.
White-Beam.
Orange flowering.
Winter Cherry.

On the 15th.

Single Velvet Rose goes off.

On the 22d.

Lavender and Morjoram blow.

On the 26th.

Damask, red, moss, and double Velvet, Roses go off.

On the 28th.

Rosa-Mundi, and Rose without Thorns, go off.

On the 31st.

White Rose goes off.

These were all the flowering Shrubs observed by me.

GARDEN FLOWERS.

On the 2d.

Convolvulus Minor blows.
Garden Poppy.
Single Rose Campion.
Double Larkspur.
Candy-Tuft.

Common Marigold.
Pansies continue blowing.

On the 5th.

Lupines blew, and white blow.
Purple Toads-flax.
White, and blue Campanula.

On the 9th.

Double-scarlet Lychnis blows.
Tree Primrose.
White Lilly.
Willow-Bay.
Scarlet Bean.
French Marigold.

On the 11th.

Yellow Lupin blows.
Tree-Mallow.
Amaranthus Cat's-tail.

On the 19th.

Striped Lilly blows.
Fairchild's Mule.
Double rose-Campion.
African Ragwort.

On the 23d.

Whole Carnations blow.

On the 24th.

Double-white Stock in bloom.

In the Fields Scabious, St. John's Wort, Trefoil, Yarrow, Bugloss, Purple Vetch, Wild-thyme, Pale Wood-Orchis, Betony, and white Clover, flowering on the 1st. Large blue Cranesbill the 9th; Ragwort, Mothmullein, and Brambles, the 20th; Knapweed all the month. There was rain (more or less) 13 days out of the 31, this month; and 17 days out of 30 in June preceding.

I was too late for the post on Saturday, so I continue on Monday. It is now 6 in the afternoon, and the thermometer is mounted to 80, though the wind is at N. E. by N. The gay Lady Essex is dead of a fever during her lying in; and Mrs. Charles York last week, with one of her children, of the sore throat. Heberden, and (I think) Taylor, attended her; the latter had pronounced her out of danger; but Heberden doubted about her. The little boy was at Acton, and escaped the infection.

Everybody continues as quiet about the invasion, as if a Frenchman, as soon as he set his foot on our coast, would die, like a toad in Ireland. Yet the king's tents and equipage are ordered to be ready at an hour's warning. Nobody knows, positively, what is the damage, that Rodney has done,[1] whether much or little: he can only guess himself; and the French have kept their own secret, as yet. Of the 12 millions, raised for the year, eight are gone already, and the old party assure us, there is no more to be had for next year. You may easily guess at the source of my intelligence, and therefore will not talk of it. News is hourly expected of a battle in Westphalia, for Pr. Ferdinand was certainly preparing to fight the French, who have taken Minden by storm.

I hear the D. of N. is much broke ever since his sister Castlecomer died, not that he cared for her, or saw her above once a year; but she was the last of the brood, that was left; and he now goes regularly to church, which he never did before. Adieu? I am ever yours.

I hope Mrs. Wharton's native air will be more civil to her, when they are better acquainted: my best compliments to her. I am glad the children are well.

[1] This alludes to the Bombardment of Havre-de-grace, by Admiral Rodney, in the month of July in this year; the French having collected several large flat-bottomed boats there, for a threatened invasion on some part of the British territories.—[*Mit.*]

END OF VOL. II.

www.ingramcontent.com/pod-product-compliance
Lightning Source LLC
Chambersburg PA
CBHW032316280326
41932CB00009B/826
* 9 7 8 3 7 4 4 6 8 5 5 0 4 *